Disher, Maurice
Victorian Song

'On such a night the sea engulph'd
My father's lifeless form.'

VICTORIAN
SONG

FROM DIVE TO DRAWING ROOM

by

Maurice Willson Disher

DECORATED WITH 'FRONTS'
FROM BALLADS AND
PIANO PIECES

PHOENIX HOUSE LTD
LONDON

TO EVELYN

* * *

*

Printed in Great Britain by
C. Tinling & Co., Ltd., Liverpool, London and Prescot
for Phoenix House, Ltd., 38 William IV Street
Charing Cross, W.C.2
First published 1955

PROGRAMME

MUSIC COVERS

Music for Remembrance

ORDINARILY song consists solely of words and music. Any history of it would be about authors and composers with singers and pianists thrown in. Which country and which century should be awarded the highest praise may be in doubt, but we are all agreed that Victorian England, even with the aid of America during the same period, cannot carry off the prize. Why pick on it then? The reason is that there is a lot more than words and music when we listen to some such tunes.

Memory is heavily involved. Numbers of ballads out of all reckoning stir our most venerable generation to thoughts of its origin, and there is not yet a generation so brand new as to be free from the influence of nineteenth-century music altogether. The silliest snatch of old doggerel may have the sway over our feelings that we now know as evocative, calling up visions like a witch's spell, and the worst may possess this power more strongly than the best. The secret is unknown to respected musicians, who are very poor judges of popular songs. Ask them to please the widest possible public and they drive us to fury by choosing the "Londonderry Air". All they can hear is music when the rest of us are listening to the rhythm of our lives. Singers, as distinct from people who sing, are not much better; they know so little of emotional unreason that a soprano will reject some dramatic tale which goes straight to the heart, because it is supposed to be told by a man.

Brushing aside both poetry and music as naught, I have studied 'all that to the soul belongs' instead. Soul was very much the Victorian song-writer's personal property. Other topics, from mothers-in-law to alcoholism, might serve for comic relief, but the main entertainment had to be soul no matter how many side-shows spiced it. Varying moods merely emphasized how deadly this earnestness could be: nostalgia had "Home, sweet home" for permanent model, and agonies of separations grew longer and longer until they lasted for ever and a day. Still there is no need to be definite about soul. How far it soared above brass tacks that

9

gallant and adventurous huntsman and soldier Whyte-Melville demonstrated when he wrote "Mary Hamilton", music by Mrs Wilberforce, which had a great vogue in its own day though hastily dropped in ours:

There's a bonnie wild rose on the mountain side,
            Mary Hamilton;
In the glare of noon she hath droop'd and died,
            Mary Hamilton,
Soft and sweet is the evening show'r,
Pattering kindly on brake and bow'r,
But it falls too late for the perish'd flow'r—
            Mary Hamilton.

There's a lamb is lost at the head of the glen,
            Mary Hamilton,
Lost and missing from shieling and pen,
            Mary Hamilton . . .
The shepherd sought it in toil and heat,
And sore he strove when he heard it bleat,
Ere he wins to the lamb, it is dead at his feet—
            Mary Hamilton.

The mist is gath'ring ghostly and chill,
            Mary Hamilton;
And the weary maid cometh down from the hill,
            Mary Hamilton,
The weary maid, and she's home at last,
And she trieth the door, but the door is fast,
For the sun is down, and the curfew's past—
            Mary Hamilton.

Too late for the rose, the ev'-ning rain—
            Mary Hamilton,
Too late for the lamb the shepherd's pain—
            Mary Hamilton . . .
Too late at the door the maiden's stroke,
Too late the plea when the doom hath been spoke,
Too late the balm when the heart is broke—
            Mary Hamilton.
            Mary Hamilton . . .

You may do your damnedest to guess what the maid has been up to before she cometh weary down from the hill, after which you

can have another severe mental tussle to decide why Mary Hamilton
has to be admonished so often and with such elegant variety of
punctuation; the fact remains that as it concerns soul, practical
details are irrelevant.

To do the subject full justice we must start by sampling the
zest of the preceding age for songs about strong drink, and at the
end we may note how the succeeding age, gasping for fresh air,
went fey in hysteria over what lovesome things gardens were
'God wot'. Now that we are out of sympathy with the Edwardians
we incline towards the songs belonging to the maudlin century in
between these two outbursts of glee. We may not understand why
there was so much insistence on distress—physical for the comic,
spiritual for the serious—but we are willing to put ourselves in a
responsive frame of mind in order to imagine the Victorian musical
evening as a thing of fragrance instead of fug.

Nevertheless, we may not hope to hear what our forebears
heard, for though the words and music are the same we have
changed radically. The difference is not in radio or other con-
trivances for making life difficult; it is best summed up in an
entry that has caught my eye by chance in Crabb's *Synonyms*.
Concerning 'devil' he says that associations connected with the
name render its pronunciation in familiar discourse offensive to
the chastened ear. We no longer possess a chastened ear.

I

The Musical Evening

‹+·+›

Hope, youth, love, home—each human tie
That binds, we know not how or why—
All, all that to the soul belongs,
Is closely mingled with old songs.

Eliza Cook

'Bring your music' . . . perhaps those words are still used, but if
so they are spoken to a musician. Not so many years ago they
were regularly addressed by everybody to everybody else. There
was a widespread belief that all, capable or incapable of singing,
must sing. Goodfellowship upheld it. To rebel was to hurt the
feelings of kind friends willing to suffer horrible noises in a good
cause.

The similarity of what millions experienced as the result of
that custom now astonishes us. Among old friends of like age
it may be taken for granted, but why should anyone twenty years
younger have duplicate reminiscences? The same songs are
recalled, hundreds upon hundreds of them, which will not sound
exaggerated when you yourself start listing them, and whatever
chorus you sing three or four generations can sing, no matter where
you travel in this country or almost anywhere in the lands of our
tongue.

On comparing notes we find that there were reluctances and
persuasions that might have been ordered by set rules. We seem
to recollect the same people: the sentimental tenor, the stern
baritone, the formidable bass, the hero worshipper who copied his
idol, the man with one song and one song only, the lady who went
for top notes with no means of reaching them, the parents who
believed in their child, and the hog who stuck to the piano stool.
Whole populations with a vast repertoire to choose from kept to a

small pattern which was the same wherever you went. Each musical circle repeated all other circles, so that they can be likened to wallpaper.

Nowadays we give credit for songs to professional singers—not very accurately, for one known as Gracie Fields' was Melba's—and listen to them on radio or records when we cannot swarm to see stars in the flesh. We used to care so little about songs apart from our own singing of them that we were vague about their origins in opera, drama, concert, music-hall, tap-room, barrack-room, illustrations, entertainments, revival meetings, the Highlands, the cotton-fields, the minstrels, the glee club, and the country inn. Rather later than 1900 there was a fad for singing the latest ballad by a favourite composer, but till then what mattered was not who wrote it but which member of the family was going to claim it. If it were *my* song then it was as much part of myself as the clothes I wore, or more so because it would be mine for longer. If it were somebody else's song then it had to be respected as personal property, and it generally was. Odd and preposterous as this may now seem it has one consequence as dear to us as the glass slipper in the fairy tale was to one other sentimentalist. Whenever we come across an old tune we know whose it was and spend a little time fitting it where it belongs.

As long as there are many of us with such memories, Victorian song will continue its life whether or no it is actually sung. Every reader above a certain age, though I am not at all sure what it is, will be hearing tunes whenever my text breaks into verse. Anyone old enough to remember the way we amused ourselves during the blitz will recognize a great many, for they were all trotted out again then. At every opportunity children who cannot reasonably be expected to know more than one or two out of the nineteenth-century store prove that they know nearly all. They learn a few at school, pick up some from their parents, and hear a number from radio, but the tenacity of popular music is not easily explained. Possibly all these familiar songs will always be familiar, and yet it is hard to believe that the dwindling of our delight in singing them will not take effect immediately. The difference is marked from birth, for in contrast with the old manner of up-bringing which bestowed an extensive repertoire upon an infant almost before it reached consciousness, the children I can observe are never sung to. What has happened to the lullaby? It is all very well to hanker after the tender snippet which is a debt we owe to Sir Walter Scott:

> O hush thee, my baby, thy sire was a knight,
> Thy mother a lady both gentle and bright

but a modern mother, unless married to a knight, could not sing that without libelling both herself and her child; still the tune was so pleasing that it was rapturously clapped in night-clubs of the 1920s as a new dance—by a new composer. There were scores upon scores of other lullabies, some old and some newly taken from shows, concerts, and music-halls, for a happy trait in the character of the Victorians was their habit of serving up nonsense in adult entertainment and then taking it home to pacify the children. Of course, we are always adapting ancient ballads like "Come lassies and lads" to infant needs, and even "Gossip Joan", an old ditty which reeked, has been disinfected for schools; reversing this process the radio often turns baby jingles into the latest plug for adults. But we have lost the happy knack of inventing choruses like "Diddle diddle dumpling", which an ordinary red-nosed comic sang. From John Beulah's "If I had a donkey and he wouldn't go" during the Regency, down to Marie Lloyd's "Oh, Mr. Porter, what shall I do?" in the 1890s, the beery breath of ruffians bellowed sweet simplicities fit for the mouths of babes and sucklings.

If we had to decide which was the most frequently sung of all Victorian ditties the prize would go to:

> Twinkle, twinkle, little star,
> How I wonder what you are,
> Up above the world so high
> Like a diamond in the sky

written during the Regency by Jane Taylor, whose sister Ann innocently caused much ribaldry with, "Who kissed the place and made it well?" The little star would have been one nursery rhyme among many but for the coming of mechanized amusements. It took first place when magic lanterns were equipped with a double slide, consisting of a coloured star on a square piece of glass and another coloured star on a round piece of glass fixed side by side in wooden frame, with a wire contrivance which caused the round piece to revolve when the operator turned its handle. Here was the first of all flicks. While the projection of the double star on the screen behaved like a kaleidoscope, the vicar's sister started

> Up above the world so hay
> Lake a day-a-mond in the skay

because in those days 'i' was vulgar.* Twinkle, twinkle always stopped the show, and always saved it. After some horrifying temperance slides had shown how bloody our fathers would be if they did not turn teetotal, the star turn of the magic lantern could be trusted to bring happiness back. While little girls stayed in a state of rapture, little boys tasted the first joys of bad behaviour by changing the last line into, 'Like a rabbit in a rump steak pie', though the sinful zest of this would have faded had they but recognized the tune as belonging by right to

> In the kingdom of Thy grace
> Give a little child a place.

That is symbolic. The British public sins and sings in ignorance. As the centuries go by we tend more and more to spiritual salvation and musical damnation, as anyone can tell who listens to hymns from a football colosseum.

All we ever asked of a song-writer was that his heart should be in the right place. His popularity depended not on poetry or music, for the former may be non-existent and the latter pilfered, but on his feelings. As long as he knew how to be solemn or ridiculous, tender or strong, plaintive or rousing, homesick or adventurous, sentimental or righteous, his rhyme and reason might be good, bad, or indifferent for all we cared. Most of the authors so employed are horse-poets, not after the fashion of Horse Marines but using excess of gloss or size to make up for what they lack in delicacy, like horse-chestnuts, horse-mushrooms, and horse-laughs. Horse-poetry may be told from poetry, as a rule, by counting apostrophes, which is strange when you consider that though intended to go to music they can be seen† but not heard:

* Just as in our own day 'o' was so vulgar that we had to hear about the boys of the 'oode' brigade.

† By the same token the word 'engulph'd' is never spelt thus except when meant to be sung.

Enraptur'd, charm'd, amaz'd I was,
My inmost soul was stirr'd,
I look'd . . . .

Whether the printer's founts run dry of ' ' ' ' ' ' ' ' or not the style of ev'ry mem'ry flow'd ev'nly 'twixt ev'ning's slumb'ring flow'rs must be pr's'rv'd. There are also many ; ; ; but these are signals that the voice must not be dropped.

The only songs that make do without apostrophes and semicolons are those that do without words. I am not thinking of Mendelssohn's so much as of the tacit text in descriptive music. The theory that unsung songs are sweetest was thoroughly exploited by composers of the quadrilles and fantasias that mix with songs in every Victorian cabinet, and win admiration for their 'coloured fronts', which give some preliminary assistance to pictures in sound of history in the making. All major reports in the Court Circular were thus celebrated upon some thousands of pianofortes; princely christenings and royal weddings inspired quadrilles, frivolous subjects became lancers, and military conquests reflected their glory upon full orchestra in mighty scores that drew heavily upon the public's richly stored musical memory. "Rule Britannia" signified embarkation, "A life on the ocean wave" the voyage, and "British Grenadiers" columns on the march before war started in earnest with bugle-calls, bagpipes, the big drum, discords easily recognized as native music, and a hymn here and there in varying degrees of solemnity according to whether the narrative had got as far as night bivouac or the field of death. Long before Tchaikowsky adopted the pattern in "1812" every bandmaster knew how it could be done, and every audience responded as though to a masterpiece. Not only history but geography could be taught in this way, for there were Edinburgh quadrilles and Nicaraguan valses. Publishers adorned their song fronts half-heartedly compared with the reckless expenditure they lavished on splendours to catch the eye of amateur pianists.

B

II

The National Anthem

"THEN HAIL VICTORIA", "A British Cheer for England's Queen", and dozens of others like them, expressed devotion to her. They were such poor stuff that efforts to sing them did not last long. The shelf in the music cabinet which should have been theirs was occupied instead by a rival royal family. Why, she may have asked, should the Stuarts have all the good tunes? Throughout her reign loyalty to them might still be heard, no matter how fictitiously, in "Here's a health unto his Majesty":

> And he who will not drink his health,
> I wish him neither wit nor wealth
> Nor yet a rope to hang himself

which was echoed by John Dyer's equally popular, "Here's a health to the King":

> And he who will this health deny,
> Down among the dead men let him lie.

The advantage lay with the Jacobites, because they could be light-hearted. Duty to the Hanoverians required solemnity in "Loyal Songs", one of which contained the lines:

> Send flying death enwrapt in lead,
> Your chain and shot with double head,
> From bellowing lungs thro' pervious air . . .

to denote what atmospheric conditions favour the free passage of cannon balls when fired. As this was published with a stirring engraving it gives us fair warning not to expect poetry from the supporters of the Georges. Nor was it supplied.

But when the threat of rebellion arose in 1745 the needs of music to excite patriotic feelings became urgent. At a reasonable

guess we may suppose that His Majesty's Servants, the actors at
Drury Lane and Covent Garden, had orders to lift up voices in
praise of King George and make it perfectly clear that he was the
king they had in mind. Only in this way can we account for the
signs of haste in the paean they provided themselves with. They
had no need of a composer, as new words were regularly fitted to
old tunes for theatrical numbers, and they had no need of a poet
either in this particular emergency. There are no certainties concerning it except that it was sung as a duet and published as "A Loyal
Song, Sung at Both Theatres", at a date clearly indicated by its
topical allusions. It began with "God save great George our King",
before continuing in the now familiar strain until the last verse,
which caught a fleeting moment:

> O grant that Marshal Wade
> May by his mighty aid
> > Victory bring.
> May he sedition hush
> And like a torrent rush
> Rebellious Scots to crush.
> > God save the King.

Until 1745 General George Wade had been directing the making of
roads in the Highlands. At the approach of the Clans he was so
speedily relieved of his command that he had a very brief career
as the hope of the United Kingdom. Therefore the belated legend
that our National Anthem was the work of Henry Carey, author of
"Sally in our Alley", is not likely to be true, since he died in 1743.
He might have been asked for it, in which case I can imagine a
stage-manager's panic on hearing, just when the band was ready
to strike up, that Carey had hanged himself. No professional hack,
even of the meanest sort, would have rhymed king with king in
the first and second lines and again in the third and seventh lines,
and few would have dared to match victorious or glorious with over
us, or arise with enemies, or reign with king. Somebody with a
sure sense of the stage and no literary fastidiousness whatsoever
licked a stub of pencil, with these immortal results. There is a rival
claim put forward by Richard Clark in his *Account of the National
Anthem*, published in 1822, on behalf of John Bull, Doctor of
Music, in the reign of James I. Mr Clark, lay-vicar of Westminster
Abbey, announced in 1841 that he had prepared the manuscripts of

Bull for publication, but as the volume did not appear we cannot be sure of Clark's testimony, for antiquarians are an odd lot.

More may be learned from the next attempt to concoct a "Loyal Song" out of materials that lay ready to hand. Both the music and the refrain were taken this time from "Over the hills and far away", which had been sung at Drury Lane frequently in Farquhar's *The Recruiting Officer* to this verse:

> Over the hills and over the main,
> To Flanders, Portugal and Spain;
> The king commands and we'll obey,
> Over the hills and far away

before Gay took it for *The Beggar's Opera* and a nursery rhyme borrowed it. It was now made to serve as a denunciation of rebel clans in search of prey:

> With these a vain Pretender's come,
> And perjur'd traitors, dupes to Rome,
> Determin'd all, without delay,
> To conquer, die, or run away
> O'er the hills and far away

after which it was plain that both theatres had better make do with 'Great George our King' instead. Much of the first version has been retained despite all the many attempts to improve upon it. In 1811 a new opening verse was published, but though partly correct in rhyme it erred in making no religious appeal:

> Fame! let thy trumpet sound;
> Tell all the world around
>   Great George is King.
> Tell Rome and France and Spain
> Britannia scorns their claim
> All their vile arts are vain
>   Great George is King.

Another new verse at the end gets into difficulties with, 'O grant him long to see, Friendship and unity, Always increase', while in America Samuel Smith came forward with 'My country, 'tis of thee . . . Of thee I sing'. When Victoria ascended the throne her loyal subjects gladly went back to 'Send her victorious' throughout her reign, after which Masefield wrote a version with lines like 'Where the ships swing' which could not be sung, and A. A. Milne showed goodwill with:

> And make the income tax
> Optional

than which no line of verse has ever been hailed with greater unanimity. Just to show how very difficult it is to fit any humour to this tune, I must record that schoolboys in my day never managed any parody apart from 'God save our old tom cat, feed him on bread and fat', and there it stopped.

In spite of all temptations we still stick to the version of the 1740s—years also memorable for having left on Victorian song the tender imprint of Jacobite idolatry. "Charlie is m' darling" welcomed the Young Pretender ashore; naturally it was not published till a much later date, when it appeared in the collected works of two authors independently, so proving that neither had invented it. No doubt "Flora MacDonald's Lament" is private:

> She look'd at a boat with the breezes that swung,
> Away on the wave like a bird on the main,
> And aye as it lessen'd, she sigh'd and she sung,
> 'Fare-weel to the lad I maun ne'er see again'

but one more ballad with two authors to claim it may be accepted as the spontaneous outburst of a people:

> Better lo'ed ye canna be,
> Will ye no come back again?

At this time, Jane Elliot, still short of her twentieth birthday, wrote words for a masterpiece of piobaireachd. It was not in Gaelic, the language proper to the pipes, but it was Gaelic at heart:

> I've heard the lilting at our yowe-milking,
> Lassies a-lilting before the dawn of day;
> But now they are moaning on ilka green loaning—
> The Flowers of the Forest are a' wede away.

> At buchts, in the morning, nae blithe lads are scorning,
> The lassies are lonely, and dowie, and wae;
> Nae daffin', nae gabbin', but sighing and sabbing,
> Ilk ane lifts her leglen and hies her away.

In hairst, at the shearing, nae youths now are jeering,
  The bandsters are lyart, and runkled and gray;
At fair, or at preaching, nae wooing, nae fleeching—
  The Flowers of the Forest are a' wede away.

At e'en, at the gloaming, nae swankies are roaming
  'Bout stacks wi' the lassies at bogle to play;
But ilk ane sits drearie, lamenting her dearie—
  The Flowers of the Forest are a' wede away.

Dule and wae for the order sent our lads to the Border!
  The English, for once, by guile wan the day;
The Flowers of the Forest, that foucht aye the foremost,
  The prime o' our land, are cauld in the clay.

We hear nae mair lilting at our yowe-milking,
  Women and bairns are heartless and wae;
Sighing and moaning on ilka green loaning—
  The Flowers of the Forest are a' wede away.

It was so deeply felt as to solemnize national mourning still.
Jane Elliot said that she had Flodden Field in mind but that is
not convincing; what she felt was the sorrow of Culloden and its
butchery, a horror that loyal souls had to accept as victory. Her
lament was full of Jacobite sympathy: that may explain why the
title and refrain were taken by Alicia Rutherford for "I've seen
the smiling of fortune beguiling":

I've seen the forest adorned the foremost,
  Wi' flow'rs o' the fairest, both pleasant and gay;
Sae bonnie was their blooming, their scent the air perfuming,
  But now they are wither'd and a' weed away.

which amounts to blasphemy in lowering sacred to profane. Other
Scotswomen adopted Jacobite sentiments for many years to come
with notable additions to minstrelsy, including this, written and
composed by Mrs Groom:

If I ferry you o'er, if I ferry you o'er,
Will you bring back the laddie we all adore?
There's a gallant band ready with sword in hand,
    To win back his own for him fairly.
Oh! ferry me o'er, ferry me o'er,
I'll bring the bonnie lad hame once more;
Oh! ferry me o'er, ferry me o'er,
    I'll soon return with our Charlie.

You would hardly think a century had elapsed since the Bonnie
Prince had left Scotland for ever; and when critics speak of nineteenth-century Jacobites as mere sentimentalists I think of these
songs and wonder.

Yet in the summer of 1740 the best of all the "Loyal Songs"
in honour of the Hanoverians was written by a Scottish poet aided
and abetted by another Scot:

> When Britain first, at Heaven's command,
>   Arose from out the azure main,
> This was the charter of the land,
>   And guardian angels sung this strain:
>   Rule Britannia, rule the waves;
>   Britons never will be slaves.

The comma that ought to precede Britannia was even then
omitted, but it was the Victorians who turned rule into rules
and will into shall, thus spoiling the dramatic effect it had as
climax to a masque. The idea began in the aspiring brain of David
Mallet, who preferred this surname to the one he was born with,
which was Malloch. He had obtained the post of under-secretary
to Frederick Prince of Wales, after the heir apparent had quarrelled
with George II and set up a Court of his own at Cliveden. In
order to provide entertainment there at a garden fête, Mallet
collaborated with James Thomson, then basking in the fame won by
his poem *The Seasons*, even though this was slightly dimmed by the
record he set up with the most preposterous line ever uttered in
tragedy:

> O, Sophonisba!   Sophonisba, O!

These two poets chose King Alfred to be the hero of their masque
because he, like their royal master, suffered from 'universal defec-
tion', to use their term for the complaint. They exhibited the
Saxon's lonely condition in exile, after his defeat by the Danes,
before the news of victory is brought to his retreat by the Earl of
Devon. You could hardly call this a plot, but it served to introduce
songs by Dr Arne about heroes who never despair but stand
ready to serve their sinking land when heaven calls upon them
to do so. Finally a blind and aged bard is led on to mark the
climax with, 'When Britain first, at Heaven's command, arose from

out the azure main'. There are five more verses which we have
not cherished. As the song is historic here they are:

> The nations not so blest as thee,
>   Must in their turn to tyrants fall;
> While thou shalt flourish, great and free,
>   The dread and envy of them all.
>
> Still more majestic shalt thou rise,
>   More dreadful from each foreign stroke,
> As the loud blast which tears the skies,
>   Serves but to root thy native oak.
>
> Thee haughty tyrants ne'er shall tame:
>   All their attempts to bend thee down
> Will but arouse thy generous flame;
>   But work their woe and thy renown.
>
> To thee belongs the rural reign;
>   Thy cities shall with commerce shine:
> All thine shall be the subject main;
>   And every shore it circles, thine.
>
> The muses, still with freedom found,
>   Shall to thy happy coast repair:
> Blest isle! with matchless beauty crown'd,
>   And manly hearts to guard the fair.
>   Rule Britannia, rule the waves;
>   Britons never will be slaves.

Purcell's "Britons strike home" ends with 'record yourselves in
Druids' songs', which shows how the meaning of 'Briton' had
changed. Anyhow English audiences responded when the masque
was staged at Old Drury. After Thomson's death, Mallet brought
it out under his own name, first as an opera with no change of title,
and then as a musical drama called *Britannia*. Mallet's private
character was typical of those who extol virtue.

III

Sorting Out Subjects

+++

The good old Duke of York,
He had ten thousand men,
He march'd them up to the top of the hill,
And he march'd them down agen.
And when they were up they were up,
And when they were down they were down,
And when they were only half way up
They were neither up nor down.

THERE IS A LOT to be learnt from the familiar jingle. It does,
no matter how often denied, refer to an actual event in military
history.* The good old Duke, brother of the Prince Regent, had
planned to bar the way of the French Revolutionary forces by a
bold manoeuvre that would unite his army with the Austrians.
Their Archduke overslept himself on the day appointed, and as no
under-officer had any right to order the advance, the ten thousand
men mentioned in the song found themselves in insufficient strength
to give battle. The Duke of York marched them down again to
the beat of drums that would sound for over a century in the
favourite song of British infantry, regulars or volunteers. If any
enterprising hack had cared to put his name to it the verse would
have been his for ever, which gives us fair warning how easily this
can happen, but as it was never published throughout its heyday
we know its author to be The Army.

Usually it is the other way round. Ballads marked 'traditional'
may have poet and composer when trouble is taken to find them.
It does take trouble, for no matter how vast the quantities of sheet

---

* Not that it was altogether original. Two hundred years earlier a Pig's Coranto,
or newsletter, contained a verse to say how the King of France with forty thousand
men went up a hill and came down again. Soldiers may have kept singing it in between
whiles: it has the genuine sound of an old Army good-humoured grumble.

music pulped during the paper shortages of two world wars, the lumber rooms and glory holes of old homes can still disgorge cartloads of it—disdained by the mice and rats which devour the stuff it is wrapped in—and most of it is worthless to such an extent that only about one page in a hundred deserves as much as a second glance. It may be rubbish now but during the great plague of pianos, when each instrument hungered insatiably for ballads, baring its keys to clutch at them as though no inferno of notes could appease its open maw, every crotchet and quaver came into force. The day-by-day manufacture of fresh fodder for eager throats amounted to a major industry. But that was not enough; whatever could be found to suit current tastes in the output of previous generations was regularly republished. According to our tastes much of the best was ignored and much of the worst resurrected, but those who sang them were the best judges of that. We must take out for examination whatever was in their cases, and form a notion of what the fuss was all about by trying to hear that enormous concourse of untrained voices as a whole—or whatever the word is that will suit this prodigious social phenomenon.

What we sang became Victorian when we sang it. There was so little difference to our ears between ancient and modern, between old and ye olde, between Annie Laurie* and Mary of Argyle. There is a theory that all popular tunes are variations on "Three Blind Mice", in which case it doesn't seem to matter where any of them come from, but there is another theory that they all descend from the original version, in Arabic or Aramaic, of the chant we know as, "We won't go home till morning", antiquated enough, heaven knows, without any lies of this sort. To reasonable souls like myself latitude is here more important than longitude, meaning that while the tracing of songs back to remote ages leads to no better results than straws in the hair, much can be learnt from spreading them sideways to see how few are the groups they divide themselves into. It may be a clumsy game, since paper is so heavy as to take a lot of lifting after the first hundredweight or so; but since we must understand the Victorians, assortment is necessary in order to discover where they led and where they lagged. At the outset it is plain that the spirit we name after the queen existed before she did. Moral fervour and sentimentality,

* Written by William Douglas of Kirkcudbright before my time. Mary of Argyle is Mid-Victorian.

neat or blended, had been swelling visibly for a long time past, even before they suddenly took effect on song directly the nineteenth century started. How one style went out of fashion as another came in, because of this change, should become clear as soon as the sheets are shuffled. Imagine them spread around you, stack by stack, eyed by your wife in despair as she asks when next the room will be fit for dusting, and as you beg for yet another reprieve, this is how your stooks and sheaves will be labelled:

Lampoons

Take the pile under this label first because it is the smallest. On top is the tune of "We won't go home till morning", as used in France for "Malbrough s'en va-t-en guerre, ne sait quand reviendra" which wishes him a splendid and speedy funeral. In 1781 the nurse of the Dauphin was heard singing it as she rocked the cradle; the court of Versailles took it up, it spread to Paris and throughout France. Whenever Napoleon mounted his horse before battle he hummed it. At St Helena he began it only to stop and murmur, 'What a thing ridicule is! It fastens upon everything, even victory.' What an overworked tune it is. When London journalists had been entertained in Paris, they sang "For he's a jolly good fellow" to their leading host whether he thought the tune was in good taste or not. When another host spoke they sang again; nor could the next be spared the compliment, nor the next nor the next . . . until, hours later, the words imperceptibly changed to "We won't go home till morning". I have never been able to abide 'musical honours' since.

England's classic lampoon is "Lillibullero", which Lord Wharton wrote to Purcell's tune to rouse Protestants against James II; the words, declaring that Ireland shall be ruled by an ass and a dog, have lost their interest, but the music survives as a military quickstep and as one of the catchiest bits of *The Beggar's Opera*. In Victorian England political jingles were regularly addressed on the halls to Gladstone no matter what he did, but with no domestic scandal to commend him to the mob he was outsung by 'Charlie Parnell's naughty shape went scooting down the fire escape' or 'Charlie Dilke upset the milk'. For the ordinary purposes of entertainment the last lampoons were those sung by knockabouts at Christmas to disparage feminine allure in their vicinity. On the hollow pretence of extemporizing the rhymes they would warble a time-honoured tune while inviting young men in the audience to say where their sweethearts came from. Supposing the answer asked for it, this is what would be received:

> I wouldn't have a girl from Birmingham, from Birmingham,
>   from Birmingham,
>   (pause for reflection)
> I've 'eard summat funny concernin' 'em,
> So I wouldn't have a girl from Birmingham.

Personal lampoons, banned from the stage ever since Gladstone objected to Gilbert's *The Happy Land* at the Court Theatre in 1873, flourish in such places as Broadcasting House privately, on the subject of directors-general.

Weather Reports

As you would expect, the first profane song to be sung in England was about the weather. "Summer is icumen in" was made suitable for Mid-Victorian song-and-supper rooms by changing icumen into acoming. Shakespeare put in his word whenever *Twelfth Night* was acted with "The rain it raineth every day". Then there was a Regency song by Jacob Cole which ran:

> What daily complaints of the weather are told,
>   'Tis too wet or too dry or too hot or too cold.
> The sot sits all day with his mug to his nose,
>   Then complains that the weather is muggy and close.

Nothing else was said of the subject until, "It ain't gonna rain no mo' " in the 1920s. The inference is that in between whiles respectable people considered the English climate no fit matter for jest. And we are rapidly coming to agree with them.

Drinking (and eating)

Since "I cannot eate but lytyll meate" and "The Leather Bottel" got printed, each generation added to our stock of drinking songs. Their numbers swelled, until all Englishmen seemed to be raising their voices in praise of wine, beer, or spirits under the leadership of George III's roystering sons. Their catches and glees are all lively, but in bulk a little monotonous. Still it is amusing to watch how a snatch in the Jacobean tragedy of *The Bloody Brother; or, Rollo, Duke of Normandy:*

> Then let us swill, boys, for our health,
> Who drinks well loves the commonwealth,
> And he that will to bed go sober,
> Falls with the leaf, still in October

grows into the glee which was sung a hundred years later:

> He who goes to bed and goes to bed sober
> Falls as the leaves do and dies in October;
> But he who goes to bed and goes to bed mellow,
> Lives as he ought to do and dies an honest fellow

and then into a verse of "Come, landlord, fill the flowing bowl", after another interval of a hundred years:

> The man who drinketh small beer,
>   And goes to bed quite sober,
> Fades as the leaves do fade
>   That drop off in October;
> But he who drinketh strong beer
>   And goes to bed quite mellow,
> Lives as he ought to live
>   And dies a jolly good fellow.

Following the whirlwind of drinking songs which subsided in 1800, there was prolonged attention to other topics such as love. Half way through the nineteenth century temperance had a brisk innings, to which Champagne Charlie replied along with Tommy Dodd, Burgundy Ben, and the Rollicking Rams, very much after the fashion of the late eighteenth century though in the social scale a good octave lower; this also applies to R. A. Eastburn's "Little Brown Jug", the only one of the lot to be beloved by children, who took kindly to the idea of:

> If I'd a cow that gave such milk
> I'd clothe her in the finest silk

and they chirruped it at their parties with results apparent to social reformers.

Food songs, known to the eighteenth and twentieth centuries, were little to the taste of the nineteenth. True, Herbert Campbell sang, "They call me a poor little stowaway" in the 1880s but that is a tale of gluttony with no relish for the quality of vast quantities consumed.

Hunting

With "Old Towler" and "A-hunting we will go" at the head of its long list, the eighteenth century is the richest in hunting songs, though their bane is monotony. Early Victorian efforts suffered from the influence of Shakespeare's "What shall he have that killed the deer?", with the consequence that most of the hunting done at the piano usually employed bow and arrow. The note of actuality was restored by Whyte-Melville, who paid for his pleasure in the chase with his life. Then came the masterpiece, John Woodcock Graves's "D'ye ken John Peel?", often accepted as an antique until his countryside celebrated the centenary of his death in 1954. These verses scribbled to an old tune, over a drink after the funeral of a friend, many miles from any dealer in music, have won an affection so great that no poet has ever surpassed it.

Old chairs, clocks, bells, and oaks

When the bottle found no more favour with composers during its spell of disfavour between 1800 and 1850, all the praise formerly lavished upon it had to find an outlet elsewhere. That is why, since I can find no other reason, a passionate adoration was suddenly felt for any number of chairs. We can all sing Eliza Cook's outburst, 'I love it, I love it, and who shall dare to chide me for loving that old arm chair?', to which there was no answer, because a referendum would have shown a whole electorate in favour. If it were not grandmother's chair it was grandfather's clock or a clock in a steeple. There was thus a link with bells—evening bells or bells in our birthplace. Anyone who argues that this list could be extended indefinitely should be challenged to find one vocal table to set beside all those vocal chairs; and why should all those lovers who simper over mills that never sheltered them ignore the barns that always served for courtship, rain or fine? Streams naturally go with mills, and also with the valleys so persistently loved in song. There is no counting the ballads that have titles of the "Sweet Emma of the Vale" order.

Spinning-wheels come into the list—fortunately, for they remind me of an inn, midway between Stratford-on-Avon and the Tweed, where a hostess used to introduce us to Ann Hathaway's wheel with the words, 'Very sad, that affair of hers with Bobbie Burns'. Trees are more puzzling still, for the plane with all its rhymes has been overlooked while worship is bestowed upon the old oak, though this last item made its first appeal for public favour as "The Sapling Oak", composed by Stephen Storace,* who died at the age of thirty-three in 1796. He was as gifted as his sister, Anna Selina Storace. That is worth mentioning before I add that "The Sapling Oak" belongs to James Cobb's *The Siege of Belgrade*, a favourite piece at Drury Lane and the Lyceum long after the composer's death:

> The sapling oak lost in the dell,
> Where tangled brakes its beauties spoil,
> And ev'ry infant shoot repel
> Droops o'er the exhausted soil.
> At length the woodman clears around
> Where e'er the noxious thickets spread,
> And high reviving o'er the ground,
> The forest's monarch lifts his head

which serves to show that woodmen are not all villains, but this one would have been if 'noxious thickets' had included the semi-sacred ivy, revered in 'Be our love like the ivy' and other ballads like it.

Birds and Flowers

That the rose and the nightingale move us to melancholy is mostly due to the habit of lifting up our voices in song. Without this we might not imagine that the one blossoms merely to fade and the other leans its breast against a thorn. Historians who tell

---

* Storace is best remembered for "With humble suit and plaintive ditty", a tune he took from a Neapolitan beggar. It was still to be heard some thirty years ago in amateur revivals of his *No Song No Supper*, an operatic trifle written by Prince Hoare.

how Philomela was raped by her brother-in-law, and how her sister Procne caused him, in revenge, to feast on the flesh of his own son, declare the metamorphoses of Philomela into a nightingale and Procne into a swallow to be the embellishment of poets. It was a skylark which prompted Shelley to 'Our sweetest songs are those that tell of saddest thought', and the same thought occurred to the music-hall bard who wrote, "Like a bird with a broken wing".

Dirges

Since Shakespeare's clown sings, "Come away, come away, Death," in the midst of comedy, the dirge is plainly a normal method of giving pleasure. Victorians agreed with this sentiment. While carefully refraining from calling them an unctuous crew of morbid sentimentalists, I must for the sake of accuracy define the philosophy of their songs as a belief that life was a good excuse for dying, since many recommend death so unreservedly as to stop not far short of incitement to suicide. In a more robust style infant voices of the twentieth century shared the same outlook in the popular ballad, expressing the satisfaction of a corpse in a coffin during a good funeral, "Ain't it grand to be bloomin' well dead?"

Finality-Mongering

'Goodbye for ever', and similar utterances, have such a very Victorian sound that any previous *cri du coeur* to the same effect must be noted. There was a sample of much earlier date, with a Miss Abrams named as composer, which ran:

> And must we part for evermore?
> Hard fate such friends to sever,
> So faithful so true.
> Go and may bliss betide thee,
> Each guardian angel guide thee,
> For evermore adieu.

Byron's request to the Maid of Athens, 'ere we part, give, oh give me back my heart', was set to music, but for the lack of any reference to evermore it hardly counts. Kathleen Mavourneen was told in 1834 that it might be for years or it might be for ever with a disqualifying doubt. Miss Abrams alone saves Tosti and his contemporaries from the blame of having invented it.

Grief

Far from attempting a survey of all the world's sorrow as it has expressed itself in rhyme, I wish solely to indicate one of the earliest songs that served the Victorians for a model. This is "Auld Robin Gray":

> My faither could na work, my mither could na spin;
> I toil'd day and night but their bread I could na win;
> Auld Robin maintain'd them baith, and with tears in his e'e,
> Said, 'Jenny, for their sakes will you marry me?'
> My heart it said na, for I look'd for Jamie back;
> But the wind it blew high, and the ship it was a wrack;
> The ship it was a wrack—why didna Jenny dee?
> Oh, why do I live to say, 'wae's me?'

This appeared anonymously in 1771. Lady Anne, daughter of James Lindsay, Earl of Balcarres, married Sir Andrew Barnard in 1793. He died in 1807. She told Scott in 1823 that she wrote that famous ballad.

Swagger Songs

Already it is plain that what may not be said may often be sung. The point is thrust home by the ballads that enable bass or baritone to fling his weight about. Boastfulness, mocked in life or on the stage, became admired in these orgies of ultra-masculinity. There is a classical fragment about a *hybrias*, or braggart, which Thomas Campbell, the most respectable and law-abiding of poets, translated as "The Song of Hybrias the Cretan":

> My wealth's a burly spear and brand,
> And a right good shield of hides untann'd
>   Which on mine arm I buckle.
> With these I plough, I reap, I sow,
> With these I make the sweet vintage flow,
>   And all around me truckle!

c

But your wights that take no pride to wield
A massy spear and well-made shield,
    Nor joy to draw the sword:
Oh! I bring those heartless, hapless drones,
Down in a trice on their marrow bones,
    To call me king and lord.

In a setting by Colborn this had a great vogue not only among those who bellowed but those who were bellowed at.

Travellers and Hermits

While enjoying a light-hearted fling at solitude, Dr Johnson wrote one of the best songs in the language. Boswell put it into print and William Kitchener, M.D., set it to music in a manner worthy of Handel:

Hermit hoar in solemn cell,
    Wearing out life's evening grey,
Smite thy bosom, sage, and tell,
    Which is life and which the way, which the way?
Thus I spoke, and speaking sigh'd,
    Scarce repress'd the starting tear,
When the hoary sage replied,
    Come, my lad, and drink some beer.
Come, co-o-o-o-me, co-o-o-o-ome, and drink some beer.
    Drink some beer.

Long after that had ceased to be sung, travellers and hermits, gypsies and monks, either separately or in pairs, joined the stock characters of song. Reeve's "Friar of Orders Grey":

What baron or squire, or knight of the shire
Lives half so well as a holy friar?

was one of many who adopted the outlook of Dr Johnson's hoary sage; it was the traveller who represented abstinence. In the end Longfellow's "Excelsior" made such a thorough job of it that the subject became his copyright, since nobody dare tackle it afresh.

Nostalgia

Homesickness and regrets for days that are no more now seem typical of Victorian England. In origin they are Irish or Scottish or both, unless "By the waters of Babylon" is, not unreasonably, brought into the quest. That there is some strain of musical affinity between the Irish and the Scottish is suggested by the number of tunes claimed by both, and these tend to be nostalgic. "Limerick's Lamentation" has the same tune as that of an old ballad which was adapted by Allan Ramsay—father of Allan Ramsay, the painter—to his poem, "Lochaber no more", in 1728. The very name is full of yearning. No other can be substituted for it, so that an exile says, "Lochaber no more", no matter where his lost home may be. Yet Ramsay's lover ends his supposed lament with, 'And then I'll leave thee and Lochaber no more', which is out of keeping with the tradition he founded; as the verses move us less than the refrain of three words the part is greater than the whole:

> Farewell to Lochaber and farewell my Jean,
> Where heartsome with thee I have mony day been,
> For Lochaber no more, Lochaber no more,
> We'll may be return to Lochaber no more.
> These tears that I shed they are a for my dear,
> And no for ye dangers attending on weir,
> Tho' bore on rough seas to a far bloody shore
> May be to return to Lochaber no more.
>
> Tho' hurricanes rise, and rise ev'ry wind,
> They'll ne'er make a tempest like that in my mind,
> Tho' loudest of thunder on louder waves roar,
> That's nothing like leaving my love on ye shore;
> To leave thee behind me my heart is fair pain'd,
> By ease that's inglorious no fame can be gain'd,
> And beauty and love's ye reward of ye brave,
> And I must deserve it before I can crave.
>
> Then glory my Jeany maun plead my excuse,
> Since honour commands me how can I refuse,
> Without it I ne'er can have merit for thee,
> And without thy favour I'd better not be;
> I gae then my lass to win honour and fame,
> And if that I should luck to come gloriously hame,
> I'll bring a heart to thee with love running o'er,
> And then I'll leave thee and Locherer no more.

"A Scot's Musical Entertainment" composed by Allan Ramsay was given at the Little Theatre in the Haymarket at this time with several favourite songs sung by a Mr Lauder wearing the kilt.

Morals and Maniacs

With all due respect to the unco' guid, I find it impracticable to separate the songs with a moral purpose from those which show relish for insanity. When "The Gambler's Wife" and "The Drunkard's Child" are compared with "The maniac", they all leave the impression that some baritone is having a good time (as Sir Henry Wood used to say) regardless. To startle, horrify, or terrorize the audience, with or without excuse, was the height of the Victorian baritone's ambition. And since people did not walk out on him, we must conclude that to be startled, horrified, and terrorized was the height of the audience's ambition. There was nothing new in this. All our forebears took madness to be a normal means of entertainment, as you can tell from their visits to lunatic asylums in the course of ordinary sight-seeing. Where Shakespeare left off in *King Lear* poets of succeeding generations began assiduously to pile on the agony. Here is "Mad Tom", composed by Purcell to please the wits of the Restoration, which may be usefully compared to labours of a similar kind two centuries later:

> Forth from my dark and dismal cell,
> Or from the dark abyss of Hell,
> Mad Tom is come to view the world again,
> To see if he can cure his distempered brain.
> Fears and cares oppress my soul,
> Hark how the angry furies howl,
> Pluto laughs, and Proserpine is glad,
> To see poor angry Tom of Bedlam mad.
>
> Thro' the world I wander night and day
>   To find my strangling senses,
> In an angry mood I met Old Time
>   With his Pentateuch of tenses,
> When me he spies away he flies,
> For time will stay for no man;
> In vain with cries I rend the skies,
> For pity is not common.

Cold and comfortless I be, help, help, O help or else I die.
        Hark! I hear Apollo's team,
          The Carman 'gins to whistle,
        Chaste Diana bends her bow,
          And the boar begins to bristle.
        Come Vulcan with tools and tackles
        To knock off my troublesome shackles,
        Bid Charles make ready his wain
        To bring me my senses again.
        In my triumphant chariot hurl'd
        I range around, I range around the world.
'Tis I, 'tis I, 'tis I, Mad Tom, drive all, all, all, all before me,
While I to my royal throne I come, bow down, down, down, bow down,
      down, down, down, down, bow down my slaves and adore me,
        Your sov'reign lord, Mad Tom
And tho' I give law from beds of straw and drest in a tatter'd robe
The mad can be more a monarch than he that commands the vassal globe.

Content

Since the singer likes to play upon people's feelings, not many poems in praise of content have been set to music. One of the first successes in this category was "The Miller of the Dee". Another was scored by "The Splendid Shilling", the work of James Hook, composer to Vauxhall Gardens at the beginning of the nineteenth century, who is remembered now for his tune to "The Lass of Richmond Hill", a poem of disputed authorship. He usually looked for words to his son Theodore, who owes his fame less to versification than to practical joking and to his willing response, when asked whether he subscribed to the Thirty-nine Articles, 'Make it forty'. Another reason for remembering James Hook is in the last line of his "Within a mile of Edinboro' Town", which gives us a verb peculiar to infancy when Jenny says she canna, canna, winna, winna, mauna, 'buckle to'. To get back to the business in hand here is "The Splendid Shilling" according to the song:

      O how happy is the man
        Has health and can command a shilling,
    A friend, a sweetheart and a can,
      A book and house to dwell in.

With him the day is light and gay,
    The night is never dreary,
With friend and lass, with book and glass,
    He's happy, snug and cheery.

'Happy the man who . . . in silken or in leathern purse retains a splendid shilling' is what John Philips wrote in the time of the Restoration.

Emigration

Here is a category that Victorians made entirely their own. Eagerness to emigrate, reluctance to emigrate, compulsion to emigrate, and regrets at having emigrated, were continually poured out by them in song. The range is wide. There is the Cockney lament for a deported sweetheart with the refrain, 'All round my hat I vears a green viller' (which recalls Desdemona's 'Sing all a green willow'). There is bull-dozing, "Cheer, boys, cheer". The American song,* now labelled Irish, of emigrants about to return: "I'll take you home again, Kathleen", was by Thomas F. Westendorf. It was said to have been inspired by the grief, known to him in reality, of a wife suffering from an incurable illness:

I'll take you home again, Kathleen,
    Across the ocean wild and wide,
To where your heart has ever been,
    Since first you were my bonny bride.
The roses all have left your cheek,
    I've watched them fade away and die;
Your voice is sad whene'er you speak,
    And tears bedim your loving eye.
Oh! I will take you back, Kathleen,
    To where your heart will feel no pain;
And when the fields are fresh and green,
    I'll take you to your home again.

Negro Minstrels

At the outset of his career Charles Dibdin played a comic negro at Drury Lane in 1768. Twenty years later he wrote a coon song:

---

* Victoria's American cousins are, whether they would have liked it or not, considered throughout these pages as Victorians, which they were in their feelings —only more so.

> One negro, wi my banjer,
> Me from Jenny come,
> Wid cunning yiei
> Me savez spy,
> De buckra world one hum,
> As troo a street a stranger
> Me my banjer strum.

The first song of the kind to leave its mark on our history was "Jump Jim Crow", originally the chant of a negro porter on a quayside of the Ohio, who would put down his load at intervals in order to kick up his heels and sing:

> Wheel about, and turn about,
> And do just so;
> Ebry time I wheel about,
> I jump Jim Crow.

This struck the fancy of T. D. Rice on landing from a river steamer to keep a date at the Louisville theatre. In exchange for a tip he borrowed the porter's shapeless cap and old tail-coat, dressed himself in them, appeared on the stage blacked-up, and scored a hit there and everywhere else all up and down the Eastern States. Other comedians imitated him. Leaving this highly profitable business behind him for rivals to exploit, he crossed the Atlantic to craze Europe. In 1836 he appeared at the Adelphi in *A Flight to America; or, Twelve Hours in New York*. The up-to-date version of his song, 'arranged with appropriate symphonies and accompaniments' by Jonas Blewitt, reveals how it had become one of those topical numbers which were always in demand. Some verses dealt with, 'Jim Crow's Peep at the Balloon':

> If I have speechy wid de moon,
> She ax of tings dere price
> I hab an answer cut and dry,
> Dar's rising in de Rice.

Paris also went wild about him and the porter's poem had to be translated:

> Je tourne, re-tourne, je caracole,
> Je fais des sauts;
> Chaque fois je fais le tour,
> Je saute 'Jim Crow'.

The mania passed, his wife and children died, he ended in poverty; but nobody forgot his song.

Comic Songs

Wit is one thing, we are always being told, and humour another. Both can be distinguished in old songs that could not be properly called comic. What calls for this label is neither the thoughtful laughter of the one nor the broader animal spirits of the other but an insistence on jokes. In this sense it began in clown's ditties like those of Grimaldi. What he made of "Tipitywitchet" with its hiccup, sneeze, yawn, cry, and laugh, may be guessed. The word mag, derived from magpie, means chatter:

This very morning handy,
    My malady was such,
I in my tea took brandy,
    And took a drop too much.
        (Hiccups) Tol de rol.

But stop! I mustn't mag hard,
    My head aches, if you please,
One pinch of Irish blackguard,
    I'll take to give me ease.
        (Sneezes) Tol de rol.

Now I'm quite drowsy growing,
    For this very morn,
I rose while cock was crowing,
    Excuse me if I yawn.
        (Yawns) Tol de rol.

I'm not in cue for frolic,
    Can't up my spirits keep,
Love's a windy cholic,
    'Tis that makes me weep.
        (Cries) Tol de rol.

I'm not in mood for crying,
    Care's a silly calf;
If to get fat you're trying,
    The only way's to laugh.
        (Laughs) Tol de rol.

This was a pantomime song. As such it links itself with patriotic ballads in prodigious numbers, topical duets to suit every year or every week of the winter holidays in every year, a series of simple ditties about food, a spell of choruses intended for tongue-twisters, a lot of solemnity to serve the turn of the *basso profundo*, and some nauseating sentimentality to be incongruously expressed by a fairy queen because she is a soprano. Yet the most renowned of all pantomime songs, repeatedly called for by early Victorian 'gods', was none of these. There is no ignoring it. "Hot Codlins", meaning roasted apples, was originally the peculiar property of Joseph Grimaldi. The gallery got into so regular a habit of demanding it that they went on demanding it for thirty years after his death. *Mother Goose*, at Covent Garden in 1806, included its first performance, and ever since Archie Harradine revived it in *Late Joys* underneath the Arches at Charing Cross, it is doubtful whether we have heard the last of it yet. It runs:

> A little old woman her living she got
> By selling hot codlins, hot! hot! hot!
> And this little old woman who codlins sold,
> Though her codlins were hot, she felt herself cold;
> So to keep herself warm she thought it no sin,
> To fetch for herself a quartern of ——
> > Ri tol, etc.

> This little old woman set off in a trot,
> To fetch her a quartern of hot! hot! hot!
> She swallowed one glass and it was so nice,
> She tipp'd off another in a trice;
> The glass she fill'd till the bottle shrunk,
> And this little old woman they say got ——
> > Ri tol, etc.

> This little old woman, while muzzy she got,
> Some boys stole her codlins, hot! hot! hot!
> Powder under her pan put, and in it round stones;
> Says the little old woman, 'These apples have bones!'
> The powder the pan in her face did send,
> Which sent the old woman on her latter ——
> > Ri tol, etc.

The little old woman then up she got,
All in a fury hot! hot! hot!
Says she, 'Such boys, sure, never were known,
They never will let an old woman alone'.
Now here is a moral, round let it buzz,
If you mean to sell codlins, never get ——
                                Ri tol, etc.

Whatever may be thought of this celebrated relic now, it reads riotously amid the *Casket of Comic Songs* which reprinted it while barring every other thing that might not prove 'a source of instructive and innocent recreation' to the family circle. This was a time when pantomime authors experimented with the new idea of using children's tales as plots. While *Cinderella* was furbished up with Dandini from Rossini's opera, *Robinson Crusoe* was derived not from Defoe but from a preposterous French melodrama, with an over-populated isle and a villain named Will Alkins who has remained naturalized into Will Atkins. When an operetta in Paris had a heroine called Red Riding Hood who was pursued by an aristocrat, he was imported as a Christmas luxury, so that instead of a King Wolf with fangs we have had a biped with rapier ever since; but wicked as he is he cannot refrain, in the forest glade, from singing "Rock'd in the cradle of the deep", which is more devout than many a hymn.

Loving and Jilting

About love the less said the better, since there is too much to be said, but that is not true of love songs. About most of them there is nothing to be said, partly because poets make the worst lovers and partly because composers can rarely recognize a love poem when they see one. One or more centuries are usually required for the right words in this category to find the right tune. "My Sweet Sweeting", which Henry VIII wrote in the sixteenth century, found favour with choral societies when Fraser-Simson, at the outset of a career which led to *The Maid of the Mountains*, chose it for a glee in the last year of the nineteenth. More inspiration seems to have been derived from being jilted.*

* American songs incline to let the maid be jilted as in "I'd leave ma happy home for you, oo, oo, oo, oo." Her English equivalent says, "I wouldn't leave ma little wooden hut for you, oo, oo."

The hardiest of all, "Lady Greensleeves", points to this:

> Alas, my love, ye do me wrong,
>   To cast me off discourteously

which for length of life finds its closest rival in

> Oh, do not leave me, oh don't deceive me,
>   Why should you treat a poor maiden so?

To offset these there is a trifle, nearly as old, that distils the wisdom of the heart. It is quoted in Marlowe's *The Jew of Malta:*

> Love me little, love me long,
> Is the burden of my song,
> Love that is too hot and strong
>   Burneth soon to waste.
> Still I would not have thee cold,
> Nor too backward, nor too bold;
> Love that lasteth till 'tis old,
>   Fadeth not in haste.
>
> Winter's cold or summer's heat,
> Autumn's tempest on it beat,
> It can never know defeat,
>   Never can rebel.
> Such the love that I would gain,
> Such love, I tell thee plain,
> Thou must give, or woo in vain,
>   So, to thee farewell.

In all good faith I began to copy this as the declaration of a lover, only to discover, in the last line, yet another jilt.

What with his pugging tooth, greasy Joan, and man's ingratitude, Shakespeare set his mind on too many things to write amorously except to his patrons, and for a long time the best composers in the land, Purcell and Arne, paid tribute to his daisies pied, yellow sands, and winter winds. Schubert gave us the music for, "Hark! Hark! The lark at heaven's gate sings"—slightly inclined to love since it tells my lady sweet it is time to get up—whereupon Bishop rivalled it with another of Shakespeare's larks, from "Venus and Adonis", where you would not expect to find a lyric:

> Lo! here the gentle lark, weary of rest,
> From his moist cabinet mounts up on high,
> And wakes the morning. . .

This found a rival in 1897 when H. G. Pélissier, the young though bulky leader of a pierrot troupe, published his lovely setting to lines hidden (page 320) in the indigestible folio of Davenant's *Works*, 1673:

> The Lark now leaves his wat'ry Nest
> And climbing, shakes his dewy Wings;
> He takes this Window for the East;
> And to implore your Light, he Sings,
> Awake, awake, the Morn will never rise,
> Till she can dress her Beauty at your Eies.

It is the singing of these three larks which gives force to Davenant's account of his begetting. His mother was the landlady of an inn at Oxford where Shakespeare used to spend a night on his ride from London to Stratford-on-Avon. Without any regard for the reputation of the good lady, her son boasted that he wrote with the pen of Shakespeare, and while listening to "Awake" I incline to believe him.

The best way to start a row almost anywhere is to state the plain fact that when it came to love songs Shakespeare was never a match for Ben Jonson. People who are a little weary of "Drink to me only with thine eyes" overlook:

> O so white! O so soft! O so sweet is she!

and the subtle affrontery of "Still to be neat":

> Lady, it is to be presumed,
> Though art's hid causes are not found,
> All is not sweet, all is not sound.

Even so, the best of glorious Ben's amorous verses are so very good that it will take musicians another century to discover them. Jacobean poets gave us love in such variety that their lines have been set and reset continually. Jonson's apt pupil, Herrick, an old goat in his prying ogles and snuffles, is exhibited as the soul of delicacy in the tender treatment of the Victorians. "To Anthea" was demurely set by J. L. Hatton in Prince Albert's day, and Charles Edward Horn won their hearts not exactly with "Cherry ripe, ripe, ripe, I cry" but the slightly altered refrain which Madame Vestris sang:

> Cherry ripe, cherry ripe, ripe I cry,
> Full and fair ones, come and buy.
> If so be you ask me where
> They do grow, I answer, 'There
> 'Where my Julia's lips do smile,
> 'There's the land of cherry isle'

so that nobody can read it now without in fancy singing it* as the composer rewrote it to suit his tune. With "Gather ye rosebuds while ye may", set by Henry J. Lautz with English and German words, it is the same. All the royalists warble. Sir Charles Sedley's

> Phillis is my only joy,
>   Faithless as the winds or seas,
> Sometimes forward, sometimes coy,
>   Yet she never fails to please

got its setting from John W. Hobbs, and a dozen others are so happily wed that the maiden names of their tunes, so to speak, are never mentioned. George Wither, a poet who lived from 1588 to 1667, and entangled himself hopelessly in the Civil War by fighting on both sides, included in *Fair Virtue, the Mistress of Philarete,* a song with the refrain:

> If she be not so to me
> What care I how fair she be?

Raleigh is credited with, 'If she undervalue me what care I how fair she be?' but neither wrote, 'If she be not fair to me what care I how fair she be?'

Whether "There is a lady sweet and kind" is earlier than the seventeenth century starts an argument with no satisfactory ending. One version I have found is a glee for four voices in *The Harmonist,* volume VIII, c. 1800, where the composer is given as Ford, who published it along with "Since first I saw your face I resolved to honour and renown you" and other madrigals in *Musicke of Sundrie Kinds,* 1607. The text in *The Harmonist* has a word or two other than those we know:

---

* In common with many of the best lyrics it seems to have been stolen. Compare Thomas Campion's "There is a garden in her face":
> There cherries grow which none may buy
> Till 'cherry ripe' themselves do cry.

There is a Lady sweet and kind
Was never face so pleas'd my mind
I did but see her passing by
And yet I love her 'till I die,
Her gesture, motion and her smiles
Her wit her voice my heart beguiles,
Beguiles my heart I know not why
And yet I love her 'till I die.
Cupid is winged and doth range,
Her country so my love doth change
But change she earth or change she sky
Yet will I love her 'till I die.

There is no truth in the widespread belief that the poem is Herrick's and the tune Purcell's. (Incidentally Purcell has always been a name of joy to me ever since a bright young shop-assistant corrected me with, 'Is it Purchell you mean?')

Bawdry

Rather than bowdlerize I omit obscenity. My respect for the authentic is shocked by texts of "She was poor but she was honest" which would have their readers believe they are enjoying the worst. The original, which possessed literary merit as a burlesque of poetic solemnity, is unprintable. My memories of it belong to the Grey Brigade of London volunteers after the South African War, memories which helped me to enjoy an inspired spy story of a thousand secret Germans disguised as a British regimental reunion who gave themselves away: when they sang they *sang*.

IV

Rationing the Sea

Should thunder on the horizon press,
Mocking our signals of distress,
E'en then dull melancholy
Dares not intrude: he braves the din
In hopes to find a calm within
The snowy arms of Polly.

Charles Dibdin

WHILE SHUFFLING SHOALS of old sea songs, bestowed upon us by
Neptune's sons with a prodigality as reckless as the spawning of
herrings, I am impressed by the fairness of the British public in
giving a chance to as many salt-water composers as possible. You
might expect big whales to be nourished at the expense of small fry.
Not a bit of it. Popularity has been shared out so evenly that one
famous sea song is allowed per head. Charles Dibdin's work as a
whole was cherished long, but if I am right in my guess that
today he is represented on the active list by "Tom Bowling" alone,
then it is plain that the system of rationing does exist and is still
valid in some queer way.

Shakespeare has his sea song, "The master, the swabber, the
boatswain and I", about Kate who preferred a tailor; and Congreve
has his, "A soldier and a sailor, a tinker and a tailor", about Joan
who gives the sailor his revenge. As Purcell wrote the music for
the one in 1690 and John Eccles the music for the latter in 1693,
we might regard this as an example of the 'reply', that happy
exchange of ideas among poets and composers. But the oldest sea
song on Victorian pianos was Martin Parker's sixteenth-century
"You gentlemen of England", adapted by Dr John Callcott, author
of *A Musical Grammar*, who died insane in 1821 after adding to
our gaiety with catches and glees. The chorus remains whatever
happens to the rest:

47

> You gentlemen of England
>   That live at home at ease,
> Ah little do you think upon
>   The dangers of the seas.
> Give ear unto the mariners
>   And they will plainly show
> All the cares and fears
>   When the stormy winds do blow.

When the stormy winds do blow, when the stormy winds do blow,
When the stormy winds do blow, when the stormy winds do blow.

Chorus:
When the stormy winds do blow, when the stormy winds do blow,
When the stormy winds do blow, when the stormy winds do blow.

Both Drury Lane and Covent Garden memorized the refrain with
wild applause, and we have been grateful ever since for its holiday
from mental effort. For a long time Dr Callcott had a second
string to his bow in "To all you ladies now on land, we men at sea
indite", written by Charles Sackville, Earl of Dorset, on the eve
of the battle in 1665 when Opdam, the Dutch admiral, was blown
up with all his crew—witnessed by the poet as he thought of:

> Let's hear of no inconstancy,
> We have enough of that at sea.

While the words live on we forget the tune along with Callcott's
setting for Campbell's "Friend of the brave", concerning how the
heart its trembling homage yields on stormy floods and carnage
cover'd fields. Campbell's quota is, "Ye mariners of England"
which stole the stormy winds that blow for its refrain. John
Gay has a proud place in the record with Richard Leveridge,
a composer of quality. In 1720 they invented the sentimental Jolly
Jack Tar in "Sweet William's Farewell to Black Ey'd Susan",
where he is matched by a heroine who waves a lily-white hand:

> All in the Downs the Fleet was moor'd,
>   The streamers waving in the wind,
> When Black Ey'd Susan came aboard,
>   'Oh, where shall I my true love find?
> 'Tell me, ye jovial sailors, tell me true,
> 'Does my sweet William sail among your crew?'

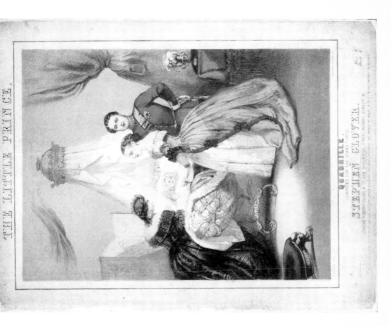

The Throne and its defenders

Be sure the hand most daring there
Has wiped away a tear

Another of the eight verses alludes to a legend not then in its final form:

> Believe not what the landsmen say
>   Who tempt to doubt thy constant mind;
> They'll tell thee sailors, when away,
>   In ev'ry port a mistress find:
> Yes, yes, believe them, when they tell thee so,
> For thou art present wheresoe'er I go.

It was Dibdin who changed this reference from 'mistress' to 'wife in every port'. But we cannot come to his turn yet awhile for the sea was the English singer's glory when he was still a child. It was in 1760 that *The Universal Magazine* published the warlike zest of an actor:

> Come, cheer up, my lads! 'tis to glory we steer,
> To add something more to this wonderful year;
> To honour we call you, not press you like slaves,
> For who are as free as the sons of the waves?
>> Heart of oak are our ships,
>> Heart of oak are our men:
>>> We always are ready,
>>> Steady, boys, steady,
> We'll fight and we'll conquer again and again.

If it is surprising to learn that David Garrick wrote this, it is just as typical of the times that the composer should be Dr William Boyce, an authority on cathedral music to which he contributed anthems of his own, notably "By the waters of Babylon". None but antiquarians hum his amorous numbers, which are kept secret like the indiscretions of an ecclesiastic, though his "The Fair for Ever" deserves to be sung. Anyhow, these two worthies started the vogue of the o-come-all-ye's (whose influence Macaulay did not escape by writing attend-all-ye instead). All trades lent a hand at making verbal and musical imitations of storms; even seafarers were represented. William Falconer had served as second mate on trading vessels and suffered shipwreck before he wrote, "Fierce and more fierce the tempest grew", a poem of some length which was sung in full. It was heartily welcomed, though the *Nautical Dictionary* which he compiled might have come in useful:

D

> Now some to strike top-gallant-yards attend,
> Some travellers up the weather-back stays send,
> At each mast-head the top-ropes others bend:
> The parrels, lifts and clue lines soon are gone,
> Topp'd and unrigg'd, they down the backstays run;
> The yards secure along the booms were laid,
> And all the flying ropes aloft belay'd.

By the time Falconer had gone to sea again in 1769, never to return, the Jolly Jack Tar and his songs provided the British public with its favourite entertainment. Only an expert knows what victories were then celebrated, for the next naval event to leave a permanent mark was the inglorious capsizing of the *Royal George* off Spithead in 1782, as described in Cowper's "Toll for the brave, the brave that are no more", which added to the misery of music lessons at school from generation to generation.

In an atmosphere thick with such imaginary spume and spray, sensed at second-hand, Charles Dibdin revealed his unfailing gift of melody in operettas so easily that in 1773, when he was aged twenty-five, these numbered nine. The next year the Haymarket presented his most lasting success, *The Waterman*, with its fresh-water classic:

> Then farewell my trimbuilt wherry,
>   Oars and coat and badge farewell,
> Nevermore at Chelsea ferry
>   Shall your Thomas take a spell.

as first favourite with a close runner-up:

> And did you not hear of a jolly young waterman
>   Who at Blackfriars Bridge us'd for to ply,
> And who feather'd his oars with such skill and dexterity,
>   Winning each heart and delighting each eye.

though the gardener in the story held his own with horticultural numbers such as

> Cherries and plums are never found
>   But on the plum and cherry tree;
> Parsnips are long, turnips are round,
>   So Wilhelmina's made for me.

Tinkers, grinders, gypsies, shepherds, huntsmen, hop-pickers, and dozens of other earthbound clods tuned Dibdin's merry note till the death of his brother Tom, a sailor, moved him to write, "Poor Tom, a Sailor's Epitaph", the sheer hulk of whose form was of the manliest beauty:

> For though his body's under hatches,
> His soul is gone aloft.

From then on critics awarded no more praise for his happy knack of making you smell the hay and feel the mud and bask in the sun ashore. Admiration was reserved for his portraits of the sailor in his courage, generosity, simplicity of heart, unworldliness, warmth of affection, love of present enjoyment, and thoughtlessness of tomorrow. All seafarers, from Admiral of the Fleet to the cabin boy of a merchantman, acknowledged its truth. For his services in encouraging recruits he was awarded a government pension but the task of extolling fecklessness came naturally—he was idealizing the temperament possessed by himself without ever spending more than a day or two at sea. The main difference was that whereas his own infidelities were notorious, his Tars were chaste:

> The moon on the ocean was dimm'd by a ripple,
> Affording a chequer'd delight;
> The gay jolly tars pass'd the word for the tipple
> And the toast—for 'twas Saturday night:
> Some sweetheart or wife that he loved as his life
> Each drank, while he wished he could hail her;
> But the standing toast that pleased the most
> Was—The wind that blows, the ship that goes,
> And the lass that loves a sailor!

In "Poor Jack", one of Charles Dibdin's many neglected songs, occurs the liveliest of all his phrases. We have all heard about the sweet little cherub who sits up aloft, but when we look for it in the first verse what we find is 'a Providence' instead—lifeless when compared with the later refrain:

> Why, I heard our good chaplain palaver one day,
> About souls, heaven, mercy, and such;
> And, my timbers! what lingo he'd coil and belay,
> Why, 'twas just all as one as High Dutch:
> For he said how a sparrow can't founder, d'ye see,
> Without orders that come down below;

> And many fine things, that prov'd clearly to me,
>   That Providence takes us in tow:
> For, says he, do you mind me, let storms e'er so oft
>   Take the top-sails of sailors aback,
> There's a sweet little cherub that sits up aloft,
>   To keep watch for the life of poor Jack.

If ever genius flowed from song-writer's quill it did so when those last lines were penned. They gave birth to a new kind of angel.

When *The Songs of Charles Dibdin* at last appeared in a collection which could claim to be comprehensive, the editor stated in a footnote that Dibdin's tunes for verses by other authors had been omitted. As this is of importance I quote his words, 'The plan of the present publication necessarily excludes these beautiful airs, their poetry not being Dibdin's'. Because of this his claim to "The British Grenadiers" has been overlooked, although the list of his works includes *The Mirror; or, Harlequin Everywhere*, the pantomime in which it was first sung. Perhaps a little piece called *The Grenadier*, which Dibdin wrote six years earlier for Sadler's Wells, had a bearing on it, but even without this clue the evidence points to the same authorship as "Tom Bowling". When the music is examined, not as we know it now but in the original, there is a resemblance where each fifth line begins with repetitions of one note—'His form was of' and 'But of all the world's great heroes'. In *Harlequin Everywhere*, one of Dibdin's acknowledged songs runs:

> That figure on the wheel you see
> I'd have you understand

which provides one example among a great many more of his habitual use of lines cut to this length.

William Shield, his closest rival, is now represented among sea songs by his setting of Prince Hoare's "Arethusa", a typical o-come-all-ye about a four-to-one engagement:

> 'Bear down, d'ye see, to our admiral's lee.'
> 'No, no', says the Frenchman, 'that can't be'.
> 'Then I must lug you along with me,'
>   Says the saucy Arethusa

which sounds cheerful to us but not to Bret Harte in "The Luck of Roaring Camp", when the English miner sings it to the defence-less infant. In London the composer was so envied that when Astley, wanting more noise for a battle in his circus, called out, 'We must have shields', his grossly offended band walked out. So many composers flung themselves at a piano directly they heard news of a naval victory that maritime history was made to music; songs of the sea chased each other from the press so closely that some were rather too close. Here is a snatch of Dibdin's "Tack and Half Tack";

> Jack joins the jest, the gibe, the jeer,
> And heaves the pond'rous plummet;
> By the mark seven!
> And now, while dang'rous breakers roar,
> Jack cries, lest we bump ashore,
> 'Quarter less four!'

and here are two snatches of Shield's "The Heaving of the Lead", which proved so popular in the Royal Navy that captains had to order their men to stop singing it:

> While off the lead the seaman flung,
> And to the pilot cheerly sung,
> 'By the mark seven!'

> The lead, once more, the seaman flung,
> And to the pilot cheerly sung,
> 'Quarter less five.'

These comparisons are of added interest because resemblances keep recurring throughout the progress of Victorian song. No matter what the subject may be—blacksmiths, arm-chairs, old oak trees—every prospect that pleases is bound to have a companion picture. Where ships are the subject they come in fleets, mostly afloat in the reigns of the Four Georges and mostly wrecked in the reign of Victoria, when the sea provoked an awful lot of pessimism.

The words of "In the Bay of Biscay, oh" were by Andrew Cherry, and there are few verses in the language that have been more frequently memorized. The composer was John Davy, whose fame became obscured because of the Victorian custom of pitching his number into the score of *The Waterman*. He also composed "Will Watch", the last fight of a fam'd smuggler against the excise men, or 'Philistines', as they were very properly called; it gradually faded out, leaving nothing but the name of Will Watch as a household word to worry antiquarians. Some more ocean-going lines that lasted just long enough for inclusion here are well worth quoting. Carter was a composer who went in for realism with "The Sea Fight":

> Ram home your guns and sponge them well,
> Let us be sure the balls will tell,
> The cannons' roar shall sound their knell.
> Not yet, nor yet, nor yet.
> Reserve your fire I do desire.
> Broadside, my boys.   See the blood in purple tide
> Trickle down her batter'd side.

and as musician to Thomas Hurlstone's farcical *Just in Time* at Covent Garden in 1792, Carter was still grim:

> But a cannon ball swept him one day in full flight,
>   From the quarter deck into the sea;
> So he died as he liv'd for his country and right,
>   And may that be the end too of me.
> Cannons may roar, echo'd from shore,
>   For the grave of a sailor's the sea.

There was salty stuff in "The Old Commodore", Reeve's setting of Lonsdale's words:

> Here I am in distress, like a ship water-logg'd,
> Not a tow rope at hand or an oar,
> I'm left by my crew and may I be flogg'd
> But the doctor's the son of a whore.

When it came to his turn Lewis, nicknamed 'Monk' because of the notoriety he enjoyed with a horrid novel of that title, wrote "The Disabled Seaman", to a tune by Dignum, which begged for alms because of the loss of arm and eye in battle, and his heart to Nancy who had married Frizzle, the barber. There were many songs in the cheerful style of "Come, push the can of grog", words by Hart, music by Blewitt, but these retired before the cheerless

style of G. A. Barker's "The White Squall", which opens with
a bright sea, each sail set, each heart gay, only to end:

> For the white squall rides on the surging wave,
> And the bark is gulph'd in an ocean grave

sombrely repeated four times. Bryan Waller Proctor, writing under
the name of Barry Cornwall, published a volume of songs in 1832;
his "The Sea", in a setting by the Chevalier Sigismund Neukomm,
Haydn's pet pupil who was waving his baton at the Congress of
Vienna when Napoleon rudely shattered its musical festivities,
began in zest:

> The Sea, the Sea, the open Sea!
> The blue, the fresh, the ever free!

but remembered what was expected of it before the end:

> And Death where . . . ever he comes to me,
> Shall come, shall come, on the wild unbounded sea.

   Unhappiness made such a steady bid for approval that in
John Percy's "Wapping Old Stairs" even illicit love caused no
protests:

> Your Molly has never been false, she declares,
> Since last time we parted at Wapping Old Stairs,
> When I vow'd that I still would continue the same,
> And gave you the 'bacco box mark'd with my name.
> When I pass'd a whole fortnight between decks with you,
> Did I e'er give a kiss, Tom, to one of your crew?
> To be useful and kind with my Thomas I stay'd,
> For his trowsers I washed, and his grog, too, I made.

The most diligent search through all the scores upon scores
of sea songs to honour the Jolly Jack Tar will not yield another
as eloquent of his life as that. It was still hummed by seamen until
they no longer remembered sail, and snatches of it would share the
reminiscent mood along with "What shall we do with a drunken
sailor?" and this mention of a harpy which I cannot trace in print:

> She bore down upon us to see what we wor'
> And under her mizzen false colours she wore

until sea-shanties became the personal property not of the modest old salt but the breezy, swaggering, hearty, overwhelming baritone.

"The Anchor's Weigh'd" makes you feel the sorrow of long partings in the days of sail—except, that is, when it is sung by drunkards on pleasure boats, with whom it was a favourite. It was composed by John Braham, a Jewish tenor who charmed Napoleon and roused audiences at the greatest opera houses of Europe, then returned to London, built the St James's Theatre, lost his fortune, and died at the age of 82 in 1856, still renowned. I cannot forbear to quote this from his obituary:

> The only spot upon Braham's character was his *liaison* with Signora Storace, but this, we believe, has been much misrepresented. He left five sons and one daughter. The eldest son (by Signora Storace) . . .

But what I had in mind when mentioning his one surviving song was that for many years there were two. Even in my boyhood we still sang his "The Death of Nelson", words by S. J. Arnold, from their opera, *The Americans,* at the Lyceum in 1811:

> 'Twas in Trafalgar's Bay, we saw the Frenchmen lay,
>   Each heart was bounding then.
> We scorn'd the foreign yoke, for our ships were British oak,
>   And hearts of oak our men!
> Our Nelson mark'd them on the wave, three cheers our gallant
>   Nor thought of home and beauty.   seamen gave,
> Along the line the signal ran, 'England expects that everyman
>   'This day will do his duty.'

It is good stirring stuff, but we keep Braham to his ration with "The Anchor's Weigh'd". Arnold also wrote the words of "A life on the ocean wave" but this is now attributed to Epes Sargent, who lengthened it.

Authorship is not always apparent at first sight, since publishers worked on the principle that the more popular a song the less important its poet and composer. "Ben Bolt" was issued and re-issued without mentioning that it had been written by Thomas Dunn English, who remained unknown when his verse was a favourite among millions:

Oh! don't you remember sweet Alice, Ben Bolt,
  Sweet Alice with hair so brown;
She wept with delight when you gave her a smile,
  And trembled with fear at your frown.
In the old churchyard in the valley, Ben Bolt,
  In a corner obscure and alone,
They have fitted a slab of granite so gray,
  And sweet Alice lies under the stone.

Ben was, of course, a sailor, since nobody else could have over-looked Alice so casually, and the earliest edition I have seen is decorated with ships in full sail to support this as plea of justification. Svengali hypnotized poor Trilby into singing it at the Haymarket in 1895, and "Ben Bolt" was published as "The Trilby Song"—still without the name of the author though he was then living. Copies of "Britannia, the pride of the ocean" bear portraits of the actor who sang it in the drama of *Black-Eyed Susan*, but no acknowledgment to David Taylor Shaw. It was popular in all lands because of the way it lent itself to changes of the first word to any name ending in 'ia'—Helvetia excepted—despite its declaration 'No land can compare unto thee'. Three cheers for the red, white, and blue suit any number of flags.

Evidence for my theory of one sea song for each poet and composer could be extended. Part of the explanation is that all had a go at the Navy and the subject brought out the best in them, unlike the soulful themes which brought out the worst. Put down any name famous in English popular song since Nelson's day and a sea song usually comes to mind.

Verses enough to keep several composers busy were bountifully supplied by Dibdin's two illegitimate sons, who used his surname. Charles Isaac Mungo Dibdin, the elder, was long remembered for a knight of gay and gallant mien who cried, "Fair lady, come ride with me" only to be answered with her guitar:

Tink a tink, tink a tink, tink a tink ting
The bee proffers honey but bears a sting

Tom, the younger, was also known later by one song, "The Snug Little Island", more particularly for one line:

A right little, tight little island.

He had been paid five guineas to write a piece for Sadler's Wells in 1797 called *The British Raft*, to ridicule the 'grand Gallic machine of that description which we were told was preparing to transport troops from France for the invasion of this country'. The performance opened the season on Easter Monday, when Tom was appearing at Maidstone before an audience partly composed of local volunteers under Lord Romney and partly of his lordship's political opponents. When one side called for an encore of "God Save the King", the other side tried to shout it down. Amid the tumult Tom came on in a smock to sing "Snug Little Island" and caused both crowds to repeat it again and again:

> Daddy Neptune one day to Freedom did say,
> 'If ever I liv'd upon dry land,
> 'The spot I should hit on would be little Briton'.
> Says Freedom, 'Why, that's my own Island'.
>   Oh! what a snug little Island,
>   A right little, tight little Island;
>   All the globe round, none can be found
>   So happy as this little Island.

> Julius Caesar, the Roman, who yielded to no man,
> Came by water, he couldn't come by land!
> And Dane, Pict, and Saxon, their homes turn'd their backs on,
> And all for the sake of our Island.
>   Oh! what a snug little Island,
>   They'd all have a touch at the Island,
>   Some were shot dead, some of them fled
>   And some stay'd to live on the Island.

> Then a very great war-man, called Billy the Norman,
> Cried, 'Hang it! I never liked my land;
> 'It would be much more handy to leave this Normandy,
> 'And live on your beautiful Island'.
>   Said he, ' 'Tis a snug little Island,
>   'Shan't us go visit the Island?'
>   Hop, skip, and jump—there he was plump,
>   And he kicked up a dust in the Island.

Though Tom Dibdin's "Tom Tough, or Yo, Heave Ho " was still being reprinted in the 1880s, most of his work soon died—even his comic opera, *The Cabinet*, the talk of the town when it was sung at Covent Garden in 1802. This is strange, because it was served by the leading composers, Reeve, Moorehead, Davy, Corri, and Braham. It made such a stir that at least one song, music by Moorehead, deserves quotation:

> Tell me sweet bird, ah! tell me why
> Thy plaintive strain should words deny
> To soothe a lover's agony?
> Thy answer seems to be, 'O fie,
> 'What words e'er lack'd Orlando's eye
> 'To speak in sweetest melody?'

Between them the brothers wrote about five hundred pieces for the theatre, mostly burlettas, pantomimes, and other musicals, which means that their songs numbered thousands. To Tom belongs the blame for changing burlesque that did burlesque into the thing the Victorians knew by that name, which was the plot of any well-known story told incongruously and pointlessly. Tom's *Don Giovanni; or, A Spectre on Horseback*, at the Surrey in 1817, contained a parody of his father's "Jolly Young Waterman" in

> Come, who's for a row with the jolly young watermen,
> Who at Blackfriar's Bridge cheerily ply?

which was funny solely because the singer was dressed as a gondolier.

V

Eighteenth-Century Legacies

❖❖❖❖❖❖❖❖❖❖❖❖❖❖❖❖❖❖❖❖❖❖❖❖❖❖❖❖❖❖

Oh ponder well! Be not severe
To save a wretched wife:
For on the rope that hangs my dear
Depends poor Polly's life.

The Beggar's Opera

AT FIRST GLANCE eighteenth-century poets seem to be unpopular in the Victorian repertoire, but only at first glance. How much persuasion lies in a good tune is made clear by the verses which survived the change of one century to another when the rest of their authors' lines were forgotten. There is no better example than *The Beggar's Opera*. Its progress from decade to decade was accompanied by shrieks from outraged moralists whose feelings were respected everywhere else. Macheath, as long as he was in good voice, was allowed to defy respectability. All thefts were forgiven the thief who sang, "Let us take the road"; similarly all Dr Pepusch's thefts were forgiven because he stole good tunes— in this case Handel's Royal Guards March, played on parade for forty years.

John Gay owes still more of his nineteenth-century popularity to Handel. Together they brought out *Acis and Galatea* at the Haymarket in 1732, a pastoral which contains "O ruddier than the cherry", "Would you gain the tender creature?" and "I rage, I melt, I burn", that bear the stamp of an unregenerate world in their titles. The rest of Handel's songs come from bewildering sources. One from a light opera has become sacred under the title of "Largo". Another has been taken from Biblical oratorio to enliven our beanfeasts for the sake of its triumphant acclamation, "See the conquering hero comes". Though Dryden had written something similar, the credit for the words belongs to Dr Thomas Morell; they formed part of his libretto for *Joshua* until a still better moment was found for them in *Judas Maccabaeus*—originally presented without them at Covent Garden in 1746 to celebrate the battle of Culloden. There is another tangle for unravelling in Handel's opera of *Semele*, originally written by Congreve in 1710 but not staged until some years later. Nowadays it is remembered as the source of

> Where'er you walk cool gales shall fan the glade,
> Trees where you sit shall crowd into a shade

—words so full of loving solicitude that we are slow to recognize them as a quotation from Pope's "Pastorals" in honour of the current passion for landscape gardening.

Since Italian opera, German opera, English operetta, and sacred oratorio all came alike to Handel, complexity has caused "I rage I melt, I burn" to be ascribed to *Samson*, while one or two of his songs seem to have been misplaced altogether. It is disconcerting to read on copies of "Droop not young lover" that it has been edited and 'adapted' by William Hills; the fit is as perfect as the mating of Haydn and Anne Hunter in:

> My mother bids me bind my hair
>   With bands of rosy hue,
> Tie up my sleeves with ribbons rare,
>   And lace my bodice blue.
> 'For why', she cries, 'sit still and weep,
>   'While others dance and play?'
> Alas! I scarce can go or creep,
>   While Lubin is away.

Arcadian shepherds and shepherdesses of courtly entertainments are changing into lovers of flesh and blood, fit for ordinary people to sing about. Many strains go to the making of Victorian song and this is one of them, possibly the best of them, even though it would never excel the model set by Henry Carey at the very beginning. His "Sally in our alley" is so immaculate a work of art that we would like to think we have it as he designed it; yet his tune was scrapped round about 1760, some twenty years after his death, and a traditional air belonging to "A Country Lass" substituted. That is an outrageous piece of vandalism, but nobody would have it otherwise. Here are his verses in a ballad of too rare a beauty to be shortened:

Of all the girls that are so smart,
    There's none like pretty Sally:
She is the darling of my heart,
    And she lives in our alley.
There's ne'er a lady in the land,
    That's half as sweet as Sally;
She is the darling of my heart,
    And she lives in our alley.

Her father he makes cabbage nets,
    And thro' the streets does cry 'em,
Her mother she sells laces long,
    To such as please to buy 'em:
But sure such folks could not beget
    So sweet a girl as Sally;
She is the darling of my heart,
    And she lives in our alley.

When she is by I leave my work,
    I love her so sincerely;
My master comes like any Turk,
    And bangs me most severely:
But let him bang his belly full,
    I'll bear it all for Sally,;
She is the darling of my heart,
    And she lives in our alley.

Of all the days that's in the week,
    I dearly love but one day,
And that's the day that comes betwixt
    A Saturday and Monday;
For then I'm drest in all my best,
    To walk abroad with Sally;
She is the darling of my heart,
    And she lives in our alley.

My master carries me to church,
    And often I am blamed,
Because I leave him in the lurch,
    As soon as text is named:
I leave the church in sermon time,
    And slink away to Sally;
She is the darling of my heart,
    And she lives in our alley.

When Christmas comes about again,
    Oh! then I shall have money;
I hoard it up, and box and all,
    I'll give it to my honey;
And would it were a dozen pounds,
    I'd give it all to Sally;
She is the darling of my heart,
    And she lives in our alley.

My master and my neighbours all,
    Make game of me and Sally,
And but for her I'd rather be
    A slave and row a galley;
And when my seven long years are out,
    Oh! then I'll marry Sally;
And then we'll wed, and then we'll bed,
    But not in our alley.

Young lovers at a fair had inspired Carey. He was neither the first nor the last to catch a rhythm in living speech but his example, for all its success, was rarely followed. His son, George Saville Carey—named after his grandfather, George Saville, Marquis of Halifax, whose amour founded this line with its tragic heirloom of genius—possessed the gift of song but not the knack of relating it to life. Here is one verse of his which had a setting composed by Aylward:

Oft I have seen at early morn,
    All tempting to the view,
A rose bud on some lofty thorn,
    Adorn'd with glitt'ring dew.
A symbol 'twas of that dear fair
    Whose beauties rank'd so high;
From mortal reach 'twas planted there,
    To blush, to charm and die.

However rarely his works were read at the time Victoria came to the throne, Pope was at least a name. Shenstone, in utter neglect, had no mention in the largest lending library—but he had a song, still being republished in Albert Oswald Wynne's setting to the last year of Victoria's reign. What adds to its appeal is the way the poet has put his whole life into it:

How pleased within my native bowers,
  Ere while I passed the day!
Was ever scene so decked with flowers,
  Were ever flowers so gay?
How sweetly smiled the hill, the vale,
  And all the landscape round!
The river gliding down the dale,
  The hill with beeches crown'd.

But now, when urged by tender woes,
  I speed to meet my dear,
That hill and stream my zeal oppose,
  And check my fond career.
No more since Daphne was my theme,
  Their wonted charms I see;
That verdant hill and silver stream
  Divide my love and me.

They did indeed! Shenstone inherited a small estate in Shropshire called Leasowes. When he had spent his entire fortune on transforming it into a far-famed marvel of landscape gardening, he fell in love. Having no means left for marriage, he spent the rest of his days nursing a broken heart and subduing duns at his door.

If Fielding has but one or two titles in the family album it was not for want of trying. In his early days as a playwright and manager he wrote many musical numbers, picking up tunes here and there as he pleased. With "A-hunting we will go" he has been lucky, since there are a dozen others of the same type, equally rousing but ignored because we can have too much of a good thing. All begin with the time of day as he does:

The dusky night rides down the sky,
  And ushers in the morn

as though daybreak were an historic event. There is more hunting than Fielding in it except for:

The wife around her husband throws
  Her arms and begs him stay,
'My dear it rains and hails and snows,
  'You will not hunt today'.
But a-hunting we will go

'Poor Ernestine! Your misfortune makes my bedchamber the temple of purity.'

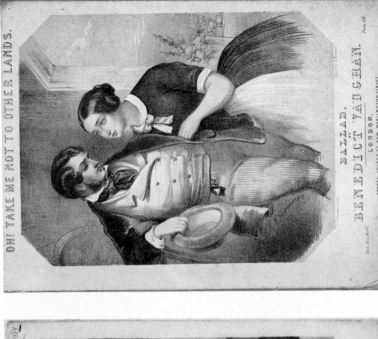

'A charm from the skies seems to hallow us there.'

and we must look to his other songs for more personal evidence of his spirit. This next one he wrote, to a tune he named "The King's Old Courtier", twice. First it cropped up in his *The Grub Street Opera* of 1731:

> When mighty roast beef was the Englishman's food,
> It ennobled our hearts and enriched our blood;
> Our soldiers were brave and our courtiers were good.
>   Oh! the roast beef of England,
>   And old England's roast beef!
>
> But since we have learnt from all-conquering France
> To eat their ragouts as well as to dance,
> Oh, what a fine figure we make in romance!
>   Oh! the roast beef of England,
>   And old England's roast beef.

In his *Don Quixote in England* (1734) Sancho Panza grows so fond of beef and beer that he refuses to return to Spain, whereupon the heroine sings the three opening lines as above and then adds to them, with a slight but invigorating change in the refrain:

> Oh, the roast beef of old England,
>   And old England's roast beef!
> Then, Britons, from all nice dainties refrain,
> Which effeminate Italy, France and Spain;
> And mighty roast beef shall command on the main.

With additional verses it was published under Leveridge's name as composer. Some extra lines condemning 'coffee, tea, or such slip-slops' may be authentic but we must look with suspicion on anything so unlike Fielding as the coyness of:

> O, then they had stomachs to eat and to fight,
> And when wrongs were a-cooking to do themselves right,
> But now we're a h'm—I could—but goodnight.

What resemblance Fielding's work bore to the Old Courtier—preserved in the Percy Reliques—may be judged from this beginning to its comparison between a genuine courtier and a fake:

E

> Here is an old song, made by an old ancient pate,
> Of an old worshipful gentleman who had a great estate,
> Who kept an old house at a bountiful rate,
> And an old porter to relieve the poor at his gate,
>   Like an old courtier of the queen's
>   And the queen's old courtier.

Violent hands were laid on this by W. H. Murray, manager of the Theatre Royal, Edinburgh, in 1826, when he used the tune for his, "The brave old country gentleman, all of the olden time", and sang it himself in public. Some few years later a publisher of Holborn, named Charles Purday, brought out a close imitation with the refrain, 'Like a fine old English gentleman, one of the olden time'. There was an action in the King's Bench, brought by Murray's publisher, but it was non-suited after the jury had been thrown into disagreement by Henry Bishop's evidence that the tune had been taken from "The last rose of summer". The judge saw that some of the words were new and wished there were more of the old, which is not surprising when we find what Murray and Purday have left us:

> He laid him down right tranquilly,
>   Gave up his latest sigh;
> And mournful stillness reign'd around
>   And tears bedew'd each eye,
>   For the good old English gentleman.

In part "There was a jolly miller" has a similar history, since it began as an old tune—this one belonged to a thieves' rhyme— set to new words by a playwright and lengthened for use at concerts. The author was Isaac Bickerstaffe, an officer of Marines who wrote twenty pieces for the London stage between 1770 and 1785, before he was banished, guilty of the deed without a name, to some unknown spot, where nobody heard of him again. All the leading composers had helped with his scores, but his outstanding success was this from *Love in a Village* at Covent Garden in 1762:

> There was a jolly miller once
>   Liv'd on the River Dee,
> He work'd and sung from morn till night,
>   No lark more blithe than he;

> And this the burthen of his song,
>   For ever used to be,
> 'I care for nobody, not I,
>   'If nobody cares for me.'

One verse is enough in the play. In later years a second was added about quaffing ale while grinding corn, a third about the way his mill is like parent, child, and wife, and a fourth about his boast that no lawyer or doctor has ever had a groat of his money. The only other item from *Love in a Village* to rival this in Victorian drawing-rooms was:

> No age, no profession, no station is free;
> To sovereign beauty mankind bends the knee;
> That power, resistless, no strength can oppose,
> We all love a pretty girl under the rose.

Arne was the composer; all the compliments he is regularly paid cannot keep much of his work, apart from "Rule Britannia", alive. "Water parted from the sea", the favourite air from his opera of *Artaxerxes*, is a curiosity because Keats quoted it, on his last voyage, when waves washed into his cabin through the planks.

Arne's settings for Shakespeare's lyrics, which are given to schoolboys now, kept a professional status to the end of the nineteenth century. His gifts were inherited by his son Michael, the composer of "Hieland Laddie", which belongs to great occasions, as we heard when it was played by massed pipes and drums at the Victory Parade of the second World War. Whatever hope there was for Michael evaporated when he built himself a laboratory at Chelsea, studied chemistry, zealously prosecuted experiments in hopes of discovering the philosopher's stone, and ruined himself. But he found time for "The lass with the delicate air".

Many eighteenth-century songs have now been mentioned. Some have been mournful, and to these must be added, "Robin Adair", although the complaint here is 'What made my heart so sore?' not suicidal grief.* The dominant mood of that age is gaiety.

* No early edition of "Robin Adair" has come my way. *The Oxford Dictionary of Quotations* ascribes it to Lady Caroline Keppel, 1735—?

If there is a different impression it is because succeeding generations who hugged the belief, 'most musical, most melancholy',
picked out the sad and scrapped the gay, including festive glees
and catches like "The Alderman's Thumb". This was the work of
that rousing, sadly neglected, composer Dr Henry Harrington;
who died at a ripe old age in 1816. He provided it for the Harmonic
Society which he founded:

> What a noise and what a din,
> How they glitter round the chin.
> Give me fowl, give me fish,
> Now for some of that nice dish.
> Cut me this, cut me that,
> Send me crust, send me fat.
> Some for titbits pulling, hauling,
>   Legs, breast, wings, head,
> Some for liquor scolding, bawling,
>   Hock, port, white, red.
> Here 'tis cramming, cutting, slashing,
> Here ye grease and gravy splashing.
> Look, sir, what you've done!
> Zounds, sir, you've cut off the Alderman's thumb.

And why should we be deprived of this, copied from a collection of 1811 without names to words or music, which tells the
legend of the Toby Jug*:

> Dear Tom, this brown jug, that now foams with mild ale,
> (In which I will drink to sweet Nan of the Vale),
> Was once Toby Filpot, a thirsty old soul,
> As e'er cracked a bottle, or fathom'd a bowl,
> In boozing about 'twas his praise to excel,
>   And among jolly topers he bore off the bell.
>
> It chanc'd, as in dog-days he sat at his ease,
> In his flow'r-woven arbour, as gay as you please,
> With a friend and a pipe, puffing sorrow away
> And with honest old stingo was soaking his clay,
> His breath-doors of life on a sudden were shut,
> And he died full as big as a Dorchester butt.

* From Reginald Haggar's *Staffordshire Chimney Ornaments* I learn that this
originally appeared in the Rev. Francis Fawkes' *Original Poems and Translations*,
1761.

His body, when long in the ground it had lain,
And time into clay had dissolv'd it again,
A potter found out in its covert so snug,
And with part of fat Toby he form'd this brown jug
Now sacred to friendship, to mirth, and mild ale,
So here's to my lovely sweet Nan of the Vale.

Dr Callcott, who helped to found the Glee Club, wrote many glees of the jovial kind which had a lot of fun in the music as well as in the words, a hint of which may be dropped by mentioning that all references to the Welshman in what follows were deep bass:

When Arthur first in Court began to wear long hanging sleeves
He entertained three serving men, and all of them were thieves.
The first he was an Irishman, the second was a Scot,
The third he was a Welshman and all were knaves I wot.
The Irishman lov'd usquebaugh, the Scot lov'd ale call'd Blue Cap,
The Welshman he lov'd toasted cheese and made his mouth like a
                                                            mousetrap.
Usquebaugh burnt the Irishman. The Scot was drown'd in ale.
The Welshman had like to be choak'd with the mouse but he pull'd her
                                                            out by the tail.

There was richness in these jests, but few of them survived as vigorously as this seventeenth-century one by Jenkins, still familiar today:

A boat, a boat, unto the ferry
For we'll go over to be merry,
To laugh and quaff and drink good sherry.

"Catch on a pinch of snuff", by S. Paxton, was a witty mixture of singing and sneezing. Dr Aldrich, Dean of Christ Church in 1689, author of *Artis Logicae Rudimenta*, scholar, architect and musician, composed a glee called, "Hark! the bonny Christ Church bells", which is a work of art though it ends comically with, 'There's ne'er a man will leave his can till he hears the mighty Tom'.

Then there was Dr Kitchener who composed the setting for Johnson's "Hermit", and also the catch from Piozzi's *Johnsoniana:*

> If the man who turnip cries
> Cry not when his daddy dies,
> 'Tis a proof that he would rather
> Have a turnip for a father.

Lord Mornington, the father of the Duke of Wellington, was another gifted amateur who delighted in glees. His happiest trifle was:

> Here in cool grot and mossy cell,
> We rural fays and fairies dwell,
> Tho' rarely seen by mortal eye,
> When the pale moon ascending high
> Darts thro' yon limes her quiv'ring beams,
> We frisk it, frisk it, frisk it, frisk it,
> near these crystal streams.

Cheerfulness came first at the meetings of music clubs. Shield, who could be grim elsewhere, brought this to the board:

> When we dwell on the lips of the lass we adore
> Not a pleasure in nature is missing.
> May his soul be in heav'n, he deserves it I'm sure,
> Who was first the inventor of kissing.

Shield should not be separated from his favourite librettist, John O'Keeffe, for they wrote enduring stuff together. The former died in 1829 at the age of 81, the latter in 1833 at the age of 85, after many years of blindness. Only the antiquarian bothers about their comic operas sufficiently to admire their lightness of touch, gossamer compared with what we have been having ever since, but an ever rolling stream of formidable baritones revelled, without a thought for whose it was, in their swagger song, "The Wolf":

> While the wolf in nightly prowl
> Bays the moon with hideous howl,
> Gates are barred in vain resistance,
> Females shriek but no assistance,
> Silence or you meet your fate.
> Your keys, your jewels, cash and plate.
> Locks, bolts and bars soon fly asunder,
> Then to rifle, rob and plunder.

In cold print it may leave us unmoved, but when bawled straight at us by gaping mouth, under bristling moustache and bulging eyes, the frenzied attempt to make our flesh creep created sensations every timorous audience enjoyed. Another song by Shield and O'Keeffe, treasured by people who have never heard of their partnership, is "Old Towler", which is usually printed as by authors unknown. It has a touch of realism which the opponents of hunting might approve of were they to hear the verses right through:

> Bright Chanticleer proclaims the dawn,
> And spangles deck the thorn;
> The lowing herds now quit the lawn,
> The lark springs from the corn.
> Dogs, huntsmen, round the window throng,
> Fleet Towler leads the cry;
> Arise the burthen of their song,
> This day a stag must die.
> With a hey ho chivey, hark forward, hark forward tantivy,
> Arise the burthen of their song, This day a stag must die.

> The cordial takes its merry round,
> The laugh and joke prevail;
> The Huntsman blows a jovial sound,
> The dogs snuff up the gale:
> The upland winds they sweep along,
> O'er fields thro' brakes they fly;
> The game is roused, too true the song,
> This day a stag must die.

> Poor stag, the dogs thy haunches gore,
> The tears run down thy face;
> The huntsman's pleasure is no more,
> His joys were in the chace.
> Alike the sportmen of the town,
> The virgin game in view;
> Are full content to run them down,
> Then they in turn pursue.

One other song by O'Keeffe and Shield must be quoted because it is the forerunner of much work in the same style. The chamber-maid in *Fontainbleau; or, Our Way in France*, Covent Garden, 1798, sings:

When drest in all my finest things,
My gold repeater, bracelets, rings,
            In toilet glass,
            A lovely lass,
I view so gaily glancing;
            I can't tell how,
            But ne'er till now
I felt my heart a dancing.

Out of all the festive ditties joyously sung in Dr Johnson's time
only one survives on the tip of everybody's tongue. This is not
because of any superior merit but because it cannot be detached
from its place in *The School for Scandal*. We can all sing Verse One
of "Here's to the maiden of bashful fifteen" although uncertain of:

Here's to the charmer whose dimples we prize;
    Now to the maid who has none, sir:
Here's to the girl with a pair of blue eyes,
    And here's to the nymph with but one, sir.

Let the toast pass——
Drink to the lass,
I'll warrant she'll prove an excuse for the glass.

When Sheridan revelled, no stag party sat round a table without
songs and choruses; admirable drinking songs, full of melody and
wit, were written and sung by men of quality. Tom Moore's first
success was with translations of Anacreon, which won for him the
name of 'Anacreon Moore'. He sang them himself in a voice of
such charm that he was welcome at the exclusive Thatched House
Tavern where the Prince Regent sat among the tippling dukes, his
brothers, listening to harmonious exhortations to drink and be
merry. "Give me the harp", the words translated by Thomas
Moore from Anacreon, was composed by Sir John Stevenson as a
chorus glee, with accompaniment for 'two performers on one
pianoforte'. As such it was sung with great applause at the Irish
Harmonic Club on 4 May, 1803, in Dublin. It fairly represents the
old world of song before the nineteenth-century saddened it:

Give me the harp of epic song
Which Homer's fingers thrill'd along
But tear away the sanguine string
For war is not the theme I sing.

Proclaim the laws of festal rite,
I'm monarch of the board tonight
And all around shall brim as high
And quaff the tide as deep as I!
And when the clusters' mellowing dews
Their warm enchanting balm infuse,
Our feet shall catch th' elastic bound
And reel us thro' the dances round.
Then Bacchus! we shall sing to thee
In wild but sweet ebriety
And flash around such sparks of thought
As Bacchus could alone have taught.

As the eighteenth-century way of life faded, the singers of England resolved on the survival of the saddest in what they sang. There was a massacre of the merry without any regard for merit, which demonstrated that they looked neither for poetry nor melody but feeling. Here is the clue to all that follows in this history.

Look into the Victorians' repertoire and see what survived in it from an older fashion. Cherubini, born in 1760 and still composing at the age of 80, was not for them, however great his popularity in other countries: his opera of *Anacreon* proved where he belonged. Very few indeed of the airs and graces composed by himself and his contemporaries for the delight of Marie Antoinette gained a place in our great-grandparents' vocal albums. Out of all that delicate tinkle, always about to bow before the minuet, only one outlived the kings and emperors—the saddest of them all.

Its title is, "O Richard, O my King, the world has forsaken thee", and it belongs to the theatres of Paris when castles were regularly represented in the scenery of performances that pleased courtiers, usually ending in conflagrations that caused towers to topple like a child's toy bricks, until the mob in grim reality borrowed the idea and upset the Bastille after the same fashion. At the height of the Revolution "O Richard, O my King" left its mark on history. At Versailles there was a banquet to celebrate loyalty to the old order. The king, accompanied by Marie Antoinette with the Dauphin in her arms, paraded past the tables. The band struck up that fatal song. The tricolour was trampled underfoot, white cockades suddenly appeared, swords were drawn and glasses drained to the pledge of defiance to the changing order.

Starving women, hearing of it, forced Lafayette to lead the people's army against Versailles.

A general who had opposed Lafayette in America wrote the English words of the song. It belonged, in the original version of "Richard Coeur-de-Lion", written by Sedaine, composed by Grétry, to Blondel in the scene where the minstrel makes his legendary journey to the castle where his royal master is imprisoned. At Drury Lane in 1786 General Burgoyne gave the song to a soprano in order, so he said, to add to the interest of the situation. Publishers a hundred years and more later issued it to baritones, but by then it was just another plaintive ditty without a single ghost in silk breeches standing by, steadying himself with his sword to the floor as a plebeian bullet drains his life away.

VI

With Melancholy Expression

++

Oft in the stilly night,
  Ere slumber's chain has bound me,
Fond mem'ry brings the light
  Of other days around me.
The smiles, the tears, of boyhood's years,
  The words of love then spoken,
The eyes that shone, now dimm'd and gone,
  The cheerful hearts now broken!
When I remember all the friends so link'd together,
I've seen around me fall like leaves in wintry weather,
I feel like one who treads alone,
  Some banquet hall deserted,
Whose lights are fled, whose garlands dead,
  And all, but he, departed.

Tom Moore

IF WE MUST FIND a definite origin for Victorian song, it is in the quarrel between the Prince Regent and Tom Moore. Until then the flowing bowl that delights the soul had been Tom's theme. As an exile from royal favour he devoted the next thirty years of his life principally to Irish Melodies, the music selected from the ancient ballads by Sir John Stevenson, Mus. Doc. From the first number in 1807 to the last in 1834, they had a success so vast that it has always been taken for granted. They set a new fashion for what should be sung not only in the home but in the opera house. With these poems as model, almost any plain journeyman could, and did, set himself up as a poet for the piano.

Moore's Irish Melodies proved a misleading title, it robbed Stevenson of his due for we never hear of their composer until a new setting is provided. Naturally the stress at first was on nationality: those that were best known expressed the patriotic melancholy of, "The harp that once through Tara's halls", "The Minstrel Boy", "Erin! oh Erin", "Tho' the last glimpse of Erin", "Dear Harp of my Country", and "The Meeting of the Waters", culminating in the tenderness of the lament, "She is far from the land where her young hero sleeps". It was not many years before the publication of this that Robert Emmet had been executed*, not many before the woman he loved had died of a broken heart in exile; since it moves us still, how great must its spell have been then?

But not all of the Irish Melodies gave so much thought to country. Some were of everyday experience like growing old. Many were love songs. "Believe me, if all those endearing young charms" was spiced with unconscious humour when it came to describing the beloved's features as likely to become 'dear ruins', for the purpose of winning her heart. What they all had in common, if we ignore "Come send round the wine" as an Anacreonic hangover, was nostalgia. The form was so simple that imitation was child's play, and it was regularly copied for both Church and stage: the tune of "Oft in the stilly night" was plagiarized for a hymn without any of its devout admirers suspecting that it was not original. Easy as the musical style was to copy, the pattern of the verse was easier still, and the model of the sentiments that Moore employed when he forgot Ireland, was a peeled onion. Roses can always fade or blossom alone, fondest hopes can always be blasted, and despair invoked by ordinary or extraordinary objects:

> I never nurs'd a dear gazelle
>   To glad me with its soft black eye,
> But when it came to know me well
>   And love me, it was sure to die.

It is difficult to believe that Moore did not mean such straining after misery to be read as nonsense, but the context in *Lalla Rookh* is serious enough.

Yearnings for distant places or bygone times became more and more profitable. Naturally there were other founder members of this saddening society, and though none can compare with Moore a word must be said for John Tobin, a poet of the drama with a gift for coining such phrases as, 'Foil'd at last and by a woman'. In

---

* After heading the unsuccessful rising of 1803 in Dublin, Robert Emmet escaped to the Wicklow Mountains but returned to visit Sarah Curran and was captured.

The Honey Moon, at Drury Lane in 1805, he introduced a song with music by Tom Cooke which ended:

> But should he view without a tear
>   My altering form, my waning bloom,
> Then what is left me but despair
>   What refuge but the silent tomb?

This comedy contains the famous remark that the man who lays his hand upon a woman, save in the way of kindness, is a wretch whom 'twere base flattery to name a coward. It seems a pity to add that it is not uttered in all earnestness. Anyhow, Moore wrote a song like Tobin's to music by the Hon. Augustus Barry:

> If all your tender faith is o'er,
>   If still my truth you'll try,
> Alas! I have but one proof more,
>   I'll bless your name and die.

The view that a lover could die whenever he cared to lay him down had been held for a long time but it was never so common as now. Sheridan made things worse in verses, set by the Duchess of Devonshire, for the drama of *The Stranger,* acted everywhere:

> I have a silent sorrow here,
>   A grief I'll ne'er impart,
> It breathes no sigh, it sheds no tear,
>   But it consumes my heart.
> This cherish'd woe, this lov'd despair,
>   My lot for ever be,
> So, my soul's lord, the pangs I bear
>   Be never, never known by thee.
>
> And when pale characters of death,
>   Shall mark this alter'd cheek;
> When my poor wasted, trembling breath
>   My life's last hope would speak——
> I shall not raise my eyes to heav'n,
>   Nor mercy ask for me:
> My soul despairs to be forgiven,
>   Unpardon'd, Love, by thee.

How many songs Sheridan wrote may never be known. He dashed them off whenever they were wanted; no such task was too mean for him, not even patriotic doggerel for pantomime, though he left it to another hack to take one of the happiest lines from *The Critic*—'An oyster may be crossed in love'—and elaborate it into a duet for Grimaldi with a property oyster suffering in like manner:

Oyster: OH!   *Clown:*   OH!
Oyster: Oh, gentle swain, your knife resign,
            Nor wound a heart so soft as mine.
Clown: Who thus my pity tries to move?
Oyster: An oyster who is cross'd in love.
Clown: Ye Gods! An oyster cross'd in love!
            Then quit your cruel nymph for now
            A far more tempting claims your vow.
            She's form'd for pleasing all beholders,
            For 'tis a fine cod's head and shoulders.
Oyster: Ah! Cease! Nor tempt a faithful fish.
Clown: She waits you on a Wedgwood dish.
Oyster: No! No! For soon my death shall prove
            That oysters can be true in love.
Clown: The hardest heart 'twould surely move
            To see an oyster cross'd in love.

Since that is based on Sheridan's idea a spark of his genius enlivens it, which is more than can be said of a song written by himself and composed by Shield:

> Mark'd you her eye of heavenly blue,
> Mark'd you her cheek of roseate hue,
> That eye in liquid circles moving,
> That cheek abash'd at man's approving,
> The one love's arrows darting round,
> The other blushing at the wound,
> Her eye darting, her cheek blushing, at the wound

which is enough to make anyone glad to get back to plain misery.

Out of all these lovelorn lays only one survived the Regency, owing to the floods of newly shed tears supplied afresh by each new generation. This one, written by 'Monk' Lewis, lives on while all his sensational novels, nerve-shattering melodramas, and awe-inspiring stage spectacles are undeniably dead. We still sing:

> But the miller's lovely daughter
>   Both from cold and care was free;
> On the banks of Allan Water
>   There a corse lay she

though somehow the sad ballad no longer sounds the same. You are not surprised when a young person who has been listening to it asks, 'Why "of course" lay she? Did she *have* to drown herself?'

You patiently explain that the poetic word for corpse used to be, out of respect for Shakespeare who still spells it this way in modern editions, corse. Upon which the young person replies that dead bodies cannot be aggrandized with the silent 'p' as though they were comptrollers.

No purpose can be served by continuing the argument. Since she cannot tune in to the versifiers of Victorian song that is the end of it. Even those of us who can manage to do so must first adjust our sight or hearing, somewhat after the fashion of swimmers who prepare themselves for fish-spearing under water. Similarly, just as frogmen think their efforts worth while because of the discovery of a different sort of existence, so the diver for pearls of words and music finds himself well rewarded.

"On the banks of Allan Water" with music by 'Lady C. S.' is good for a start, with its melancholy tale of a miller's daughter who drowned herself for love. Considering with what rudery millers' daughters introduced themselves into English poetry, as every reader of Chaucer knows, it is remarkable how firmly a later tradition established them as objects of tragedy. Mills, mill-ponds, and mill-streams became closely associated with lost virginity, until a reaction set in a century later to the refrain of:

> . . . she lived beside the mill.
> Deep and sad were the waters
> But she was deeper still.

If we are covering too much ground by taking in one stride more than a century it is simply to make sure of travelling in the right direction. We must wade through floods of sentiment to reach the dry land of the twentieth century, where we may decide that our present condition is too dry and plunge back again. What is the reason for this difference between our mute selves and our very vocal forebears, who continually sang about anything that affected their feelings? All the succeeding pages will be needed to answer the question, no matter how great the temptation may be to state some such simple fact as that we play a great deal more golf and tennis. It is worth observing, for example, that "Allan Water" was not written by anyone suffering from melancholia or undue

sensitivity towards human frailty but by a writer who had won
a well-deserved notoriety for horror-mongering. 'Monk' Lewis
demonstrated, even before the nineteenth century dawned, how
thoroughly the British public could indulge in the sensation of
being shocked. 'Even Satan's self with thee might fear to dwell',
Byron wrote, 'and in thy skull discern a deeper hell.'

What Moore did for Ireland, Carolina Baroness Nairne did for
Scotland. Her maiden name was Oliphant, which is a little con-
fusing for it was Thomas Oliphant, who as author of the English
words of "The Ash Grove" and "Men of Harlech", may be
regarded as the bard of Wales. She was born in 1766 at the House
of Gask in Perthshire; at the age of 40 she married her second
cousin, Major William Murray Nairne, who became Lord Nairne
when the Jacobite peerage was revived by Act of Parliament.
While editing *The Scottish Minstrel* in the 1820s she herself wrote
eighty of the songs it contained, though her adherents have put
her name to some others, like "Charlie is my darling", which
she heard in the Highlands. The mistake arose because she published
all anonymously, including her own "Caller Herrin' ", "The Land
o' the Leal", and "Wi' a hundred pipers and a' ". The House of
Gask, her old home, had to be pulled down; she had it rebuilt
and died there in 1845, leaving a posthumous publication, *Lays
from Strathearn*, which won for her the title of 'Flower of Strathearn'. This song was hers, though the version we know is Irish:

> Oh, the auld house, the auld house,
> What though the rooms were wee!
> Oh, kind hearts were dwelling there,
> And bairnies fu' o' glee;
> The wild rose and the jasmine
> Still hang upon the wa',
> Hoo mony cherish'd memories
> Do they, sweet flowers, reca'?

> Oh, the auld laird, the auld laird,
> Sae canty, kind and crouse,
> Hoo mony did he welcome to
> His ain wee dear auld house?
> And the leddy too, sae genty,
> There shelter'd Scotland's heir,
> And clipt a lock wi' her ain hand
> Frae his long yellow hair.

During the Regency "The Bluebells of Scotland" was sung at
Drury Lane by Mrs Jordan, an actress of wit and talent who won
the heart of the future King William; it was published as having
been composed by her. None of the happiest inspirations of great
celebrities equalled its success; Sir Walter Scott himself, with
Sir John Stevenson's help, had no such luck with this from
Marmion:

> Where shall the lover rest,
>   Whom the fates sever,
> From his true maiden's breast,
>   Parted for ever;
> Where, through grooves deep and high,
>   Sounds the far billow,
> Where early violets die
>   Under the willow.
> Eleu loro, Eleu loro,
>   Soft shall be his pillow.

or with this, made by Sir John Stevenson into a glee for three
voices, from *The Lord of the Isles:*

> Merrily, merrily goes the bark,
>   Before the gale she bounds,
> So darts the dolphin from the shark,
>   Or the deer before the hounds.

and though Bishop composed a setting for the song from *Quentin
Durward* there is little to be said for its refrain, 'Where is County
Guy?' It was not until 1891 that Scott had a rousing success with
verse on the stage; in *Ivanhoe*, libretto by James Sturgess, score by
Sullivan, at the English Opera House in Cambridge Circus, the
best lyric was the authentic, "Ho! jolly Jenkin, I spy a knave a-
drinking". On top of that Scott had another posthumous triumph
when Cowen composed a rousing setting for 'The Border Ballad'.
But Scott was too much of the literary gentleman, except in
"Bonnets of Bonnie Dundee", to catch the manner of the natural
warbler. When it comes to Burns the difficulty of quotation is
not where to begin but where to stop. "O, wert thou in the cauld
blast", in Mendelssohn's setting, has a breath-taking beauty when
arranged as a duet for women's voices, and finds singers worthy
of it. Dislike of the buxom Prince Regent led to hankerings after

F

the mere wraith of Bonnie Prince Charlie, and these created a
revival of Jacobite songs followed by a vogue of any Scottish songs,
among which the one I prize most is "Huntingtower":

> When ye gang awa', Jamie,
> Far across the sea, laddie,
> When ye gang to Germanie,
> What will ye send to me, laddie?

There are many verses. When he has teased her about his wife and
bairnies three, and she has reproached him with, 'Lang syne ye
should hae telt me this, laddie', he makes amends:

> Saint Johnstoun's bower and Huntingtower
> And a' that's mine is thine, lassie.

In the midst of this craze for Scotland an enterprising publisher
issued a sheet bearing this inscription: 'O Weel May the Keel Row,
a celebrated Scottish Song sung by Mrs Waylett with universal
applause at the Theatres Royal'. Being unaware that a keel is a
Tyneside collier's boat, somebody had endeavoured to improve
the sense in phrases that have been copied ever since:

> As I came down the canongate the canongate,
> As I came down the canongate I heard a lassie sing,
> O weel may the Keel row the Keel row the Keel row
> O weel may the Keel row the Ship that my love's in.

> My love he wears a Bonnet, a Bonnet a Bonnet
> A snawy rose upon it a Dimple in his chin
> Oh merry etc.
> And now I learnt her lover, her lover her lover;
> Had landed from the Rover, and join'd her in this strain,
> O merry etc.

All through the nineteenth century, when every children's party
danced to it, it was still called 'Scotch', even when printed with
a revised text eloquent of Newcastle:

> Oh, who's so like my Johnny,
> So leash, so blythe, so bonny,
> He's foremost 'mongst the mony
> Keel lads of coaly Tyne.

He sits and rows so tightly,
Or in the dance so sprightly,
He cuts and shuffles lightly,
   'Tis true were he not mine.

Oh weel may the keel row,
The keel row, the keel row,
Oh weel may the keel row
   That my lad's in.
He wears a blue bonnet,
Blue bonnet, blue bonnet,
He wears a blue bonnet
   And a dimple in his chin.

As for some modern attempts to placate Northumbria with, 'As I came down the Sandgate', I can but pay tribute to the temerity of publishers who meddle in a border foray between two of the hardiest races on earth. Still more recently a would-be translator has tried his hand with "Weel may the boatie row", and yet London children see no difficulty in the original whatsoever. By continuing straight on from, "Here we go gathering nuts and may" to "We'll may the keel row", they imagine themselves spreading the may in a row by some sort of keel. Not even Burns's "Auld Lang Syne" has been more warmly welcomed south. There is only one other song of Northumbria in the list—"Come you not from New-castle?", with its much quoted refrain:

Why should I not love my love?
   Why should not my love love me?
Why should not we together roam?
   Since love to all is free?

Come to think of it, at the last moment, this may refer to the grand old coaching town, now completely altered, of Newcastle-under-Lyme.

Compared with the constant cosseting of Irish and Scottish airs, Welsh ballads have not been zealously cared for, despite some handsome volumes of Cambrian Minstrelsy published in Edinburgh. 'Only in Wales can a whole city burst into song', was the phrase used by my father when he came back from Carmarthen after the Investiture of the Prince of Wales; an inkling of what he meant can be gained from a broadcast from any small Welsh chapel.

In thankfulness for the thrill I have felt, as though from thrushes, whenever their soprano notes sound over the air, I rescue this trifle that has won my heart:

Of noble race was Shinkin
    Thrum thrum thrum thrum thrum
      The line of Owen Tudor
    But hur renown was fled and gone
      Since cruel love pursu'd hur

Fair Winny's eyes bright shining, thrum etc
    And lilly breasts alluring
    Poor Shinkin's heart with fatal dart
      Have wounded past all caring

Hur was the prettiest fellow, thrum etc
    At stool-ball, ounce or cricket,
    Hunting chace, or nimble race,
      Guds plutt how hur could prick it.

But now all joy defying, thrum etc
    All pale and wan hur cheeks too,
    Hur heart so aches hur quite forsakes
      Hur herrings and hur leeks too.

No more must dear Matheaglin, thrum etc
    Be top'd at gued Mungumrey,
    And if love sore smart one week more
      Adieu cream cheese and flumery.

VII

Songs That Reached the Heart

✦✦✦✦✦✦✦✦✦✦✦✦✦✦✦✦✦✦✦✦✦✦✦✦✦✦✦✦✦✦

Mid pleasures and palaces,
Though we may roam,
Be it ever so humble
There's no place like home.
A charm from the skies
Seems to hallow us there,
Which seek through the world
Is not met with elsewhere.

John Howard Payne

FLOWERS HAD TO WITHER, hearts to be shattered, birds to fall with broken wings, children to be orphaned, orphans to starve, chairs to be left empty, and sailors to drown, whenever they were the subjects of Victorian song. At a guess I should say that this morbidity was due first to over-eating and then to dozing in armchairs by the hearths of blazing fires. Away from the glow of coals, the warmth of curly rugs, and the unrest of a bulging stomach eased by port, there was no such wallowing in maudlin sentiments about the satisfactions to be found only in death: in the songs sung at tavern concerts there was far less of it. More often than not our tastes in song indicate the opposite of what we are, to justify which I affirm that the names associated with "Home, Sweet Home", are at best those of incorrigible wanderers and at the worst of a downright homewrecker. Sir Henry Rowley Bishop, its composer, was notorious. Poetic justice has now taken its revenge, and one of the worst tunes he ever wrote is cherished, possibly because of its utter misery, while the things that prove his talents have one by one crept silently to rest. At his best he was one of the sweetest of melodists.

Precisely at the moment when the public was weary of Anacreonic noise and din, as well as the nymphs and dryads who went with it, Bishop broke away from the training of his Italian master and decided to be natural. At twenty years of age, in 1806, he had composed music for ballets about Bajacet and Narcisse, but before the year was out he was providing incidental music for ordinary dramas. Drury Lane recognized his youthful genius in 1809 by mounting his opera *The Circassian Bride;* there was a wildly enthusiastic audience, but barely had the excitement died down when Old Drury perished in flames that destroyed every scrap of his music. Melodramatically it might be argued that his more serious ambitions went with it; though he did compose the opera of *The Maniac* at once, a sober scrutiny of the facts makes it plain that his early fame came too soon for the state of opera. It was not very grand yet (although it soon would be) and when he wrote music for a masterpiece the librettist was too inexperienced even for that easily pleased generation. The *mélodrames* for which Bishop wrote incidental music had been imported from the ruffianly Boulevard du Crime in Paris, and were billed in London as afterpieces. But Bishop was quite content to be composer to the Theatre Royal, Covent Garden, not then an opera house, for fourteen years. For *The Miller and His Men* in 1813 he wrote a score which showed that his genius was, so the critics reasonably said, in its fullest vigour, and the millers' glee, "When the wind blows", outlasted the century. The play itself gained immortality as first favourite in our toy theatres, since small boys relished its explosive finale; and this is one of rare instances where the play has lived longer than the music Bishop wrote for it. His 'interpolations' in Shakespeare have been neglected, often in favour of inferior work, because he proved less of a help than a hindrance.

Life was too easy. Even when no longer able to invent fresh tunes as quickly as he could put pen to paper, he still could earn very nearly enough to pay for his wild, mainly amorous, extravagances; and as amorousness makes of extravagance a necessary virtue, he was in constant and urgent need of funds. He was still at Covent Garden in 1823 when an American actor, John Howard Payne, who had won a great success with *Brutus; or, The Fall of Tarquin,* in which the great Edmund Kean appeared at Drury Lane, managed to persuade the management that his latest scribblings, entitled, *Clari; or, The Maid of Milan,* were fit to be acted. Why this village girl, abducted and kept in luxury by a duke, should pass as a maid, and why her address should be Milan, since it comes into the story only as a distant view on the backcloth, are as inexplicable as why anyone should have thought the plot worth a place on the stage. It justified itself because it contained the most nostalgic of all the songs written in a nostalgic age. Bishop accepted the command to set it to music, and it may be merely by chance that he left Covent Garden shortly after "Home, Sweet Home" had thus been plugged.

Yet he found worse tasks. For the sake of ready money he took to mending, patching, and darning anybody else's work, and did it so well that he gave the public an acquired taste for musical ole clo', which fairly describes the hash of melodramatic dialogue, interlarded with odd numbers by himself, and fragments from the foreign opera under whose title the performance was given. News came to London of the success of Rossini's *Cenerentola* long before there was a chance of obtaining the score: a few scraps were obtained with a programme and some news-cuttings, to reveal how the plot turned upon the courtship by a prince while changing places with his valet, Dandini. Patchwork joined all these, with the nursery tale as background, into *Cinderella; or, The Fairy Queen and the Glass Slipper* at Covent Garden in 1830—and Rossini's Dandini has, in the British institution of Christmas pantomime, remained an integral part of the authentic fairy story ever since. The opera of 1830 is recorded in the repertoire of our toy theatres—without the music.

This year of 1830 marks the end of the period when Bishop had earned his reputation, and the beginning of his resolve to exploit it. His first step was to become musical director of Vauxhall Gardens, where the most fragrant of all his songs was sung:

> Jane, my pretty, pretty Jane,
>   Never, never look so shy,
> But meet me, meet me in the evening
>   While the bloom is on the rye

which may not look particularly enchanting in silent print but is as tender as spring when heard. Whether he ever wrote a better tune is doubtful, but he went on writing a great many worse. He seems to have composed this one under the influence of love, for at the time he was thinking temporarily of fidelity. His first wife had had a lot to put up with. His second, Anne Riviere, a student at the Academy, found fame the moment she became Mrs Bishop, and she would also have found fortune but for the self-same reason —he was too costly to support, not because he was unsuccessful but because he liked the sound of gold coins falling in continual cascade. She left him, in order to pay for the upbringing of their children by singing abroad. Anyone who looks forward to a moral ending must be disappointed. Honours continued to be showered upon the old reprobate's head. Professorships, degrees, freedoms, concerts of his works, never stirred him to any worthy response, while he steered steadfastly towards bankruptcy. In 1842 the Queen bestowed on him a knighthood, and the military bands at the levee played only works of his composing. He was at his happiest in the glee "The chough and crow to roost are gone, the owl sits on the tree".

Payne, the author of "Home, Sweet Home", died in 1852 after spending most of his life in Europe and Africa, ending as American consul in Tunisia. Bishop died in 1855. Their song was picked up like a torch by Malibran, who responded to demands for it half-way through an opera in New York, after which the performance was allowed to continue. Adelina Patti, who made the song her own, was born of Italian parents in Madrid, and brought up in America, where the beauty of her voice made her a diva in her teens. Her first husband was a French marquis, her second an Italian, and her third a Scandinavian baron. Her favourite residence was her castle in Wales. Wherever she sang might be called her home. At the Albert Hall in 1911, long after her retirement, she again sang "Home, Sweet Home", with extra top notes that an innocent might have thought had been put there for her to crack. She cracked the first as well and truly as a stone under a hammer. There was applause. She went on cracking them, and at each crack the joy of the audience grew more and more delirious: they knew that the most Victorian of all Victorian songs would never be the grand climax of such another occasion again.

As though one "Home, Sweet Home" were not enough, its refrain was repeated in Julian Jordan's "The song that reached my heart"—a compliment paid by a song to a song:

> She sang a song, a song of home,
>   A song that reach'd my heart.
>   Home, home, sweet, sweet home.
> She sang the song of "Home, Sweet Home",
>   the song that reach'd my heart.

Without wishing to be trivial I feel forced to point out how fortune, when Victoria was crowned, favoured songwriters whose names began with a B. With Bishop we must pair Thomas Haynes Bayly, whose mission in life did not end, as we are apt to think nowadays, with the writing of the line, 'Absence makes the heart grow fonder', though many an industrious life in letters has achieved still less. He also wrote, to Bishop's tune:

> The mistletoe hangs in the castle hall,
> The holly-branch shines on the old oak wall;
> And the baron's retainers so blithe and gay,
> Are keeping their Christmas holiday.
> The baron beholds with a father's pride
> His beautiful child, young Lovel's bride;
> While she, with her bright eyes seems to be
> The star of the goodly company.
>   Oh, the mistletoe bough! Oh, the mistletoe bough!

This was introduced, as the Popular Ballad, into *The Mistletoe Bough; or, The Fatal Chest*, by Charles A. Somerset, at the Garrick, Whitechapel, in 1834. It was sung by a comic retainer who raised a laugh by claiming to be its composer. In the play, as in the ballad, the heroine hides in the chest, where she dies—a story that has become part of the apocrypha of English history, though in Samuel Rogers's poem "Ginevra", of even date, it is Italian:

> I'm weary of dancing now she cried,
> Pray tarry a moment, I'll hide, I'll hide.
> But, Lovel, be sure thou'rt the first to trace
> The clue to my secret hiding place.
> Rely on it, dearest, I'll be the first man,
> Each tower to search, and each nook to scan;
> And soon will I trace thee to where thou dost hide,
> For I'm weary without thee, my own dear bride!
>   Oh, the mistletoe bough! Oh, the mistletoe bough!

In the last act she appears as a ghost in order to accuse the villain of locking her in, and he dies by his own hand. All this is lacking in our Merry Christmas ballad:

> They sought her that night and they sought her next day,
> And they sought her in vain till a week passed away,
> In the highest, the lowest, the loneliest spot,
> Young Lovel sought wildly but found her not,

And years flew by, and their grief at last
Was told as a sorrowful tale long past,
And when Lovel appeared the children cried,
See! the old man weeps for his fairy bride.
          Oh, the mistletoe bough! Oh, the mistletoe bough!

At length an oak chest that had long lain hid,
Was found in the castle; they raised the lid,
And a skeleton form lay mouldering there,
In the bridal wreath of the lady fair.
Oh! sad was her fate; in sporting jest
She hid from her lord in the old oak chest;
It closed with a spring, and her bridal bloom,
Lay withering there in a living tomb.
          Oh, the mistletoe bough! Oh, the mistletoe bough!

Not many songs that attempt a tale of this length are able to sustain the interest after the first verse. Bayly undoubtedly had the power to make an audience listen. With a more prolonged endeavour he would have made his mark as a popular writer. What prevented him was the fever of a spendthrift. In his youth he tried the Law and the Church before discovering his bent for free-flowing verse. Fortunately his wife had a tidy income. Unfortunately he made short work of it, along with fairly large fees of his own earning, and died in 1839 at the age of 41. While his twenty plays are of no account—although the title of one of them, *You Can't Marry Your Grandmother*, was a catchword—in song he has almost the standing of an immortal. His, "We met, 'twas in a crowd, and I thought he would shun me", has a tune of his own which was not exactly shunned by Brahms, and his "She wore a wreath of roses the night when first we met" was easily first favourite among parodists, proper and improper; its tune was by Joseph Philip Knight, composer of "Rock'd in the cradle of the deep". In the style of drama Bayly gave us, "Oh no, we never mention her"; in fantasy he tried, "Fly away, pretty moth" and "I'd be a butterfly", both to his own settings, but his finest memorial must be "Isle of Beauty", for it is played by massed bands of the Guards at the Cenotaph on the Day of Remembrance. How many in that vast crowd could name the tune? It is by a little-known composer, C. S. Whitmore;

Shades of ev'ning close not o'er us,
  Leave our lonely bark awhile,
Morn, alas! will not restore us
  Yonder dim and distant Isle;
Still my fancy can discover
  Sunny spots where friends may dwell;
Darker shadows round us hover,
  Isle of Beauty, fare thee well!

'Tis the hour when happy faces,
  Smile around the taper's light;
Who will fill our vacant places?
  Who will sing our songs tonight?
Thro' the mist that floats above us,
  Faintly sounds the vesper bell,
Like a voice from those who love us,
  Breathing fondly, 'Fare thee well!'

When the waves around us breaking,
  As I pace the deck alone,
And my eye in vain is seeking
  Some green leaf to rest upon;
What would I not give to wander
  Where my old companions dwell;
Absence makes the heart grow fonder,
  Isle of beauty, fare thee well.

Though numbered among songs that are remembered by one line
it is worth printing for its own sake, if only as a jog for anybody's
memory of last glimpses of England down Channel. Bayly's
'Mid Ocean' song, "The Pilot", is noteworthy as a foreshadowing
of "Rock'd in the cradle of the deep", since it has the same message.
The setting is by G. S. Nelson, composer of "Mary of Argyle":

Oh, Pilot, 'tis a fearful night,
  There's danger on the deep,
I'll come and pace the deck with thee,
  I do not dare to sleep.

To this the pilot answers, 'Fear not', and puts forward reasons
that are calculated, or not, to inspire confidence:

On such a night the sea engulph'd
  My father's lifeless form,
My only brother's boat went down
  In just so wild a storm;

And such perhaps may be my fate,
    But this I say to thee:
Fear not! but trust in Providence
    Wherever thou may'st be.

If "The Soldier's Tear" were Bayly's richest gift to drawing-rooms, it was possibly because of Alexander Lee's music, for the words are not up to much:

Upon the hill he turn'd,
    To take a last fond look
Of the valley and the village church,
    And the cottage by the brook;
He listen'd to the sounds
    So familiar to his ear,
And the soldier leant upon his sword,
    And wiped away a tear

which points the moral,

Go watch the foremost ranks,
    In danger's dark career,
Be sure the hand most daring there
    Has wiped away a tear.

That held its own until the outbreak of the South African War, when it dried up.

VIII

The Poets Bunn and Ball

+‑+

Scenes that are brightest
May charm awhile
Hearts that are lightest
And eyes that smile;
Yet o'er them above us,
Though nature beam,
With none to love us,
How sad they seem.

"Maritana"

EARLY VICTORIAN OPERA sent people home to sing. Composers thought in terms of 'favourite airs' that would be immediately published* as songs and duets or pianoforte arrangements for two or four hands. The librettist took a play, or in desperation adapted a novel, and whittled it away until nothing but the plot was left. This served, appropriately or inappropriately, for one air after another, each introduced with some perfunctory excuse. The first came directly after the opening chorus; in due course the tenor would introduce himself with another, followed by a duet with the soprano, besides a concerted number to close the act. Acts II and III each began with a solo, often by somebody surveying the scene because of its splendours, and at regular intervals gave cues for songs which were otherwise irrelevant. For a hundred years this formula served some type of entertainment or another: it assisted grand opera when Victoria came to the throne, and she liked it immensely. There were protests against the frequency of her visits to the opera each week, and though many sided against her, all who owned pianos sided with her.

* *The World of Fashion, and Continental Feuilletons,* for November 1836 declared that Meyerbeer's *The Huguenots* was not by any means suited for amateurs: 'As an opera it may possess some merit on the stage, but in the drawing-room it is dull and profitless, and has by no means our recommendation', a verdict which damns most operas written since.

There are many operas of this period. Barely one book of words in the whole series is worth reading in itself. The interest lies in comparisons: while the majority are totally lacking in well remembered refrains, two or three of no great importance are packed full of them. The successes are the work of the poets Ball and Bunn. Ball, who renamed himself Fitzball to celebrate his triumphs as a dramatist in blood-and-thunder, was the author of that pressing but indeterminate invitation to Jane which inspired Bishop's best tune. Though not in the running for the post of Poet Laureate, he had his moment. It came when the Princess Victoria's birthday was to be celebrated at Kensington Palace. Especially for this occasion he wrote a drawing-room ballad, set to music by Herbert Rodwell, less out of compliment to the princess than to her mother, the Duchess of Kent:

> Her's the toil of anxious years,
> Her's the glory of this day;
> Her's a nation's grateful tears
> For the fairest flower of May.

Rather more aptly a Mrs G. B. Wilson wrote some verses, also to Rodwell's music, for the same birthday:

> Yet Britannia prophetic beholds the proud day,
> When the sceptre of freedom Victoria shall sway.
> The vision is bright as her own natal day—
> Awake, Rose of England! and smile on our lay!

In theatrical history Bunn finds a place as the manager who had Covent Garden and Drury Lane on his hands season after season in the 1840s. His origins were murky. His wife was the beautiful Mrs Bunn who had wealthy and aristocratic admirers. It was believed that he benefited financially from her visits to their castles, which is the kind of scandal that can be neither proved nor disproved, but the record of his early career in the MS of *Winston's Diary*, a celebrated theatrical document, certainly represents him as a disreputable character. He wrote a volume of verse which provoked *Punch* to refer to him as 'the Poet Bunn', until he brought out a rival weekly which ridiculed its staff unmercifully. Undoubtedly a man of spirit, and probably a thorough-paced rascal— such is the poet whose essays in nostalgia have achieved a longevity equal to that of the finest verse. When his poems appear in the libretti of Ball a line of italic introduction respectfully makes it known, 'By Alfred Bunn Esq., at the request of the Author and Composer'. It is not every day that your manager can be persuaded to adorn your very own script and at the same time be trusted not to make an unearthly mess of it.

Both these authors had served Bishop in those hotch-potches which trained them while untraining him. Both benefited Michael Balfe, the young Irish musician, violinist, and singer, whose gifts and charms had enabled him to tour the Continent in triumph at the outset of his career. Fresh from the encouragements bestowed upon him by Cherubini and Malibran, by patrons and managers, he came to London with *The Siege of Rochelle*. With a libretto by Ball it was in rehearsal at the Lyceum when a financial collapse closed the theatre. By chance Bunn had a gap to fill in his plans for Drury Lane. There it ran for three months in 1835, and kept drawing-room pianos heavily engaged with

> 'Twas in that garden beautiful
>   Beside the rose-tree bow'r,
> Thy gentle child had guileless stray'd
>   To pluck for me a flow'r;
> I heard alas! his feeble scream,
>   And flew some fear to chide,
> His little breast was stain'd with blood,
>   In these sad arms he died!
>
> You found my raiment dye'd with gore,
>   A dagger near me lay,
> I saw the man who struck the blow,
>   His name I dare not say!
> The dreadful secret still to guard,
>   My duty is I feel,
> And let me suffer as I may,
>   The grave my oath shall seal!

as well as with

> When I beheld the anchor weigh'd,
> And with the shore thine image fade;
> I deem'd each wave a boundless sea
> That bore me still from love and thee.
> I watch'd alone the sun decline,
> And envied beams on thee to shine,
> While anguish painted 'neath her spell
> My love and cottage near Rochelle.

Meanwhile Bunn, having prevailed upon Malibran to come to
England, commissioned Balfe to write the music for an opera he
had written himself called *The Maid of Artois*. Such causes, judged
according to the usual experiences of life, should have ludicrous
effects. But Bunn, far from breaking out in the kind of verses
to be expected from a practical business man, at once showed an
understanding of the prevalent nostalgia in a favourite air which
was described even twenty years later as 'The most popular song
in England that our days have known':

> The light of other days is faded,
>   And all their glories past;
> For grief with heavy wing has shaded
>   The hopes too bright to last;
> The world which morning's mantle clouded,
>   Shines forth with purer rays,
> But the heart ne'er feels in sorrow shrouded
>   The light of other days.

Though Bunn may have wished to keep Balfe to himself he had,
after one more try, to call in Ball while he himself was engaged
with Bishop on an adaptation—the polite word for theft, botching,
and mutilation—of Rossini's *William Tell* for Drury Lane in 1838.
Happier results occurred when the quartet changed partners, for
when Bishop and Ball busied themselves, most aptly, with
Rossini's *Thieving Magpie*, Balfe and Bunn begat *The Bohemian
Girl*, which enthralled audiences at Drury Lane during the Christ-
mastide of 1843, and caused not only them but their children
and their children's children to sing:

> The heart bow'd down by weight of woe
>   To weakest hopes will cling;
> To thought and impulse while they flow,
>   That can no comfort bring,
>   That can, that can no comfort bring:
> With those exciting scenes will blend,
>   O'er pleasure's pathway thrown;
> But mem'ry is the only friend
>   That grief can call its own.

Of course that is the philtre as before, and in a not very different
bottle. Far from finding the taste monotonous, the swooning

'. . . and who shall dare? . . .'

'. . . his farewell trip into the promised land . . .'

listeners were overjoyed to swallow it yet again in the same opera:

> When other lips and other hearts,
>   Their tales of love shall tell;
> In language whose excess imparts
>   The pow'r they feel so well,
> There may perhaps in such a scene,
>   Some recollection be,
> Of days that have as happy been,
>   And you'll remember me,
>   And you'll remember, you'll remember me.

Its riches also included, "I dreamt that I dwelt in marble halls", which likewise is too much part of early Victorian domesticity to be omitted:

> I dreamt that I dwelt in marble halls
>   With vassals and serfs by my side,
> And of all who assembled within those walls,
>   That I was the hope and the pride.
> I had riches too great to count—could boast
>   Of a high ancestral name,
> But I also dreamt, which pleased me most,
>   That you loved me still the same.

Every air awaits its label from psychologists who specialize in giving crude names to universal hankerings after love or glory. But besides these songs and "My birth is noble, unstain'd my crest", *The Bohemian Girl* contained, "When the fair land of Poland was plough'd by the hoof of the ruthless invader". Obviously the right of this opera to a place in history cannot be challenged. It represents hours out of all the private lives of England for over half a century.

If Balfe never again reached such a multitude of hearts it was not for lack of Bunn's assistance. Other composers of other nationalities set to music great quantities of plots by other hacks at theatres in all parts of Europe, often with lasting effect on the history of opera. London rang to the notes of songsmiths, from the Grecian Saloon in the City Road to the vast opera house in Pall Mall, where gentlemen still wore tights, *chapeau bras*, and swords. But what pleases people of taste, what pleases people without taste, and what pleases both together, are three different things.

G

The Bohemian Girl was as rapturously received at the Grecian as at the Lane because it was inspired by the feeling which was the quintessence of Victorianism. There was tender languor in Bellini's *La Sonnambula** and in Donizetti's *Lucia di Lammermoor*, and their favourite airs were taken home to be sung, but they earned no place in the family album.

Partnership between Ball and Bunn led to the next complete conquest of the public when one provided book and the other lyrics for William Vincent Wallace, a composer responsible for the setting of Hood's

> Our hands have met but not our hearts;
> Our hands will never meet again.

That strikes the right plaintive note that had somehow to be imposed on a play which Ball seized for rough treatment. It was a high-spirited melodrama named *Don Caesar de Bazan* with a hero who had originally appeared as a character in Hugo's *Ruy Blas*. Seeing how this minor part stole the limelight, two Paris hacks made him the chief character in a new romance. Here he is, while under sentence of death, persuaded to wed the gypsy Maritana so that she may have the rank of a nobleman's widow in order to be worthy of seduction by the king. Don Caesar escapes and petitions the queen, as an interested party, to preserve his life.

Why this should have been chosen as a fit subject for grief may not be at all clear, but there can be no doubt whatever that when transformed into Wallace's opera *Maritana*, it served the purpose at Drury Lane in 1845. By writing "Angels that around us hover" for the heroine, Ball struck the right note at the start, and struck it again at the opening of Act II when a boy who watches over the sleeping hero, sings:

> Alas! those chimes so sweetly pealing,
> Gently dulcet to the ear,
> Sound like Pity's voice revealing
> To the dying, 'Death is near!'

But it is Bunn who supplies the nostalgia. At the request of author and composer (so the 'book of words' informed the public) he enriched the libretto with:

* Translated for Covent Garden in 1848 as *La Sonnambula; or, The Somnambulist* by W. L. Rede. No title could be more helpful.

> In happy moments day by day,
>   The sands of life may pass
> In swift but tranquil tide, away
>   From time's unerring glass

and also with "Scenes that are brightest". In this mood Bunn
was untouchable. What Ball could do was shown at the cue, 'If
his majesty would but confer on me the happiness of falling like
a soldier':

> Yes, let me, like a soldier fall
>   Upon some open plain;
> This breast expanding for the ball . . .

which helps us to understand why humorists called him 'The
Terrible Fitzball' as a warlike hero in one of *The Bon Gaultier
Ballads*. Before parting from Wallace he joined with him in a
ballad:

> I'm leaning o'er the gate, Annie!
>   Neath thy cottage wall;
> The grey dawn breaks; the hour grows late——
>   I hear the trumpets call.
> I could not brook thy cheek so pale,
>   The sad tear in thine eye:
> This heart which laughs at war, might quail,
>   So Annie dear, good-bye.

Ball also brought his gifts to bear on Auber's *The Bronze Horse;
or, The Spell of the Cloud King*, at Covent Garden in 1835. As this
opera was 'arranged' it was Rodwell who supplied the tune to
Ball's interpolated master-stroke:

> Oft hast thou told me, Mother dear,
> Subtle man I'd cause to fear,
> Tho' a saint in yonder skies,
> Still thy warning voice I prize;
> But if he would still pursue,
> Mother dear what could I do?
> Let this little tear proclaim,
> Mother, I was not to blame.

Meanwhile the operas of Friedrich von Flotow, a German
nobleman who was said to have studied as a recreation 'the art

which his graceful talent abundantly adorns', won the favour of
Vienna and Paris though not, at first, of London. When his *Martha*
was sung in German at Drury Lane in 1849 its welcome was
half-hearted, and six years passed before Drury Lane presented
the English version which made his name in Great Britain. This
was not entirely due to any merit of his own, but to an old familiar
tune which had been interpolated because he had not provided the
prima donna with enough scope. Tom Moore's "The last rose of
summer" was added, and it served the purpose so well that it
remained part of the score not in London alone but in Vienna
as well and cannot be left out.

When Verdi turned that notorious play *La Dame aux Camélias*
into *La Traviata* in 1853, the characters sang favourite airs at each
other in the approved manner. But though this mode had not gone
out of fashion, some of its manipulators had. By composing the
music for Bunn's *The Sicilian Bride* and *The Devil's In It* (both
1852), Balfe sank very low. His next opera, written by Augustus
Glossop Harris and Edmund Falconer at the Lyceum in 1857, was
The Rose of Castille, long remembered for

> I'm but a simple peasant maid,
>   None e'er served or me obeyed,
> My humble cot and woodland range
> I would not for a palace change.

with demonstrations of queenly pride during the verses. The same
trio brought out another opera, *Satanella; or, The Power of Love*,
at Covent Garden the year following. After acting in Boucicault's
melodrama, *The Colleen Bawn*, Falconer wrote several Irish melodramas which would hardly be worth mentioning had they not
led to an Irish melody, words by Falconer, music by Balfe, in
Peep o' Day at the Lyceum in 1861:

> By Killarney's lakes and fells, em'rald isles and winding bays,
> Mountain paths and woodland dells, mem'ry ever fondly strays.
> Bounteous nature loves all lands, beauty wanders everywhere;
> Footprints leaves on many strands, but her home is surely there!
>   Angels fold their wings and rest in that Eden of the west,
>   Beauty's home, Killarney, Heav'n's reflex, Killarney.

These words, like Shakespeare's, were memorized by thousands
who could not make head or tail of their meaning; hardly anybody

could grapple with three more verses in the still more aspiring strain of

> Music there for echo dwells, makes each sound a harmony;
> Many voic'd the chorus swells till it faints in ecstasy.

But it was heard everywhere, which was rather rough on Boucicault when he turned *The Colleen Bawn*, his Killarney melodrama, into an opera, collaborating over the libretto with John Oxenford, that old hand at lyrics, and persuading Sir Julius Benedict —no mean melodist as he proved with "The Moon Hath Raised Her Lamp Above"—to provide the score. Under the title of *The Lily of Killarney* it began at Covent Garden in 1862 and toured the British Isles for years, but though its favourite airs were published and presumably tried out on many a piano, barely one of them caught the public ear. Benedict was no match for an Irish composer and Irish poet on the subject of Ireland, but it is only fair to give a sample of the poetry he had to deal with. Here, then, is what Eily O'Connor had to sing:

> I'm alone, I'm alone,
>   I watch the stars as they rise,
>   I hear the sound of my sighs,
> Mock'd by the breezes' moan.
>   All things around me seem to say
>   That I am sad and so are they,
>   But could I see my heart's delight,
>   His smile would cheer the gloom of night.

There was another opera by Falconer that wafted its airs to the plague of pianos. *Victorine*, written by him, was seen in 1859 at Covent Garden; its conductor, Alfred Mellon, was the composer. The most popular of the ballads was:

> This flower, dear maid, doth image thee,
>   Yet is more like the love
> That makes on earth a Heav'n to me
>   All other joys above.
> The parent stem on which it grew,
>   No bud save this has blown.
> As it no rival beauty knew,
>   So I love thee alone.

Operas of favourite airs reached a climax with Gounod's *Faust*, the libretto taken by Michael Carré and Jules Barbier from Goethe. It was first staged at the Lyrique, Paris, in 1859, and sung in concert form at the Canterbury Music Hall in London before being performed in H. F. Chorley's English version at Her Majesty's in 1864. In Paris the original authors, carried away by their success, took the customary course of seeing what else this chap Goethe had done. All they could lay hands on was his philosophically fictionized semi-autobiography *Wilhelm Meister*. Undeterred, as before, by his loftiness of purpose, they had the preposterous idea of making its rambling pilgrimage into a libretto. Wild as that fancy was it yet took shape, to the delicate tunes of Ambroise Thomas, as *Mignon*, first at the Opéra Comique, Paris, in 1866, and then at Drury Lane in 1870. Despite an execrable translation, the gavotte, "Yes, I am in beauty's room", charmed the drawing-rooms, while a rough translation of "Kennst du das land, wo die Zitronen blühn?" into:

> Knowest thou that fair land
> Wherein the citron grows

still exercises a spell not unlike magic. To its first hearers it was all enchantment and a dream.

IX

The Emigrant's Laureate

✦✦✦✦✦✦✦✦✦✦✦✦✦✦✦✦✦✦✦✦✦✦✦✦✦✦✦✦✦✦✦✦

Woodman spare that tree! . . .
Touch not a single bough;
In youth it shelter'd me,
And I'll protect it now;
'Twas my forefather's hand
That placed it near his cot,
There, woodman, let it stand,
Thy axe shall harm it not.

George Pope Morris

SINCE HE KEPT SINGING for seventy years Henry Russell could come in as confidently at one end of this book as at the other. Most of the time he was an entertainer: in the 1830s he was all that and more, for he made history. Consequently, he had better be given his chapter when his songs were new and actively stirring masses of people to thoughts of emigration. He was born in 1813. As a boy he was engaged at Drury Lane while so small that, when he sang before George IV, the king took him on his knee and kissed him. His youth was spent at Bologna, where he studied until qualified to take up a post as music teacher in New York. After an engagement or two in opera, he invented an entertainment which was to serve him for life. In its first form it was called *Far West, or the Emigrant's Progress*, for which he composed the music. The verses were by Dr Charles Mackay, a poet held in high esteem, who also had a brilliant career in journalism as editor of *The Illustrated London News* and as war correspondent of *The Times* during the American Civil War. His *Voices from the Crowd* and *Voices from the Mountains* have vanished even from second-hand bookstalls but we have all heard, "Cheer, boys, cheer".

Far West, or the Emigrant's Progress was first heard in the United States; when Russell returned to England in 1840 it took on a different character altogether, without any effort on his part. He was now a species of evangelist inciting his countrymen to a new species of crusade, and succeeding moreover in shipping whole populations across the Atlantic. The appeal was the more effective by beginning in the customarily nostalgic manner:

> Farewell, a last farewell,
> Land where our fathers dwell,
>   More dear by parting made,
>   Where we as children play'd;
> In meadows, gath'ring flow'rs,
> And pass'd our happiest hours;
>   Here on the beach we stand,
>   Our home our native land,
> And weep to think our feet shall tread thy happy shore,
> And our sad eyes behold thee never, never more.

But that was merely the prelude to "Cheer, boys, cheer! No more of idle sorrow", followed by, "Far, far upon the sea" to the refrain of 'Oh! gaily goes the ship when the wind blows fair'. Next comes:

> Land! Land! Land!
> How gladly through its paths we'll tread,
> With bounding step, uplifted head,
> And through its wilds and forests roam,
> To clear our farms, to build our home;
> And sleep at night and never dread,
> That morn shall see us wanting bread.
> Land! Land! Land!

At the point where an audience might begin to wonder whether or no Dr Mackay were overdoing things, the plaintive note was struck again with "Long parted have we been", but even this ended on the optimistic note of, 'They are coming with the flowers'. Not that it stopped there. "Rouse, brothers, rouse", exhorted, 'If cities follow, tracking our footsteps, Ever so westward shall point our way!' and as a grand climax, "To the West! To the West! To the land of the free!" spoke of prairies like seas where the young may exult and the aged may rest, which in 1840 was just not true.

The lack of humour which beset romantics then was noticeable

in Mackay, as in most song-writers; in "Sunshine after Rain" he
makes one of his emigrants say:

> I left my love in England,
>   In poverty and pain;
> The tears hung heavy in my eyes,
>   But hers came down like rain.

Of course there was another side to it. This was put forward by
Mrs Benedict Vaughan in "Oh! take me not to other lands",
composed by her husband:

> In England we have competence,
>   Then wherefore should we roam?
> 'Tis wild ambition lures thee hence
>   From Country, Friends, and Home.

But that, while suitable for a song, would not serve for an animated
diorama. *The Emigrant's Progress* had most of the advantages
of a theatrical production with none of the disadvantages. Where it
scored over other performances that took place on the stage was
in the fact that the Lord Chamberlain's licence was not required
for a series of songs. Such programmes were not theatrical and
therefore could be given in Lent, that season of abstinence from
all sinful self-indulgence, when anything answering to the legal
definition of a play had to close down. In the April of 1851, Russell
rented the Olympic Theatre (close to Drury Lane) and mounted
his Lenten Entertainment lavishly. Each song in Part 1, written
by Mackay, had a different scene that culminated in a view of
Niagara, while Russell chanted a very sensible poem by Mackay in
praise of the Falls. Another poet, Angus B. Reach, was called in
for a second diorama, called *Negro Life in Freedom and in Slavery*,
where slaves are taken in battle, transported in a ship which is
chased, sold by auction in Havannah, put to work in plantations,
pursued by bloodhounds and riflemen, and caught in a forest fire,
as well as exhibited in light-hearted mood at a dance. This was
severe rivalry for theatres, which were reduced to lectures or
Shakespeare readings during the fast.

How Russell passed the time once Lent was over is indicated by
an advertisement for the Lecture Hall, Greenwich, in 1846. Several
months in advance he had the honour to announce a vocal entertainment on Monday, August 17 and during the week, on which

occasion, in addition to the selection of his established songs and
scenas, he would introduce his newest compositions; he used a lot
of words in the lavish opulence of showmanship. "Mazeppa", from
Byron's poem, challenges the circus spectacle on this subject
which was then astounding the public. To offset the optimism of
"There's a good time coming, boys", he included not only "The
Pauper's Drive" but Hood's "The Song of the Shirt". There were
also "Little Pools and Great Ones", and Negro Melodies, with
anecdotes of negro life and character. He made a particular hit
with:

> I was born in Alabama,
>   My massa's name was Deal,
> He used to own a yaller gal,
>   Her name was Lucy Neal.
> My massa he did sell me
>   Because he thought I'd steal
> Which caused a separation
>   Ob myself and Lucy Neal.
> Oh! poor Lucy Neal, Oh! poor Lucy Neal.
> If I had you by my side, how happy I should feel.

Although his songs were on many subjects he maintained his appeal
for the slaves; when *Uncle Tom's Cabin* created a feverish interest
which inspired a large batch of songs, some in dramatized versions
of the novel and some at concerts, Russell composed and sang a
fierce "Little Topsy":

> Whip me till the blood pours down,
>   Ole Missus used to do it,
> She said she'd cut my heart right out
>   But neber could get to it

which was written by Eliza Cook. Her collected poems, published
at this time in four volumes, testify only to a part of her fame.
She was a power in the land as a song writer. She specialized in
dashing off to a spirited start before turning round in an attempt
to make you collapse in tears. With John Blockley as composer
she won confidence with the cheerful idea of "Many happy returns
of the day", which in other hands might be thought fit for a party,
but not in Eliza's; she aimed at asking what we would not give if
the hour could restore one who was far, far away. Similarly

when she began defiantly in the famous song which Russell
composed:

> I love it, I love it, and who shall dare
> To chide me for loving that old arm-chair

she was merely taking us off our guard in order to make us all the
more miserable. But she could be a dare-devil when she pleased.
Her sea song, music by Blockley, was "The Englishman", whose
flag may sink nailed to a shot-torn wreck but ne'er float o'er a
slave; it should be set against her "I'm afloat, I'm afloat", composed
by Russell, which amounted to a tribute to piracy. These, as well
as her "The Flag of the Free", may founder, but Russell provided
the Royal Marines with their march past when he composed "A
life on the ocean wave", to verses of Arnold, added to by Epes
Sargent, an American. Russell's son, William Clark Russell,
was a seafaring novelist whose *Wreck of the Grosvenor* is a minor
classic.

Any idea that this giant of song can be knocked off in a chapter
must be discouraged. Yet another of his memorable ballads was to
him the frolic of an idle hour. He took the poem from the volum-
inous works of Mary Botham, whose marriage to another author,
William Howitt, led to orgies of ink shed. Despite any number of
useful books this song, which Russell composed and sang, is her
one claim to immortality:

> 'Will you walk into my parlour?' said a spider to a fly,
> 'Tis the prettiest little parlour that ever you did spy;
> 'You've only got to pop your head within side of the door,
> 'You'll see so many curious things you never saw before!
>   'Will you, will you, will you, will you,
>   'Walk in, pretty fly?'
>
> 'Will you grant me one sweet kiss?' said the spider to the fly,
> 'To taste your charming lips I've a cu-ri-o-si-ty'.
> Said the fly, 'If once our lips did meet, a wager I would lay,
> 'Of ten to one you would not after let them come away'.

In the third verse the spider compliments the fly on its wings,
and in the fourth, when those wings are caught in the web, the
spider laughs, "Ha, ha! my boy, I've caught you safe at last",
which isn't the sex we expected. One more verse begins:

> Now, all young men, take warning by
> This foolish little, little, little, little fly:
> Pleasure is the spider that to catch you fast will try.

On looking up the records of Mr and Mrs Howitt I find that they
did not seem to have had such a bad time either.

Both the best and the worst of the words sung by Russell were
by George Pope Morris, an American journalist who made a habit
in New York of founding newspapers and collecting American
melodies. If he shared the contemporary enthusiasm for Campbell's
poetry, he had probably come across the lines:

> Spare, woodman, spare the beechen tree,

and if so he might well have asked himself who, outside reality,
cared the chop of an axe about beeches. Naturalists may note the
almost human contours of their branches, but gangsters of rhyme
know instinctively there's nothing like oak. Hence Morris chose
one of the sort for his famous, "The Old Oak Tree", whose glory
and renown are spread o'er land and sea; the poet's mother kiss'd
him here so forgive his foolish tear, while the relevant matter of
ownership never intrudes when he stops the woodman's work.
Still, that swayed emotions more than other products of the
same partnership, such as "My Mother's Bible"—rivalling "The
Bible was my mother's book" words by J. H. Jewell, music by
W. Wilson, also taken from St Clair's remark in *Uncle Tom's
Cabin*—and a variant of Pocahontas under the title of "The
Chieftain's Daughter":

> 'Tis ever thus when in life's storm,
>   Hope's star to man grows dim,
> An angel kneels in woman's form
>   And breathes a prayer for him.

But it was in "I Love the Night" that Morris put a strain on the
powers of Russell to say very little with a great deal of emphasis:

> But dearer far than moon or star,
>   Or flowers of gaudy hue
> Or gurgling trills of mountain rills,
>   I love, I love LOVE you,
> I love . . . I love . . . I love, I love LOVE you
> I love . . . I love . . . I love, I love LOVE you.

In his melodramatic mood Henry Russell exhibited a frenzy that
were best forgotten—but not in this book, for his sterner self,
breaking out in ballads that resemble operas in miniature, caused
long-lived emulation. For this reason I must quote his grand scena
"The Maniac" in full, since otherwise its force would not be felt.
After an *agitato* opening that almost amounted to an overture,
he grew more agitated still:

> Hush! 'tis the night watch! he guards my lonely cell,
> Hush! 'tis the night watch! he guards my lonely cell,
> Hush! 'tis the night watch, Hush! 'tis the night watch!
> Hush! hush! he comes to guard to guard my lonely cell.
> 'Tis the night watch, he guards my lonely cell.
> He comes, he comes this way.
> Yes! 'tis the night watch,
> Yes! 'tis the night watch, his glim'ring lamp I see,
> Hush! 'tis the night watch, softly he comes,
> Hush! 'tis the night watch, softly he comes, Hush! Hush!
>
> No! by heaven no! by heav'n I am not mad!
> Oh! release me, Oh! release me,
> No! by heaven, no! by heav'n I am not mad!
>
> I lov'd her sincerely, I lov'd her too dearly,
> I lov'd her in sorrow, in joy, and in pain,
> But my heart is forsaken,
> Yet ever will waken,
> The mem'ry of bliss that will ne'er come again.
> Oh! this poor heart is broken
> Oh! this poor heart is broken.
>
> I see her dancing in the hall; I see her dancing in the hall;
> I see her dancing, I see her dancing in the hall;
> I see her dancing—I see her—I see her dancing in the hall;
> I see her dancing in the hall; I see her dancing;——
> She heeds me not——
> No! by heaven, no, by heav'n I am not mad!
> Oh! release me! Oh! release me!
> No! by heaven, no, by heav'n I am not mad!
>
> He quits the grate, he turns the key;
> He quits the grate—I knelt in vain; his glim'ring lamp still,
>   still I see . . .

And all, and all is gloom again.
Cold, bitter cold, no life, no light!
Life, all thy comforts once I had;
But here I'm chained this freezing night;
No! by heaven, no, by heav'n I am not mad!
Oh! release me! Oh! release me!
No, by heaven, no, by heav'n I am not mad!
I see her dancing in the hall; I see her dancing in the hall;
She heeds me not, she heeds me not.
Come, come; she heeds me not.

For lo you, while I speak, mark how yon demon's eye-balls
                                                         glare!
He sees me now; with dreadful shriek he whirls, he whirls me
                                                    in the air!
Horror! the reptile strikes his tooth deep in my heart, so
                                               crush'd and sad!
Aye! laugh, ye fiends, laugh, laugh, ye fiends,
Yes, by heaven, yes, by heav'n, they've driven me mad!
I see her dancing in the hall, I—ha, ha, ha, ha, ha, ha, ha,!
I see her dancing in the hall,
Oh! release me, Oh! release me,
She heeds me not,
Yes, by heaven, yes, by heav'n, they've driv'n me mad!

Hard as that is to sight it would be harder still on eardrums. Yet the number of maniac songs at this period prove how popular such raving was. It did eventually pass out of date, but another of Russell's grand scenas, "The Gambler's Wife", with poetry by Dr Crofts, set the fashion which lasted the century out. After a few lines in the third person it changes to the soliloquy of the neglected wife with her child as the clock strikes one, two, three, and 'the blast howls by'. The ending restores the third person:

The Gambler came at last, but all was o'er——
Dread silence reign'd around, the clock struck four.

All that Russell sang in his long lifetime cannot be named, but it must not be overlooked that he took "The Ivy Green" from *Pickwick Papers* and set it to music worthily:

O, a dainty plant is the Ivy green,
That creepeth o'er ruins old!

> Of right choice food are all his meals I ween,
>   In his cell so lone and cold.
> Creeping where no life is seen,
> A rare old plant is the Ivy green.

Which chimes with "The Old Sexton", which Russell sang and composed:

> Nigh to a grave that was newly made,
>   Lean'd a sexton old on his earth-worn spade;
> His work was done and he paus'd to wait
>   The fun'ral train thro' the open gate;
> A relic of bygone days was he
> And his locks were white as the foamy sea,
> And these words came from his lips so thin,
>   'I gather them in. I gather them in.'

When Russell's reputation had soared so high that many authors were laying poems at his feet, he no longer monopolized the muse of his former partners. Mackay turned to the needs of drawing-rooms, where his most cherished lines were:

> Who shall be fairest? Who shall be rarest?
>   Who shall be first in the songs that we sing?
> She who is kindest when Fortune is blindest
>   Bearing thro' Winter the blooms of the Spring,

set to music by Frank Mori. Both the poetry and the music of "John Brown, or a Plain Man's Philosophy" were by Mackay; it was sung by Russell Grover:

> The hatred flies my mind
> And I sigh for human kind
> And excuse the faults of those
> I cannot love, John Brown.

Before his death in 1889 Mackay wrote "There's a land, dear land", which was unearthed for the Diamond Jubilee and kept in general use for years afterwards. It was not his fault that Edwardian enunciation turned it into "Thah's ah lahnd, d'ah lahnd".

At its height Russell's vogue was a phenomenon without an equal. Many years later it was recalled by Shaw in his criticism of

Pinero's play *Trelawny of the Wells*, at the Court Theatre in 1898. This masterpiece of the nostalgic mood overwhelmed playgoers, sentimental and unsentimental alike, when Irene Vanbrugh in the scene of the players' farewell party sang a ballad by an indefatigable pair of song-writers without a sparkle of divine light between them —music by Foley Hall, words by George Linley:

> Ever of thee I'm fondly dreaming,
>   Thy gentle voice my spirit can cheer;
> Thou wert the star that mildly beaming,
>   Shone o'er my path when all was dark and drear
> Still in my heart thy form I cherish,
>   Ev'ry kind thought like a bird flies to thee!
> Ah! never till life and mem'ry perish,
>   Can I forget how dear thou art to me?
>   Morn, noon and night, wher'e'er I may be,
>   Fondly I'm dreaming ever of thee,
>   Fondly I'm dreaming ever of thee.

According to Shaw it was significant of the difference in their temperaments that when Pinero, as a little boy, first heard "Ever of thee" he wept, whereas 'at the same tender age, I simply noted with scorn the obvious plagiarism from "Cheer, boys, cheer"'. With borrowed tune and tattered phrases Linley and Hall wrung Victorian hearts while thousands of rivals were forgotten. 'To me', Shaw continued, 'the sixties waft ballads by Virginia Gabriel'. By delving like an archaeologist it is possible to discover that she was the composer of "Parted", "A Golden Dream", "Angel Music", "Alone", "Light in the Window", "Dream, baby, dream", "Sacred Vows", "My roses bloom the whole year", "Two Little Faces", "The Tide of Time", "Resignation—heaven-born", "Are the children at home?", "Voices Calling" and "Beloved One". If one or two of those titles seem familiar, it is because they belong to other composers' songs.

'. . . lost in me . . .'

'. . . I know not where. . . .'

'It was a sight most shocking'

X

Siren to a Prime Minister

* *

In thy dark eyes' splendour
Where the warm light loves to dwell,
Weary looks yet tender
Speak their fond farewell.
Nita! Juanita! Ask thy soul if we should part
Nita! Juanita! Lean thou on my heart.

The Hon. Mrs Norton

WHY A SNATCH OF SONG, a few notes, a title, or a few words, should stick in the public throat is a clue to the public heart; it must be still more significant when we pick songs complete; if we could discern the quality peculiar to those we cherish the secret would be worth an unending series of fortunes. There was always a place in the vocal portfolio for "Juanita". Nobody particularly wanted to sing it. Yet it remained, and everybody knew both its words and its music. As time wore on a new generation was totally ignorant of its author.

Mrs Norton, grand-daughter of the author of *The School for Scandal*, had a tragic encounter in real life with backbiters whose forebears were the subject of this comedy. As Caroline Elizabeth Sarah Sheridan she was one of three sisters who were toasted almost inevitably as the Three Graces; one became the Duchess of Somerset, and another Lady Dufferin, while Caroline, at the age of twenty-one, married the Honourable George Chapple Norton, brother and heir of Lord Grantley, and such a very respectable person at first that he was a Member of Parliament and recorder of Guildford.

If you set his prospects aside, it was a queer match. She was already a successful poet. One volume of verse, *The Sorrows of Rosalie*, had appeared before the wedding; now *The Undying One*, a novel about the Wandering Jew, went into two editions in 1830.

Before the end of the year she wrote to Lord Melbourne, Prime Minister, to ask about a job for her husband. While Norton settled down as 'magistrate of Lambeth Street Police Office', the Prime Minister became a frequent visitor to the little gaily furnished house where the lovely Mrs Norton watched for him from her balcony. Here the great statesman relaxed among bright young people.

Not content with sitting pretty at Lambeth Street Police Office Norton saw in this an opportunity for raising money by bringing an action for 'Crim. Con'. This was the usual abbreviation for 'criminal conversations'—not 'criminal connection' as some modern historians suppose—and it was not another name for divorce, which was far too difficult to obtain in those moral days, but a substitute for it. As the case of Edmund Kean and Alderman Cox a few years earlier had proved, the public inclined to execrate the lover without concerning themselves with any doubt whether the husband deserved to be paid. Many, many melodramas had demonstrated that lovers were wholly to blame.

All that could be called original in Norton's plan was the flamboyant idea of pillorying a prime minister. Rulers of the land, from William IV and the Duke of Wellington downwards, were involved, and they proved to be the claimant's undoing. As usual the audience in court laughed heartily for hours although this time the husband was sent empty away. But as magistrates cannot be dismissed, and as he did not feel so shamefaced as to resign, he continued to draw his stipend as the representative of morality in its legal form at Lambeth Street Police Office.

Poems by Mrs Norton appeared at Boston in 1833. In England she began the work of a reformer in 1836 with *A Voice from the Factories*. She wrote indefatigably. In between novels and ballads for children she published *English Laws for Women in the Nineteenth Century*, and *A Letter to the Queen on Lord Chancellor Cranworth's Marriage and Divorce Bill*. She was still writing in 1870. In 1877 she married Sir William Stirling-Maxwell; a few months later she died. In *Silver Spoon*, Lord Grantley's autobiography published shortly before his death in 1954, a descendant of the author of "Juanita" makes us understand in his inheritance of her humour, why a prime minister risked his future in order to delight in her wit. One or two more of her songs outlived her:

Love not! Ye hapless sons of clay,
   Hope's gayest wreaths are made of earthly flow'rs
Things that are made to fade and fall away,
   Ere they have blossom'd for a few short hours.
          Love not! Love not!

Some hint of bitter feelings engendered by her experiences may perhaps be read into "The Murmur of the Shell", both words and music by herself:

A sailor left his native land,
   A simple gift he gave,
A sea-shell gathered by his hand,
   From out the rippling wave.
'Oh, love, by this remember me,
   'Far inland must thou dwell,
'But thou shalt hear the sounding sea
   'In the murmur of the shell'.

Ah! woe is me, with tattered sail
   The ship is wildly tossed,
A drowning cry is on the gale,
   They sink, and all are lost!
While happy yet, untouched by fear,
   Repeating his farewell,
Poor Mary smiles, and loves to hear,
   The murmur of the shell.

The tidings wrecked her simple brain,
   And smiling still she goes,
A mad girl, reckless of her pain,
   Unconscious of her woes;
But when they ring the village chimes,
   That tolled her lover's knell,
She sighs, and says she hears at times
   The murmur of the shell.

By the middle of the nineteenth century the sea was a favourite subject for pessimism, but usually it goes with a faith in Providence less questioning than that.

Today Mrs Norton is remembered solely by "Juanita". In her own day, when it ran into fifty editions without counting arrangements as duet, it had no equal in her list, though this included many a favourite such as "Maraquita", "The Love of Helen Douglas", "Avenge the Wrongs of Adam Leslie", "The Morning Star", "Sing to Me", "Voice of Music" and "The Blind Girl"—this last dedicated to her sister the Duchess of Somerset. "Delia", written by Mrs Norton, was composed by A. W. Pelzer, while her most impressive poem, "The Arab's Farewell to His Steed", was tackled by the industrious John Blockley, unerring judge of good lines. Note its first line, for it was absorbed into the language as a pleasantry uttered by young women to lovesick young men:

> My beautiful, my beautiful, that standest meekly by,
> With thy proudly arched and glossy neck and dark and fiery eye,
> Fret not to roam the desert now with all thy winged speed,
> I may not mount on thee again, thou'rt sold, my Arab steed.

Of the songs written by Mrs Norton's sister Lady Dufferin, the one that survived was "The Irish Emigrant", composed by George Barker. It was inspired by the political activities of her husband, Frederick Temple Hamilton Blackwood, born 1826, governor-general of Canada and India, ambassador to Russia, Turkey, Italy, and France, created Lord Dufferin and Ava in 1888. His work for Ireland included a book on *Irish Emigration and the Tenure of Land in Ireland* in 1867. Lady Dufferin's song ends:

> I'm bidding you a long farewell,
>   My Mary kind and true,
> But I'll not forget you, darling,
>   In the land I'm going to;
> They say there's bread and work for all,
>   And the sun shines always there,
> But I'll never forget Ould Ireland
>   Were it twenty times as fair.

XI

Composer to All the Best Poets

✦✦✦✦✦✦✦✦✦✦✦✦✦✦✦✦✦✦✦✦✦✦✦✦✦✦✦✦✦✦✦✦✦✦✦✦✦✦

Slumber baby dear, hush'd is all around,
List'ning to thy melody that comes from fairy ground.

John Blockley

As EVERY CHILD can tell there was much buying of poetry in Tennyson's England and Longfellow's America. Literary historians compare it to that earlier outbreak in the heyday of Byron and Shelley, but there is one decided difference: whereas the Georgians were content to read or recite, the Victorians had to sing. Tunes, in urgent demand, were wanted for the eloquence of Tennyson and Longfellow over chestnut tree, windmill, mountaineering, invitations to the garden, brook, breakers, Arab steed, departing swallows, and Queen of the May. Enraptured sopranos saw in all these the accepted notions of what had always been fit and proper excuses for straining after top notes. Composers, hurrying to please them, engaged in a wild free-for-all, since no copyrights existed to restrain them. All seized the same verse at the same time—there being no divergence of opinion concerning which was best—in scrums of enormous size (though no longer seen now that the scramble is past and the final score beyond dispute). Balfe, unable to invent a bad tune, has his expected place, but what are all these other names? Here, as in other chapters, the beginner has the luck, while old hands who deserve success cannot command it. Out of respect for undaunted energy, remember John Blockley who laboured incessantly at notation with—on the whole —exquisite taste in his choice of poetry but without the ability to spread beyond the confines of his own generation. He bobs up frequently in these chronicles like the inescapable apostrophe, and with about the same chance of making himself heard.

In their claims to a place at the piano, the new poems which saluted the dawn of 1837 had some old-fashioned rivals. These

were not of the best because singers are not abject respecters of
literary reputations. Keats has been barely acknowledged at all;
Shelley is allowed a hearing for "I arise from dreams of thee",
little else; Byron's farewell to Tom Moore, "My boat is on the
shore", was set by Bishop, his

> The kiss, dear maid, thy lip has left,
>   Shall never part from mine,
> Till happier hours restore the gift,
>   Untainted, back to thine

by Jausen, and several others by Alexander Lee. But all told his
contribution to drawing-room entertainment is surprisingly small
even when "So we'll go no more a-roving", set by Maude Valerie
White at a later date,* is included. As long as solid moral worth
was an important factor in artistic judgement all ranked below
Thomas Campbell, whose funeral in 1844, with eight peers of the
realm to bear his pall through Westminster Abbey, was the most
impressive that Poets Corner has ever seen—though that did not
prevent his most memorable line, 'Distance lends enchantment to
the view', from becoming the refrain of a music-hall song, with
particular reference to chorus girls. And even he, with his Cretan
and his Mariners, was outplayed by Mrs Hemans, whose plucky life,
one long struggle to make poetry pay for five children and a
feckless husband, had ended in 1826. While her "Stately Homes of
England" dwindled into a recitation for the kindergarten, her
solemn injunction, 'Not there, not there, my child' is one of those
phrases that are cemented into the English language. It comes from
her "The Better Land", composed by 'Miss Davis', who specialized in sacred songs, and then by F. H. Cowen, among others:

> I hear speak of the better land,
> Thou call'st its children a happy band;
>   Mother, oh where is that radiant shore?
>   Shall we not seek it and weep no more?
> Is it where the flow'r of the orange blows,
> And the fireflies dance in the myrtle boughs?
>   Not there, not there, my child!
>   Not there, not there, my child!

---

* James V of Scotland wrote a song beginning, "So we'll go no more a-roving",
and there is a sea-shanty with a somewhat similar refrain.

The domestic piano was a great leveller. Each sheet placed in
its holder was treasured or despised not for literary merit but for
top notes and tempo. Longfellow, returning to his duties at
Harvard after the European tour that had ended in the death of his
wife, thought of "Excelsior" as literary labour (and his readers
agreed) but directly it was set to music its popularity multiplied a
thousandfold. But that was mild compared to the joy when "The
Village Blacksmith", which he included in *Ballads and Other
Poems* in 1841, was wedded to a tune by W. H. Weiss so easy
to catch that there was never a likelihood that either words or
music would ever be forgotten; Weiss was an operatic bass, born
in Liverpool, who strung the notes that pleased us all to please
himself. Longfellow himself told the world:

> I breath'd a song into the air
> It fell to earth I know not where;
> For who has sight so keen and strong,
> That it can follow the flight of a song?

which ensured his fame, so regularly were these lines sung; Scott
anticipated him in lines about a shaft at random sent and a word
at random spoken, but as these had never been set to music they
did not hit the mark. Gounod was one of the many struck by Longfellow's arrow unavailingly, but even Balfe, who composed the
setting now favoured, is rarely remembered for his share. On the
other hand it is Balfe, not Longfellow, whose name is attached to,
"Goodnight, goodnight, beloved". They are together in several
more—"The Reaper and the Flowers", "The Green Trees
Whispered", "Anne of Tharaw", "This is the place, stand still,
my steed", "The day is done", and "Trust her not". Carl Rein-
hardt tried his notes on "The Village Blacksmith", "The Reaper
and the Flowers", and "The Rainy Day", as well as "Goodnight,
beloved", which then became:

> Goodnight, goodnight, goodnight, goodnight, goodnight,
>   Goodnight, goodnight, goodnight, beloved,

with several more goodnights after 'I come to watch o'er thee to
be near thee' had been allowed in. Jules Norman tackled "Excelsior" and "The Slave's Dream"; E. J. Westrop "A Psalm of Life";
R. Stopel "The Old Clock on the Stairs"; Franz Kullak "Stars of
the Summer Night" and "Beware, beware"; Weber, at the height

of his glory, "Footsteps of Angels". But, judging by the care taken over coloured fronts, "I stood on the bridge at midnight" was treasured most. Two versions, one by Miss Lindsay and the other by Dolores, are very handsomely decorated.

In the career of Tennyson the piano must be given the honour that is its due. It brought him popularity when critical opinion turned against him in 1855 out of dislike for the modernity of *Maud*. Medievalism was what the cultured wanted and their refusal to accept romance in plain clothes might have been adamant but for Balfe, Blockley, John Barnett, and Mrs Bliss, who knew that people could listen with pleasure to what they could not read. Balfe's "Come into the garden, Maud" soon ousted several other versions, including one by Barnett, composer of the operas *The Mountain Sylph* and *Farinelli*. Mrs Worthington Bliss, who signed herself 'Miss M. Lindsay', accompanied Tennyson devotedly, even as far as "Airy Fairy Lilian"; this had the response it deserved in the Cockney ballad of, "She ain't no airy fairy, 'igh born lady". There are any number of others. Guglielma and also Kuhf set, "Home they brought her warrior dead"; West set, "For men may come and men may go but I go on for ever"; Gale, appropriately, accompanied "The Windmill", which many a basso profundo bellowed into a swagger song with boasts—'Here a giant am I . . . with my granite jaws I devour'—likely to cause nightmares among the very young. Such strong stuff pleased the public for fifty years or more until taste veered in favour of

> So fold thyself, my dearest, thou, and slip
> Into my bosom and be lost in me

even though it does seem to be addressed to her baby by a kangaroo.

All these musicians together barely equalled the devotion to both Longfellow and Tennyson shown by John Blockley. But before trying to take his measure I begin to wonder why these two poets attracted so much music and others so little. Browning wrote, "The year's at the spring" as a lyric to be sung in his play *Pippa Passes*, and it was set by Cecile Hartog. Other composers who looked through the rest of Browning's lyrics and found "First the moth's kiss" must have shuddered at this waffle—like a mouth full of beard. Poe has been unduly neglected except for the "Annabel Lee" of A. M. Pares. No great preference for real poetry

over horse-poetry is discerned until Maude Valerie White adds to
Byron and Burns not only "What I do and what I dream" of
Elizabeth Barrett Browning, but also "Come to me in my dreams
and then by day I shall be well again" by Matthew Arnold, which
reminds us that among his poems there were many he wished to
destroy.

Having made this survey, I am in a better position to do justice
to John Blockley, who could, as long as the best poets are the subject, put music to anything. When we pick out of his list
"Excelsior", "Evangeline", almost everything else that others
chose, and "The Consecration of Pulaski's Banner", we have
merely heard the grace note. We must be prepared for the prodigies
of a man who was a genius in industry if not in inspiration.
To him the poetry of America was worthy of all respect but only
in moments spared from his simple task of providing music for all
the verse of Queen Victoria's reign. If he overlooked some trifle
he was not to blame; his horizons embraced not only the best of
this world but hymns reaching to the next.

Will power has to be exerted against the temptation to scrap
this work on Victorian song in favour of a full-length biography
of Blockley. There never has been another composer so indefatigable in his output of songs and so pernickety in his ideas of what
poets were worthy of him; and there never was another, labouring
on such a scale, of whose tunes so small a percentage can now be
recognized. By 1840 three publishers together, Cramer, Chappell,
and Duff, put their names to a formidable list of his work, which
was merely a select catalogue. It was impressive enough to make
diffident rivals wonder whether they had any right to continue in
business. Pompeii itself was on top, through the medium of Sir
E. L. Bulwer, Bart., who did the same for Granada; beauties of
Mrs Hemans, ballads by Mrs Norton, other items by Eliza Cook and
several other ladies, sacred songs by Campbell and Bishop Heber,
a treatise on singing and vocal scale, suggest the realized ambitions
of a lifetime before we are half-way.

In 1840 Blockley had occasion to add himself to his list of
best poets. It could not be helped, as the others were not available.
He had been called in as a specialist when Louisa Vining, aged two
years and eight months, acquired the habit of singing original
compositions in her sleep. First Mrs Vining, in tears, called Mr
Vining to notate the exact melody; next Louisa sang before well-

known musicians in order to extract from them misleading testimonials which seemed to refer to her sleep-singing but did not; then the evidence was placed before Blockley, who thereupon broke into verse beginning, 'Slumber, baby dear'. The young Queen, so full of fun and good nature as to be the mark of quacks, listened to it with her usual graciousness towards freaks. The result was "The Infant's Dream", poetry by John Blockley, symphonies and accompaniments written and arranged by John Blockley, as sung before her Majesty Queen Victoria at Buckingham Palace with distinguished approbation. Whether the poet ever had another hearing at the Palace has not been recorded.

Nevertheless he went on from strength to strength. What he left untouched in Tennyson is barely worth noticing. He made a 'medley' of *The Princess* which consisted of "O swallow, swallow", "Sweet and low", "Tears, idle tears", "The splendour falls", "Ask me no more", "Home they brought her warrior dead", and "As through the land". Of course he had a shot at "Come into the garden, Maud", as well as "The Brook" and "Break, break, break", among the many other verses, on which composers swarmed so thickly that his publishers had to warn the public that 'in ordering the above, orders should specify by John Blockley'. But this onerous duty of teaching wilful young singers to beware of substitutes was taken off their hands. Blockley turned publisher. First he set up shop at Park Road, Hampstead, and next in the more fitting surroundings of 3 Argyll Street, Regent Street. There he laid Tennyson on his operating table and got down to work. From *In Memoriam* he extracted "Calm is the morn" and "Flow down cold rivulet", and from *The Queen of the May* he took "Music on the wind" and "Ring out wild bells"; he did not refrain from "The charge of the Light Brigade", but his masterpiece was, "What does little birdie say?" which ran into several editions. As *Enoch Arden* was unsuitable for treatment permission was sought, and obtained, to turn it into the right kind of stuff, which was appropriately done as we can tell when we read 'poetry by F. Enoch' over the songs, "The Fisherman's Boat", "The Golden Lock of Hair", "Enoch's Farewell", "Enoch Arden's Dream" and "Enoch Arden's Farewell". With a little more encouragement Tennyson might have had all his poems written for him.

If some similarity of names caused annoyance when the Nigger Minstrels' favourite composer, Buckley, flooded the market with his "Rose by the fountain", "Old home far away", "Little blue eyed boy," "Where the moonbeams linger", "Mother's gentle voice", "Friends of long ago", and other proofs of lowlier aspirations, Blockley found the answer by raising his standards still higher and issuing a list of new and favourite sacred songs. It was dominated by his own compositions, for which he had chosen poets with his customary care—Mrs Hemans' "The Better Land", Montgomery's "Nearer home", Proctor's "Listening Angels", Keeble's "Sun of my Soul", Faber's "O Paradise, O Paradise", Heber's "There was joy in Heaven" and Newman's "Lead kindly light". On the profane level he remained indisputably high, more particularly with Martin Tupper from whom he gained, "All's for the best". He dug a ballad about "The wind and the beam loved the rose" out of *The Last Days of Pompeii*, and still found time to respond to the appeal from a rival firm to compose music for verses by J. E. Carpenter when exercising a happy knack of poetically elaborating sentiments from the novels of Dickens. For example, there is a passage in *Little Dorrit* where a handful of roses is placed on the flowing river with the reflection, 'and thus do greater things that once were in our breasts, and near our hearts, flow from us to the eternal seas'. This became in Carpenter's words to Blockley's music:

> When I deem'd they were a token,
>   Heart and flow'rs were side by side;
> Then the words were still unspoken,
>   Now I fling them to the tide.
> In the heartless world tomorrow,
>   I must still seem light and gay,
> There how many a silent sorrow,
>   Leave we floating far away.
> Bear upon thy breast, oh, river!
>   These bright flow'rs I fling to thee;
> Would the mem'ry of the giver,
>   Could *as calmly* flow from me.

As poet, composer, and publisher Blockley had thus staked his claim as the benefactor of mankind. It is when he adds to these boons by turning editor that we jib. *Blockley's Beauties* is his title for a special series which rouses us to hopes of unimaginable splendours from his own special muse only to fob us off with 'choicest morceaux' of other composers, from Auber and Beethoven

to Spohr and Weber, the poetry by Carpenter, Linley, and Charles
Trevelyan. As the music has been arranged, adapted, and inscribed
to the Hon. Mrs Norton by Trevelyan, we guess in vain how these
beauties became Blockley's.

But we must not part niggardly. If he left us nothing else we
should still be in his debt for composing and publishing Grace
Campbell's "Jessie's Dream, a story of the Relief of Lucknow":

> Aye! now the soldiers hear it,
>   An' answer with a cheer,
> As 'the Campbells are a comin','
>   Falls on each anxious ear—
> The cannons roar their thunder,
>   An' the sappers work in vain,
> For high above the din o' war,
>   Resounds the welcome strain.

In between the verses there are passages, descriptive of bagpipes, to
indicate the advance of Havelock's Highlanders. Anybody who
wished for more could buy Blockley's Fantasia for the pianoforte,
which represented the whole siege in music, incorporating a Hindu
chant, "The Campbells are coming" and "There is a green hill far
away"; all of these knit together by the master mind deserve the
title of a Blockley's beauty far more than anything by Beethoven.

XII

Cocking a Snook

I ax'd her to marry—she scornfully said,
She wonder'd how such a thought com'd in my head;
For a journeyman grocer she lov'd, Mr Figg,
And he was the man she should ved—Dash my vig!

Thomas Hudson

CLASS-CONSCIOUSNESS DIVIDES SONGS. Snobbish the cleavage may be but the cause of it is simply that while operatic airs go with the warmth of arm-chairs round the fire, the humbler blends of words and music come from tavern concerts that belong to the far less cosy life. It follows that while the elegant style soared farther and ever farther away from actuality, the squalid style tended to approach uncomfortably close to it without flinching from horrors. In such songs jokes are comic relief to tragedy. Reality is always there, often grim and horrible. These side-splitting jests make you turn to face the spectre of poverty at which they are cocking a snook.

In between the spiritual thirst of the young person in crinoline and the spiritous thirst of the cove in battered topper, there lay one common interest. Both sang of the heart, particularly the broken heart, excruciating to the one, excruciatingly funny to the other. In the eighteenth century it was the sailor who found that his sweetheart had married a tailor or a barber, and he had our sympathy; in the nineteenth it happened to tradesmen, and their complaints invited derision. Imitations of "Dash my vig!" multiplied until its joke dominated all the fun enjoyed at tavern concerts, but when Hudson was singing there in the 1820s to be jilted was only one of many comic misfortunes. His "Billy Bumpkin's peep at the Coronation" gained a hearing at the Surrey Theatre, where the verse telling how his pocket was picked became a familiar quotation:

> I lik'd the sight so well that, wit'out the slightest hesitation,
> I'd lose another sovereign to see another coronation.

Mockery might have remained mild but for Tom Hood, who put stings into it. In London, where he was born in a bookshop in 1799, he was articled to a firm of engravers, which accounts for the elaborate illustrations on his song fronts. During his struggle with hunger and ill-health he wrote poems that won a place in literature, but in song his credit stands higher still. He had the gift of making revellers laugh and think afterwards—though we may wonder why they were heartily amused by "The Lost Child":

> Why should he leave the court where he was better off
> Than all the other boys,
> With two bricks, an odd shoe, nine oyster shells,
> And a dead kitten by way of toys?

His "Skying a Copper" may not be quite so squalid:

> There was bodies all split and torn to rags,
> It was a sight most shocking,
> Here was a leg, and there a leg,
> I means (you know) a stocking

whether or no we are meant to understand that the washerwoman was killed by the explosion. But his "Ben Battle", sung with great applause according to the *London Singer's Magazine*, compels the belly laugh that leaves a headache concerning what we have been sniggering at:

> Ben Battle was a soldier bold,
> And us'd to war's alarms;
> But a cannon ball took off his legs,
> So he laid down his arms.
> Now as they bore him off the field,
> Said he, 'Let others shoot,
> 'For here I leave my second leg,
> 'And my Forty-Second Foot'.

When faithless Nelly Grey sneers, 'You cannot wear your shoes upon your feats of arms', he hangs himself:

> And they buried Ben in four cross roads,
> With a stake in his inside.

Unconscious humour in the drawing-room might approach this
with, 'I see thee still! thou art not dead though dust is mingling
with thy form', but that is by chance. Hood was not trying to
please. After marriage his endeavours to earn a living by his pen
did not tend to lightness of touch. His 'favourite anatomy song'
breathes a bitter spirit, but it was set to music by one of the most
cheerful composers of the Cockney school—Jonas Blewitt, who
had begun his career in public entertainments at the Spa Gardens,
Bermondsey, a spot dismal enough to daunt a heart less strong
than his. Between them they pleased the public with:

> 'Twas in the middle of the night,
>   To sleep young William tried,
> When Mary's ghost came stealing in,
>   And stood at his bedside.
> 'Oh! William, dear! Oh! William, dear!
>   'My rest eternal ceases,
> 'Alas my everlasting peace
>   'Is broken into pieces.
>
> 'I thought the last of all my cares
>   'Would end with my last minute;
> 'But though I went to my long home
>   'I didn't stay long in it.
> 'The body-snatchers they have come,
>   'And made a snatch at me;
> 'It's very hard them kind of men
>   'Won't let a body be.'

London minstrels played this game with zest long after hardship
had proved too much for Hood. Throwing all pretence at mirth
aside he wrote "The Song of the Shirt":

> Oh God! that bread should be so dear
> And flesh and blood so cheap

which was published by *Punch* in 1843 and sung by Henry Russell.
Hood died in 1845.

A singer so far above the Cockney level as Russell chose Hood's
verses only when they were serious, but in America his attitude was
contrary. Russell's *Virginian Melodies* are comic in a style that
demonstrates the kinship between the coon and the urchin. Of

course there would be resemblances in any language among songs of the category set long ago by "A master I have and I am his man" but there is more than that between examples made in London and those brought by Russell from Virginia:

> Boss gave him oats to feed de hoss,
> He eat 'em hisself, and master cross—
> 'What Dobbin had?' said Boss—'You flat!'
> 'Not'ing at all, and not quite dat!'
>   Walk along, John, all thro' the town.
>
> Jyhn took turnips to feed de sheep,
> But gib 'em instead green 'bacca leaf——
> 'What you do wid turnips, hungry glutton?'
> 'Keep 'em till I get some mutton!'
>   Walk along, John, all thro' the town.
>
> John lay on de railroad track,
> De engine come slap on his back;
> John didn't cry, nor wince, nor whine,
> But cried, 'Do dat again, you'll hurt my spine!'
>   Walk along, John, all thro' the town.

Without looking for parallel incidents or coincidences of any kind, that Virginian melody can be matched for a pair of snooks by a Cockney melody:

> Perhaps his lordship may fly in his airs,
> And kick John down four or five flights of stairs
> Give him a pair of black eyes to add to his beauty—
> He must bear with it all, for it's part of his duty,
>   Three females are kept,
>   So blithe and so bonny;
>   And to keep them in order
>   They now want a Johnny!
>
> Should one of the females get in a queer way,
> John his exit must make without any delay,
> Though my lord be the father—'tis common 'mongst the ton,
> They're sure to be father'd on unlucky John.
>   Three females are kept,
>   So blithe and so bonny;
>   And to keep 'em in order
>   They now want a Johnny.

Tavern songs and plantation songs jostled each other in the repertoire of Sam Cowell, an English actor's son brought up in America, who sang Cockney ballads in London before introducing them to New York. For his full evening's entertainment he wrote burlesques of *Hamlet* and *Alonzo* of such inordinate length that they must have been acted rather than just sung, but there is no record of a yawn. Ballads of this kind may be the aftermath of Hood, which seems all the more likely when we find that Cowell started with "The Lost Child" and then seized a burlesque, already popular, which made a jest of gruesome details in the ancient "Lord Lovell":

> Then he order'd the grave to be open'd wide,
> And the shroud to be turn'd down—
> And then he kissed her clay cold lips,
> While the tears came trickling down.
> Then he flung himself down by the side of the corpse
> With a shivering gulp of a guggle,
> Gave two hops, three kicks, heav'd a sigh, blew his nose,
> Sung a song, and then died in the struggle!

Once the resolve to make a mock of tragedy is removed from ordinary, everyday settings and applied to the fancy dress of medievalism, it loses its meaning. Yet the guying of Lord Lovell's grief is derived, no matter how remotely, from the idea that the cruelty of fate is a stock subject of jest, though in romantic trappings it exhibits no pointing or sharpening of wit whatsoever.

There may be seen in it the street arab's overriding impulse to adorn each image of romance with a red nose, moustache, and black teeth, but we can tell from its welcome in America that the spirit was not local. Cowell's chief success in New York was "Billy Barlow", which conforms to the humour of the human scarecrow well-known in the cotton fields. Cowell became destitute before he started singing it in drinking saloons. Civil War had been declared; he had seen soldiers going away:

> And the young women there gave vent to such woe
> You'd ha' thought they were parting from Billy Barlow.
> Oh dear, oh raggedy oh!
> You'd ha' thought they were parting from Billy Barlow.

In his childhood Cowell had heard negroes in the cotton fields and had picked up from them the lilt of refrains in such songs as "Jim Along Josey" and "Sandy Hollar", but he was first and foremost an actor, and it was by acting that he could make his one-man show last a whole evening. In print his "Runaway Cork Leg" suggests that his physical exertions must have been inspired. What keeps his memory green is "Villikins and his Dinah", a song, not his own, that had other well-known singers:

'Tis of a rich merchant who in London did dwell,
He had but one daughter, an unkimmon nice young girl;
Her name it was Dinah, scarce sixteen years old,
With a very large fortune in silver and gold.

As Dinah was a valiking in her gardin one day,
Her papa came up to her and thus he did say,
Go dress yourself Dinah in gorgeous array,
· And take yourself a husiband both galliant and gay.

Oh, Papa, oh, Papa, I've not made up my mind,
For to get mar-i-ed I don't feel inclined,
My very large fortune I'd gladly give o'er,
If I could remain single a year or two more.

Go, go, boldest daughter, the parient replied.
If you won't consent to be this here young man's bride,
I'll give your large fortune to the nearest of kin,
And you won't reap the benefit of one single pin.

As Villikins was a valiking in the gardin around
He spied his dear Dinah lying dead upon the ground,
A cup of cold pison it lay by her side
With a billy-ducks a-stating 'twas by pison she died.

He kissed her cold corpus a thousand times o'er,
And called her his dear Dinah though she was no more.
Then swallowed up the pison like a lovyer so brave,
And Villikins and his Dinah now lie buried in one grave.

Now all you young maidens take warning by her.
Never not by no means disobey your guv'ner,
And all you young gentlemen mind who you clap eyes on,
Think of Villikins and his Dinah and the cup of cold pison.

The most remarkable singer of "Villikins" was Frederick Robson, by all accounts a genius, though he rarely appeared in anything more ambitious than burlesque. But the version he introduced into *The Wandering Minstrel* at the Olympic in 1853 is inferior though he set the whole town warbling it until it penetrated courts of law, and justice herself was disturbed. Despite his success he was the victim of perpetual stage fright and died of drink. Cowell, out of sheer conviviality, had a similar ending, after leaving us one other Cockney ballad, "The Ratcatcher's Daughter of Islington". She was a seller of sprats, and she fell in love with a seller of lily-white sand:

> The Ratcatcher's daughter run in his head,
>   And he didn't know vot he was arter,
> Instead of crying, 'Vant any lily-vite sand?'
>   He cried, 'D'ye vant any Ratcatcher's daughter?'
> The donkey pricked up his ears and laughed!
>   And vonder'd vot he vos arter
> To hear his lily-vite sandman cry,
>   'Vill you buy any Ratcatcher's daughter?'

> Now they both agreed to married be
>   Upon next Easter Sunday,
> But the Ratcatcher's daughter had a dream
>   She wouldn't be alive till Monday.
> She vent again to buy some sprats,
>   But tumbled into the vater,
> And down to the bottom of the dirty Thames
>   Fell the purty little Ratcatcher's daughter.

> Lily-vite sand ven he heard the news
>   Both his eyes poured down vith vater,
> Says he, 'In love I'll constiant prove—
>   And blowed if I live long arter!'
> So he cut his throat vith a sqvare of glass,
>   And stabbed his donkey arter,
> There vos an end of lily-vite sand,
>   His donkey and Ratcatcher's daughter.

Shilling books of songs published in the 1840s contain more of such burlesque than realism. To turn from these to products of the 1860s is to discover a return to the spirit of Tom Hood. People of both periods went in for popular songs about happenings to the poor, but while one public regarded poverty from a safe distance the other got lost in it. Here is a ditty of St Giles's from a pretty little "Casket"; and what is meant by 'nightman' need not be described:

> I am the right man,
>   Be then my bride;
> A regular nightman,
>   And dustman beside.
> While cats'-meat calling,
>   You look so smart,
> I, in love falling,
>   Then lost my heart.
>   Rouse, Blowsabella,
>   Get up, my dear;
>   Come from your cellar,
>   Bob Dusty is here.

What is good fun, free from care, changes in a cheap 'songster' of 1866 to a very wry grin under the title of "Children objected to", by J. A. Hardwick:

> You may seek in the East, you may seek in the West,
> Where 'Lodgings to let' your eye may arrest,
> Each family man will find, how high he bids,
> Tho' with gloves on his hands they object to his *kids*.
> If rooms in this town you wish to obtain,
> Young fellows, directly a girl's heart you gain,
> Make this bargain tho' she may not like it when wed,
> Have no children—each sleep n a separate bed.

Turn back to the "Casket" for more hearty laughter and you will find a parody on "The Mistletoe Bough", with the refrain of "Oh the poor vorkhouse boy". While the paupers are keeping their Christmas holiday with extra soup the boy vanishes:

> At length the soup-copper repairs did need;
> The coppersmith came and there he seed
> A dollop of bones lay grizzling there,
> In the leg of the breeches the boy did vear!
> To gain his fill the boy did stoop,
> And dreadful to tell, he was boil'd in the soup!
> And ve all of us say, and say it vith sneer,
> That he vos push'd in by the overseer.
>   Oh! the poor vorkhouse boy. Oh! the poor vorkhouse boy.

Why starvation struck that poet as funny can best be explained by reference to the burlesque of Lord Lovell. No joke is a joke until it is recognized as a joke, which means that stories are usually funny because they are labelled 'funny'. Audiences brought up on Sam Cowell had been trained to laugh when a climax came to suicide or some other sort of sudden death, and had yet to understand—on the principle, 'Comedy is tragedy seen at a distance'—that the horrors which are comical when dressed up in historical costume are serious in contemporary rags.

How closely the Cockney school of versifiers kept to fact can be seen in their readiness to describe squalor at first hand with a veracity that is opposite to the moralist's desire to paint virtue and vice in bright colours. J. A. Hardwick inherited Hood's sense of humour with a razor edge. In his light-hearted moments it might make him say of "The Brand New Bobbies":

> Instead of the old flower-pot tile,
> The helmet is a better style.
> It has more room and cap-ac-i-tye,
> To hold cold mutton or rabbit pie.

But in another mood it led to "A Night in the Workhouse", published in the same songster, which causes—and is meant to cause—a shudder:

> Bags of hay laid on the floor,
> For hunted wretches on to snore,
> For one, but holding three or four,
>   All night in a London workhouse.
> In, one by one, the casuals crawled,
> In filthy tatters, raiment called,
> Like raging fiends they yelled and bawl'd,
> While by the Daddy overhauled,
> Who doled to each a slice of 'toke',
> Which eager dirty fingers broke,
> No words of thanks for that was spoke,
>   At night in the London workhouse.

Chorus:

> Swearing, yelling, all the throng,
> With jest obscene and ribald song,
> Thus passed the weary hours along,
>   Of a night in a London workhouse.

Their rags were up in bundles tied,
A check shirt was to each supplied,
With a rug and number to abide,
    All night in a London workhouse.
The roof was tiles with moisture dank,
From odours reeking, foul and rank,
Beneath stood many an iron crank,
Where tramps in weariness down sank.
A horsepail full of water stood,
For those who quaff the liquid could,
And brutes to drink it, naked stood,
    That night in a London workhouse.
Chorus:
    Swearing, yelling, etc.

There are seven verses and these give all the details:

When after twelve had lulled the din,
Nocturnal scratchings of the skin,
By some stark-naked did begin
For 'game' begot by dirt and sin,
The tin into the pail was thrust,
All thro' the night to quench the thirst,
Bred by the atmosphere accurst
    In the casual ward of that workhouse.

Although it would be difficult to find another popular song as gruesome as that, a touch of realism is present in many. 'I was doing my heavy on eighteen shillings a week' one lover carols:

Her parents they are poor, but she's a milliner,
    And earns a pound a week in the city;
A crown she gives her mother for her keep and board,
    The rest she spends in clothes to make her pretty.
She never saves a penny, but to me she says she will,
To pay the expense of marriage is a suger-coated pill;
    And should we have a family, but too soon I must not speak,
A wife and fourteen children on eighteen bob a week.

Even the horse-play in songs of the 1860s carries conviction. It is hard not to laugh on the wrong side of your mouth when a heroine who runs a fried-fish shop repels an unsuitable lover:

I called him a Johnny Raw and cried, 'Now keep your place',
And took a piece of hot fried fish and slapped it in his face.
He look'd just like a great Tom Fool but not a word he said,
I took up a bowl of batter and poured it on his head,
And then as a good wind up to make the fun complete,
I got together a mob of boys to pelt him through the street.

The scene so sharply etched becomes as vivid as personal memories
of the harsh Victorian world. A journey in a twopenny bus sung
about by James Henry Stead has the same effect. Jammed up tight
against a plump blonde whose crinoline came o'er his knee, he
couldn't quite avoid to gently press her. Then lack-a-day she ran
away, and left him with her baby. 'It's got your nose so I suppose
you're father to the baby', is all the sympathy he gets.

Flashes of wit often occur in choruses of hackneyed songs,
especially when the subject is feminine duplicity. "Minnie Bell, the
Captain's Daughter", is the tale of a charmer at Margate whose
poodle scampers into the water and is pulled out by a masher's
masculine sunshade:

> For she'd light blue eyes and golden hair,
> Tiny little feet, and a waist so rare,
> A face and form beyond compare,
>   And she was a captain's daughter.

Much the same story happens in a sixpenny hop at Islington where
a double shuffle is performed by the heroine:

> Her eyes were as black as the pips of ap ear,
> Her cheeks they were rosy—in ringlets hung her hair,
> And her name was Isabella, with a gingham umbrella,
>   And her father keeps a barber's shop at Islington.

Likewise another simpleton is caught in Burlington Arcade while
strolling up and down in the manner that gave pleasure to the
generations which had not learnt the meaning of speed:

> Although her face I did not see,
>   For the thick black fall that hid it,
> The guiding star that led me on——
>   'Twas the mauve kid glove that did it.

How to stroll was expounded by Fred French*, otherwise forgotten, in "The Beau of Wotten Wow":

> Well-fitting vest as white as milk,
> With patent shoes and socks of silk;
> Coat of velvet, shirt like snow,
> And lavender kids for Wotton Wow.
> Well shap'd hat, sometimes white,
> Twousers without winkles quite;
> Nought like fashion—that's the go,
> To men of note wound Wotten Wow.

That Blewitt should be encountered in such company proves not that he was first and last a bard of the tap-room but that he could suit his notes to any verse. In his old age he could still hear the strains from drawing-room pianos of his youthful setting for the Ettrick Shepherd's, "Bird of the Wilderness":

> Thy lay's in the heaven,
> Thy love is on earth.

Yet it was Blewitt who invented the laughing song with his (both words and music) "The Merry Little Fat Grey Man":

> There is a little man dressed all in grey,
> He lives in the city and he's always gay,
> He's round as an apple and plump as a pear,
> He has not a shilling, nor has he a care.
> Yet he laughs and he sings, and he sings and he laughs,
> And he laughs ha! ha! ha! ha! Laughs ha! ha! ha! ha!
> Ha! ha! ha! ha! ha! ha! ha! ha! ha! ha!
> Oh! what a merry merry merry merry merry merry
> Little little little little little little little little
> Fat fat fat fat fat fat fat fat fat grey man.
>
> He drinks without counting the number of glasses,
> He sings merry songs and flirts with the lassies,
> He has debts, he has duns when bailiffs draw near,
> He shuts up his door and he shuts up his ear.   *Chorus.*
>
> If the rain through the roof his garret floor wets,
> In his bed snoring snugly, the rain he forgets,
> In bleak cold December it hails and it snows,
> If the fire goes out his fingers he blows.   *Chorus.*

---

*Not to be confused with Percy French of "Phil the Fluter's Ball" and "Mountains of Mourne."

and it was Blewitt who composed, shortly before his death in 1853, the song-and-dance that had a mesmeric effect on everybody who heard it, including Charles Dickens when he was writing for *Household Words*. Its author was F. C. Perry, and its title "The Perfect Cure"—sung and danced by James Henry Stead, year in, year out. It was the usual story of a nice young maid:

> I wasted on her lots of cash,
>   In hopes her love to share.
> I with her used to cut a dash,
>   And all things went on square
> Until I caught another chap
>   Who on his knees did woo her;
> She cried as she my face did slap,
> You're a perfect cure, a cure, a cure, a cure, a cure,
>   Now isn't I a cure,
>   For here I go,
>   My high gee wo,
>   For I'm a perfect cure.

After the walk round he continued:

> I was laid up for sev'n long months,
>   Indeed I'm not romancing,
> Which brought me on Mr Antinny's dance,
>   That's why I keep on dancing.

In fool's cap and a red-and-white suit, like pyjamas, Stead kept bobbing up and down, feet together, arms to sides, before a delighted audience. It was a peculiarity of the Victorians that they could never have too much of a good thing even when not so very good either. In Blewitt's youth there was a far wider range of subjects, as you can see from his "The lamentation of Old Father Thames", written by Thomas Hudson, whose topics outnumbered those used by the whole of the next generation put together.

XIII

Week of Seven Sabbaths

⦿⟶•⟵•⟶•⟵•⟶•⟵•⟶•⟵•⟶•⟵•⟶•⟵•⟶•⟵•⟶•⟵•⟶•⟵•⟶•⟵•⟶•⟵•⟵⦿

In the gloaming, oh my darling,
When the lights are dim and low,
And the quiet shadows falling
Softly come and softly go;
When the winds are sobbing faintly
With a gentle unknown woe,
Will you think of me and love me
As you did once long ago?

In the gloaming, oh my darling,
Think not bitterly of me,
Though I passed away in silence,
Left you lonely, set you free;
For my heart was fast with longing,
What had been could never be.
It was best to leave you thus, dear,
Best for you and best for me.

Meta Orred

SOME SONGS are far more Victorian than others. Most of these
picked ones are full of despair, though not all. What they have in
common is to be found not in the words and music alone but in a
wistfulness which tugs gently at our heartstrings because its
sentiments have been given the solemnity of hymns. When saddening memories grow entangled with this the effect is like an aural
presence, a wraith. "In the gloaming", remembered as the favourite
song of a quiet voice in the past, distils the sweetness of years
when family was our whole world. Unless the mistake is made of
putting any particular meaning upon it, "In the gloaming" is the
perfect expression of Victorianism. Lady Arthur Hill, its composer,
tried again with "Let me forget thee" and "Waning Years",
without the same result.

Though unsurpassed in its special quality "In the gloaming" can be matched in sentimental appeal by a Victorian song which is even more widely remembered, namely "Alice, where art thou?" It has attracted more than one claim to its authorship, but the copies I have seen are inscribed 'written by W. Guernsey, composed by J. Ascher'. In the nineteenth century it was so well known that a greater degree of popularity could not be imagined. It was sung indoors and out of doors, quoted and parodied, ridiculed in public and admired in secret, played in pyrotechnic 'arrangements' as pianoforte duets by disciplined children or undisciplined grown-ups, chosen for brass band contests, insisted upon as cornet displays, danced to in waltzes or quadrilles, played 'by request' and encored —and yet subjected to a fairly general disdain as though the millions susceptible to its melancholy wished to assert that they were not. In all that time it was rarely, if ever, cited as a typical English song, though there was a copy of it in every home which possessed a piano. It vanished, along with shiny black horse-hair upholstery, in the usual revolt of a new generation, so thoroughly that when I wanted a copy I could not find one. In the 1950s I mugged my way through stacks of old songs in second-hand stores without finding a trace of it. Then by chance, while I was buying new music in a fashionable stores, it turned up first in a fresh collection of popular songs and next in a collection of classics by Brahms, Schubert, and Handel. There must be merit in a ballad which thus straddles the gap between community singing and chamber music. Yet if it had no other interest than that of a museum piece we should be able to appreciate the mysterious sorrows of its Gothic gloom. Perhaps the opening lines add to the pervading bewilderment, since the comment on how the birds are sleeping must come from an expert nature lover after making his round of the nests; he could hardly expect them to make their condition known by snoring, in the very moment when grief drives him frantic. Nor could the usual run of rapt musicians comprehend at one hearing who it might be who 'beameth bright', since Lyra, as the name of a northern constellation, had been out of use popularly. Anyhow, as with Shakespeare, you have only to go on listening and all will be well, whether you understand what you are listening to or not. Some soft and yet responsive trance is required to derive the maximum amount of benefit from heartbreak ending in 'Hurrah! She's dead'.

The birds sleeping gently,
  Sweet Lyra beameth bright;
Her rays tinge the forest,
  And all seems glad tonight,
The winds sighing by me,
  Cooling my fever'd brow,
The stream flows as ever,
  Yet, Alice, where art thou?
One year back this even,
  And thou wert by my side,
Vowing to love me, Alice,
  Whate'er might betide.

The silver rain falling,
  Just as it falleth now,
And all things slept gently,
  Ah, Alice, where art thou?
I've sought thee by lakelet,
  I've sought thee on the hill,
And in the pleasant wild-wood,
  Where winds blew cold and chill;
I've sought thee in forest,
  I'm looking heav'nward now,
Oh! there amid the starshine,
  Alice, I know art thou!

'With melancholy expression' had been insisted upon from the
beginning of the century; looking backwards had always been the
pet cause of it all, bereavement had constantly been harped upon,
and more and more it had been felt that thoughts should be directed
above, not overtly to religion when the words were for week-day
use, but to heav'n. In its obedience to all these rules "Alice, where
art thou?" epitomizes the settled frame of mind in the comfortable,
respectable Victorian home. Where personal dignity was confused
with personal grandeur, the cult of gravity was assisted by a
luxurious pessimism, and in order to maintain this the entertainment of the drawing-room upheld the ideal of the week of seven
Sabbaths.

With this in mind we may begin to understand why poets and
composers were so set on seeing their work laid by the side of
Sacred Music which came out in special editions, with coloured
fronts of the Holy Family, as the one permissible recreation for

Sunday. But though it might be truly said that the day of rest was to them what the Royal Academy was to painters, the full explanation of their priestlike bent is not there. The blame for this sanctimonious itch has been put upon Victoria without justification. In fairness it ought to be recognized that our songs began to sound like hymns directly the habit of using old country tunes drove professional composers out of business a hundred years earlier, and as hymn writers from the Wesleys onwards took their settings out of the same bag, singers might not be fully aware when they were in church and when out of it. Over the same period a comparable tendency in verse caused poets to preach; it is difficult to find a direct link between one and the other—melancholy music and moralizing verse—and yet they went hand in hand. It is all very well to laugh at such songs as Montgomery's:

> In lark and nightingale we see
> What honour hath humility

but Shelley's compliment to the lark as 'Scorner of the ground', and Wordsworth's 'Dost thou despise the earth where cares abound?' belong to the same school. In their defence we must feel how tired they were of their forebears' trick of bringing birds into the affairs of Venus—almost as tired as we are of our forebears' trick of using birds for sermons.

When Barry Cornwall's daughter, Adelaide Proctor, wrote "The Lost Chord", she endowed it with devotion; when Sullivan, in a mood of mourning, matched it with strains suited to church organs, they came so near an anthem that its appeal as a song is lost. Similar feeling exists in the Welsh National Anthem, translated from the Welsh by George Linley and set to music by Brinley Richards:

> Among our ancient mountains
> And from our lovely dales,
> Oh, let the pray'r re-echo,
> God bless the Prince of Wales

which gave a ritualistic effect to the turn-out of the Prince of Wales's Own Volunteers in Hyde Park unlike any other march past.

Naturally the compromise between sacred and profane was at its happiest in Christmas carols. Here John Mason Neale comes into the story. He was a clergyman with High Church convictions that repeatedly got him into trouble until, in 1857, he was burnt in effigy by zealots of the opposite extreme. Yet the Church of England had good reason to be grateful for his translation of the Crusaders' song, *Urbs Syon Aurea*, into "Jerusalem the Golden", which small boys venerated as words from the the lips of Richard Lionheart. From the time of Neale's death in 1866 joyful congregations have imagined themselves linked to antiquity by "Good King Wenceslas", the secular carol he conjured out of his own luxuriant fancy—while there are several Wenceslases in history none of these can be identified with:

> Good King Wenceslas look'd out
> On the Feast of Stephen,
> When the snow lay round about,
> Deep and crisp and even

which has a place among holly, mistletoe, crackers, and fir-tree as part of Christmas. Perhaps good Christian men wealth or rank possessing may not feel any greater desire to bless the poor on hearing how heat was in the very sod which the saint had printed, but good Christian children sing 'deep and crisp and even' with the relish for a white Christmas which belongs to Dingley Dell. More of that happy spirit bequeathed to us by the early Victorians can be discerned in "It came upon the midnight clear", written at this time by E. H. Sears, for which Sullivan composed the setting. What explains this tug at our heartstrings may be nothing more than the backwash of time, which makes us belittle the fashions of yesterday and simper over the crinolines and nosegays of the day before yesterday.

Some changes in our feelings towards bygone fads and fancies are in progress now. We may almost hear our affections turn round in their attitude to the sabbatarian gloom which once filled us with smouldering anger. Why, we used to think, should we have to listen at concerts during the week to songs that 'preached' under a mere pretence at being entertainment? The worst offender in sanctimoniousness was "Rock'd in the cradle of the deep", words by Mrs Millard, music by Joseph Philip Knight (1812-1887), which afforded such scope to the basso profundo who loved to plumb the depths of his own throat that performers of the halls would insist on introducing it into pantomimes, when

the cue for song occurred midway through their villainies as demon
king or shipwrecking activities as Davy Jones. It was just as well
that scene-shifters on the other side of the front-cloth close behind
them slammed and hammered until only the first and last lines of
this could be heard:

> Rock'd in the cradle of the deep,
> I lay me down in peace to sleep;
> Secure I rest upon the wave,
> For Thou, O Lord! hast power to save;
> I know Thou wilt not slight my call,
> For Thou dost mark the sparrow's fall;
> And calm and peaceful is my sleep,
> Rock'd in the cradle of the deep.
>
> And such the trust that still were mine,
> Tho' stormy winds sweep o'er the brine;
> Or tho' the tempest's fiery breath,
> Rous'd me from slumber, to wreck and death!
> In ocean cave still safe with Thee,
> The germ of Immortality!
> And calm and peaceful shall I sleep
> Rock'd in the cradle of the deep.

There was an ever-growing pessimism about sea voyages,
based on the sentiment 'A sailor's grave is the sea', and confirmed
by Watson Scatcherd's "Out on the lonely deep":

> No eye can see his nameless grave,
>   Out on the lonely deep,
> No tears can fall upon his tomb,
>   And peaceful is his sleep.

But there is worse to come when "The Diver", written by Douglas
Thompson to the tune of E. J. Loder, comes into the programme:

> And Mammon's the master and man is the slave,
> Toiling for wealth on the brink of the grave;
> Leaving a world of sunlight and sound,
> For night-like gloom and a silence profound:
> And fearful the death of the diver must be,
> Sleeping alone, sleeping alone, sleeping alone in the depths
>   of the sea!

Great minds, to quote our grandparents' favourite saying, think alike. "The Old Oak Tree" was rivalled by "The Brave Old Oak" (Chorley words, Loder music), and "The Village Blacksmith" by "The Jovial Blacksmith" (Oxenford, Gale), while "The Soldier's Tear" was in complete agreement with "A Soldier and a Man" (Pieri, Garland):

> A soldier stood on the battlefield,
>   His weary watch to keep,
> While the pale moon cover'd her mantle o'er
>   The souls that 'neath her sleep.
> 'Ah me!' he sigh'd, with tearful eye. . . .

Chorley is so often mentioned in popular music that a biography is warranted. He was born in 1808 at Blackley Hurst, Billinge, Lancashire, and gained a footing in London as a music critic. Like the majority of literary labourers most of his writing might have been in invisible ink for all that it matters now; his novels were published and his plays acted; his *Modern German Music* in 1854, and his *Thirty Years' Musical Recollections*, in 1862, served their day. On the other hand his ordinary hack work has lasted well, particularly his translation of the libretto of Gounod's *Faust*, which is as familiar as Shakespeare. He also translated "I am a roamer", originally written by Mendelssohn, who changed places with the author, for this number only, when setting Klingemann's *Son and Stranger* to music, with the consequence that the imitation each gave of the other has deluded nearly everybody and left all the rest of the work on the shelf. Chorley's "The Brave Old Oak", sonorously issuing from whiskers or beard, aroused a stern joy in his fifty arms so strong, the fear in his frown when the sun goes down, and his might in a wild midnight. Lovers who frolick'd there to the rebeck gay, now lie in the churchyard for gold hath its sway we all obey, and a ruthless king is he, 'but we never shall send our ancient friend to be toss'd on the stormy sea'. Nobody asked what a rebeck was while the oak stood in his pride alone:

> And still flourish he, a hale green tree,
>   When a hundred years are gone.

Chorley translated Victor Hugo's "Berceuse" in Gounod's setting, but singers stuck to 'Chantez, chantez toujours' rather than recall long afternoons at Lord's with, 'Play on, play on for evermore'.

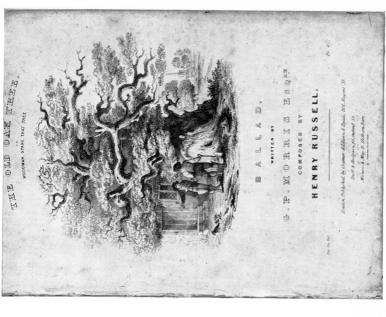

'The donkey pricked up his ears and laughed.'

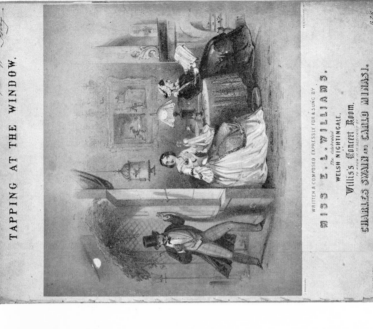

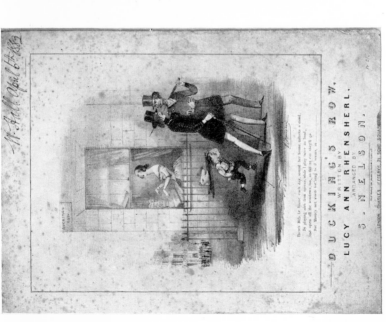

'I play twice as loud.'

It had to be re-translated straightforwardly as 'Sing on for ever-more', however formidable the prospect when the threat issued from not the most dulcet of throats.

To turn French into English was a legalized piracy then. Chorley merely dabbled in it compared with those who attained eminence by regularly stealing the unprotected work of Paris playwrights. The dramatic critic of *The Times*, John Oxenford, put his name to dozens of dramas that were his only in the sense of swag. When he wished to soar on the wings of originality he took to verse, because it is easier to invent your own rhymes than translate them, and to do him justice he gave us about as good a piece of horse-poetry as the musical evening warranted:

> I fear no foe in shining armour,
>   Though his lance be swift and keen,
> But I fear and love the glamour
>   Through thy drooping lashes seen.
> Be I clad in casque and tasses,
>   Do I perfect cuirass wear,
> Love through all my armour passes
>   To the heart that's hidden there.

After a good look at Oxenford's beard and spectacles we decided our terms of reference should be pyjamas, top and trouses, best red flannel and nightgown as far more likely, but in the end Ciro Pinsuti's tune proved too good to be taken other than seriously. In one publisher's list "White Wings" comes under Pinsuti's name, but the ballad we know was written and composed by Banks Winter:

> White wings they never grow weary,
>   They carry me over the bright summer sea,
> White wings they never grow weary,
>   I'll spread out my white wings and sail home to thee

which for a time almost rivalled Mendelssohn's "O for the wings of a dove" as a favourite for boyish treble.

Solemnity remained the true temperament of song as long as there were souls with the sensibility of Mrs Crouch. She was the poet of "Rest, troubled heart"; its beautiful melody, we are told on the copies, was actually written by Colonel Pestal, an officer in the Russian service, upon his dungeon wall the night before his

K

execution. She was the composer of "Kathleen Mavourneen", the words of which had appeared in 1835 under the name of Julia Crawford:

> Kathleen Mavourneen! the grey dawn is breaking,
>   The horn of the hunter is heard on the hill,
> The lark from her light wing the bright dew is shaking,
>   Kathleen Mavourneen, what slumbering still?
> Oh! hast thou forgotten how soon we must sever?
>   Oh! hast thou forgotten this day we must part?
> It may be for years and it may be for ever,
>   Oh! why art thou silent, thou voice of my heart?

Nor was this doleful strain a passing fancy. "Sweet Genevieve", however well meant its refrain about the hands of mem'ry weaving the blissful dreams of long ago, drew tears in many a bar parlour; George Cooper, its author, died in 1927. In America still greater popularity of a similar nature was enjoyed by "Sweet Adeline":

> In all my dreams your fair face beams

a song which insobriety made its own. One of the reasons may have been because it lent itself to alcoholic experiments in irregular part-singing, but in the main its kinship with swipes and wallop lay in its reverential approach to love.

Wickedness itself became sanctimonious. Any number of gypsies, tramps, exiles, and robbers, brought to the piano to boast vicariously of their sinful lives, made it clear that they kept on good terms with their consciences. "The Outlaw", words by H. C. Schiller, music by Edward J. Loder, exhibits a criminal who could cause no one a moment's uneasiness:

> Oh! I am the child of the forest wild,
>   Where the red deer boundeth free:
> And the mavis sings with uncaged wings,
>   To his mate in the greenwood tree.
> I range at will o'er mead or hill,
>   Or deep in the woodland shade,
> With my good yew bow in my hand I go,
> As free as the bird or the wild red roe,
> And the woods ring out with song and shout,
>   For I'm king of the forest glade.

Respectability also transformed Herrick's "To Anthea", for its 'Bid me to live and I will live thy Protestant to be', in John L. Hatton's setting, was sung in homes on Sunday among hymns. Hatton was musical director at the Princess's, in Oxford Street, in the years when Ellen Terry acted there as a child. At the time of the Great Exhibition in Hyde Park he had the daring idea of adding comedy to the concert repertoire. His success in this kind was almost unique, for on august occasions the rare occurrence of laughter would be due to songs composed by him to verses by W. H. Bellamy. "Dame Margery" had a limited existence, but long enough to inspire, as a sequel, "Simon the cellarer", who gives her a claim on our attention by mentioning her:

> Old Simon reclines in his high-back'd chair,
>   And talks about taking a wife,
> And Margery often is heard to declare,
>   She ought to be settled in life;
> But Margery has, so the maids say, a tongue,
>   And she's not very handsome, and not very young,
> So somehow it ends with a shake of the head,
>   And Simon he brews him a flagon instead.
> While, 'Oh, ho! ho!' he'll chuckle and crow:
>   'What, marry Old Margery? Oh, no, no!'

Simon was the regular encore of Sir Charles Santley, who could chuckle and crow like the ripe old character he represented until he was a ripe old age himself; and on that memorable day at the Albert Hall when Albani took her farewell and Patti came out of her retirement to sing, "Home, sweet home" yet once more, he was there to make unforgettable, to yet another generation, Hatton's legendary rascal. Far worse things have been dinned into our ears as regular encores by famous singers since. It always called forth an approving shout, and yet the joy must surely have been still greater fifty years earlier when youthful hearers found the sabbatarian gloom of a concert hall rudely disturbed by this unsoulful song. As editor of *The Songs of England* Hatton deserves thanks for volumes that are better than many works of similar purpose published later. He preserves ballads not easily found elsewhere, besides a version of the one we know as "The Lincoln-shire Poacher" which he begins:

> When I was bound apprentice
> In famous Zummersetshire

He also includes a tender love song, "Yarico to her lover", composed by F. H. Himmel, which is by that bitter satirist, Peter Pindar, whose masterpiece, "The Lousiad", had a flea on the king's plate for hero. This collection revived interest in the livelier manner of an earlier day when respectability was not so rife, and its influence was heard in new work which imitated the old, with Hatton himself leading the way. But cheerfulness still affected only a minority of what pleased the drawing-rooms, for here the idea of fun was distinct from that of concerts and entertainments.

Many of the songs so far mentioned were still being sung, and others like them were being written, as long as the nineteenth century lasted; but while nobody was in a hurry to be off with the old, everybody was ready to be on with the new. Changes came in with every fresh social development of a time when change was in the air. Cheaper musical instruments had much to do with it. Could any historian measure the effect on domestic habits of the invention of the upright piano? It caused a lot of people to stay at home; it caused a lot more to spend evenings in other people's homes; it also made a flourishing business of the 'popular entertainment' in the 1840s and 1850s, when any lecture hall or mechanics' institute which had a piano could be let regularly to singers who toured from one small town to another, sure of audiences. Some came from America to England, others went from England to America. Such refined amusement meant that the family went out as a party more often at this period than at an earlier or a later date.

Masses of songs were wanted and masses were supplied. To mention only those that are worth mentioning would create a false impression; even the mass that survives represents a crumb of the feast that was spread. Publishers prospered all the way from London Bridge and Bishopsgate to Marlborough Street, Oxford Street, and Regent Street, while Edinburgh maintained a spirited rivalry with the lot, and you need do no more than read a single list issued by any one of them to wonder where their vocal gems have gone to. Yet at the same time they constantly reprinted all that had found favour in the past half century.

It was not the entertainers but the entertained who filled publishers' pockets. Professional singers had to be wooed to sing their wares in order that multitudinous amateurs should buy not only songs but pianos to prop them on. The square piano of the Regency, a modest piece of furniture, had been a luxury of the ruling class; the newly invented oblique and upright types were made, in the shopman's language, to suit all purses. In the 'Catalogue of the reduced prices' from D'Almaine of 20 Soho Square, the piccolo pianofortes, admirably adapted for rooms of limited space wherein they can be moved about at pleasure without the risk of sustaining the slightest injury while the elegance of their appearance makes them a most attractive ornament to any apartment, cost 30 guineas. By degrees of semi-cottage or microcordon, cottage or semi-cabinet, the price rises, until for 70 guineas can be bought a pillared and leafy-legged monster that leans forward as though about to spring upon and bite the hand that opens it.

The part these played in the pursuit of happiness is revealed in a humorous ballad so directly related to reality as to risk the censure of being dubbed not very refined. This was "Ducking's Row", by Lucy Ann Rhensherl, arranged by S. Nelson:

There's Miss Le Blanc, each day, around her house collects a crowd,
By playing airs from operas, while I play twice as loud,
And open all the windows, too, as far as e'er they'll go;
But music's not worth listening to, it seems, in Ducking's Row!
Ducking's Row! Ducking's Row! Dismal, vulgar Ducking's Row!

It was published at 21 Soho Square by Charles Jeffreys, whose output as a man of business did not include the most memorable of his efforts as a poet. He is the author of "Mary of Argyle", for which Nelson composed the tune. Together they tried again, in a song of equal merit called "The Rose of Allandale", but far less successfully:

The morn was fair, the skies were clear,
No breath came o'er the sea,
When Mary left her Highland cot
To wander forth with me

In the days of sail the first thing a poet mentioned when voicing an emigrant's thoughts was the weather. Another instance of this occurred when D'Almaine, from his house in Soho Square next door, called Jeffreys in to write "A fair breeze is blowing", the farewell to her native shore of an emigrant in royal ermine, when

words were wanted for the vocal beauties of the elder Johann
Strauss. Jeffreys also wrote, " 'Tis hard to give the hand where the
heart can never be", music by Charles W. Glover, and "The song
of the blind girl to her harp", music by Stephen Glover, a very
popular composer whose other hits included the setting of J. E.
Carpenter's "The goodbye at the door".

If the prevailing mood is one of sheer insipidity, the fault may
be Tennyson's; there are tears, idle tears, diluted with still more
tears. Charles Swain wrote for Frank Mori as composer:

> A tear was on his fond cheek,
>   Sweet tears that love can bring,
> 'Twas on a Sunday morning,
>   Before the bells did ring,

as though no other explanation were needed for a good cry.
Swain's idea of fun was equally simple; "Tapping at the window",
with music by Carlo Minassi, is a young woman's complaint that
her young man taps at the window. Swain's

> I cannot mind my wheel, mother,
>   I cannot mind my wheel,
> You know not what my heart must know,
>   You know not what I feel

had music by Linley, who wrote the words of "Ever of thee",
besides words and music for "Bonnie New Moon" and "The
Orphan Wanderer" to the refrain of 'unfriended I roam bereft of a
home'. This school of thought, or lack of it, believed in saying all
they had to say in the title. "Meet me by moonlight alone", by
J. A. Wade, is a fair sample:

> Daylight may do for the gay,
>   The thoughtless, the heartless, the free,
> But there's something about the moon's ray
>   That is sweeter to you and to me.

Several of these achieved a kind of immortality; even when everything else about them is forgotten those titles will remain. "I traced
her little footsteps in the snow", originally a sentimental episode by
H. Wright, became a text for comics. "Her bright smile haunts me
still", with words by J. E. Carpenter and music by W. T. Wrighton,
haunts us just as thoroughly. Wrighton also composed:

> Every morn as true as the clock,
> Somebody hears the postman's knock

which chimes with a favourite scene in Victorian harlequinades whenever the dandy strolled up and down singing:

> Every night at half-past eight
> Somebody's knocking at the garden gate

whereupon the clown would fetch a pail of whitewash and swing it with a purpose. "Shall I, children?" Dear little innocent voices shouted, "Yes!", and the bucket was emptied over the dandy's head.

It is often the neglected songs that contain the best stuff. While "Jeannette and Jeannot", Jeffreys with music by C. W. Glover, was shelved, a few of its lines were often quoted whether or no they have an older source elsewhere:

> Oh! if I were queen of France,
>   Or better Pope of Rome
> I would have no fighting men abroad,
>   No weeping maids at home.
> All the world should be at peace,
>   Or if kings must show their might
> Why, let those that make the quarrels
>   Be the only men who fight.

To satisfy a more certain demand Jeffreys and Glover then gave us "Eva's parting words" from *Uncle Tom's Cabin*:

> Come near me all and hear me speak,
>   My voice is weak and low,
> But you must hear my parting words,
>   Dear friends, before I go.
> I love you and would have you all,
>   Remember what I say,
> And when you hear me speak no more,
>   Still think of me and pray.

Perhaps that was a little on the mournful side for some tastes; if so, relief could be sought in the half-hearted gaiety of Swain's "Merry goes the time when the heart is young", set to music by Dudley Buck, which lured the listener with its happy title into contemplation of what happens when the heart is old—much in the way that children were given chocolates containing worm-powders. The deep-seated faith that people should put up with what was good for them was carried to the point where those set on self-improvement did honestly prefer the unpleasant to the pleasant. Otherwise, how could we account for the welcome given to so many outbursts of pessimism? Setting aside all the lively lyrics of their forebears, the mid-Victorians revelled in such sombre cheer as "Look up, sad heart", written by G. H. Newcombe for the muse of Maria Piccolomini, the prima donna:

> Do the falling tear drops dreary,
> 　　Fail to ease thy ceaseless pain?
> Dost thou cry: 'I am a-weary!
> 　'O for rest and peace again?'
> Look up, sad heart, and cease thy sorrow;
> 　For thee will soon be peace and rest;
> For thee will dawn the glad tomorrow,
> 　The brightness of the haven blest.
> 　　　Look up, sad heart!

In plain English what that boils down to is, 'Cheer up, you'll soon be dead', though the sentiment was regarded as scandalous bad taste in forthright words.

For brighter notes we may turn to a musician rather better acquainted with the proximity of death, which must, of course, damp that ardour for decease as a glad tomorrow. The most spirited tune to be extracted from the vast bulk of drawing-room ballads belonging to the reign of Victoria bears the name of Poniatowski—known to history through Catherine the Great's lover, whom she made king of Poland. Prince Josef of this family commanded Napoleon's Polish contingent, and lost his life in the disastrous retreat from Leipsic. His nephew, Prince Josef, was born in 1816 in Rome. Though he spent much of his life in the study of music this was by way of relaxation. While living in Paris he brought out operas but his career was political; under Napoleon III he served as a senator until the Franco-Prussian War. From 1870 to the end of his life three years later, he lived in England and enjoyed his well-deserved popularity as a composer of rousing songs, so that a comedian in a circus pantomime—none other than The Great Macdermott in the role of William the Conqueror—

boasting of his horsey tastes, won applause by choosing Poniatowski as his favourite composer for the sake of the pun. Prince
Josef still has the distinction of having given us one of the most
English of songs. It is not simply the words but the tune of "The
Yeoman's Wedding" which conveyed his faith in existence. 'Ding
dong we gallop along, all fears and doubtings scorning' was
the answer of an exile to composers who meditated on the miseries
of life while lying snug abed.

XIV

The Novel and the Song

‧‧‧‧‧‧‧‧‧‧‧‧‧‧‧‧‧‧‧‧‧‧‧‧‧‧‧‧‧‧‧‧‧‧‧‧‧

What are the wild waves saying,
Sister the whole day long:
That ever amid our playing,
I hear but their low, lone song?
Not by the seaside only,
There it sounds wild and free;
But at night when 'tis dark and lonely,
In dreams it is still with me.

J. E. Carpenter

ONLY A FEW of the Victorian novelists made themselves known in
song. Though Dickens was represented on the concert platform by
"The Ivy Green", it did not find much favour in the home since
it lacked heart. But the songs that his novels inspired other people
to write were often sung in the belief that they were his, especially
if they reached the degree of popularity when publishers no longer
thought it necessary to print authors' names. A duet between Paul
Dombey and his sister had such apparent authenticity that a
spirited imagination could almost hear their voices. The words
were by J. E. Carpenter and the music by Stephen Glover, who
brought off successfully a feat that many of their rivals tried in
vain. *The Old Curiosity Shop* gave rise to several such efforts,
including "Little Nell", by Miss Young with music by George
Linley:

> They told him gently, she was gone,
>   And spoke of Heav'n and smil'd,
> And drew him from the lonely room,
>   Where lay the lovely child.
> 'Twas all in vain, he heeded not
>   Their pitying looks of sorrow,
> 'Hush hush!' he said, 'she only sleeps,
>   'She'll wake again tomorrow!'

Samuel Lover wrote his own songs; with him these came first, for the character he chose as the hero of *Rory O'More*, both as novel and play, began as:

> 'Now Rory, I'll cry if you don't let me go;
> 'Sure I dream ev'ry night that I'm hating you so!'
> 'Oh,' says Rory, 'the same I'm delighted to hear,
> 'For dhrames always go by contraries, my dear;
> 'Oh! Jewel! keep dhraming that same till you die,
> 'And bright morning will give dirty night the black lie.'

Whereas Tom Moore put sadness into song, Lover cast it out. No outcry against the unreality of his stage Irishman will diminish the gaiety of his joyous novels, equally joyous plays, and still more joyous verses. In his *Irish Nights*, a travelling entertainment, he sang of the man at the turnpike bar who never ask'd for his toll but scratch'd his old poll and look'd after the low back'd car:

> Sweet Peggy, round her car, sir,
> Has strings of ducks and geese;
> But the scores of hearts she slaughters,
> By far outnumbers these;
> While she among the poultry sits,
> Just like a turtle dove;
> Well worth the cage I do engage,
> Of the fair young god of love.
>   While she sits in the low back'd car,
>   The lovers come near and far,
>   And envy the chicken,
>   That Peggy is picking,
>   As she sits in the low back'd car.

Lover needs a song-book to himself. He wrote so many good things in so many moods that I must rest content with one more chorus only:

> Oh! Molly Bawn why leave me pining,
>   All lonely waiting here for you?
> The stars above are brightly shining
>   Because they've nothing else to do.

From Tom Moore's arrival to Samuel Lover's farewell, London was colonized by Irish writers. Of these Gerald Griffin had the most influence over the popular imagination, for the tales he told of his native land were turned into melodramas by a dozen enterprising hacks, although his own play, the classic tragedy of *Gisippus*, acted at Drury Lane in 1842 after his death, failed. While his novel *The Collegians* made a fortune for others on the stage as *The Colleen Bawn*, and as the opera *The Lily of Killarney*, his name rarely appeared on any work except his song, set to music by F. N. Crouch:

> I knew a gentle maid,
> Flower of the hazel shade,
>> Eileen Aroon.

Perhaps a hint from this can be detected in "Kathleen Aroon", composed by Franz Abt, but that was not the worst. Griffin's sole remaining claim to remembrance on his own merit is denied by a statement that "Eileen Aroon" is so old a ballad that in the eighteenth century "Robin Adair" was taken from it. The resemblance can be seen in:

> Dear were her charms to me,
> Dearer her laughter free,
> Dearest her constancy,
>> Eileen Aroon.

Experts on Irish folklore must decide whether this last petal may be left to one who was robbed of the laurel and the rose. He died in 1840 through caring less for his body than for his soul. No doubt he put small value on a song—unlike his contemporary, Francis Sylvester Mahoney, a Jesuit expelled from the order, who called himself an 'Irish potato seasoned with Attic salt', when he wrote verses under the pen name of Father Prout. His "Bells of Shandon", in Thomas Anderton's setting, has a verbal recklessness which might be hailed by generous critics as the beginning of modern rhyming. Of course, he was merely following the fashion set by *The Ingoldsby Legends*; even so he is a pioneer of song when he breaks away from all the modes in current use in order to indulge his fancy for 'while at a glib rate brass tongues would vibrate'. At the time his acrobatics were astonishing:

> I've heard bells tolling
> "Old Adrian's Mole" in
> Their thunder rolling
>> From the Vatican;

And cymbals glorious,
Swinging uproarious,
In the gorgeous turrets
    Of Notre Dame;
But thy sounds are sweeter
Than the Dome of St Peter
Flings o'er the Tiber
    Pealing solemnly.
Oh! the bells of Shandon
Sound far more grand on
The pleasant waters of
    The River Lee.

Religion again played a part in Irish song when Alfred Perceval
Graves wrote his classic, "Father O'Flynn", to a traditional
setting arranged by Sir Charles Villiers Stanford, a professor with
three operas to his credit and any number of pleasant songs, though
none likely to outlast:

Powerfullest preacher and tinderest teacher,
And kindliest creature in ould Donegal.

The novelist the drawing-rooms loved best was Charles Kingsley.
Long after his death in 1875 there was more life in his verses than
in those of living versifiers; what is stranger still the words were
known to be his and hardly a thought was given to the composers.
In recitation he was not much admired for "Lorraine, Lorraine,
Lorrée", which was the joy of the effervescent elocutionist rather
than those who had to listen. Plaintive appeals, not muscular
heartiness, gave Kingsley his piano-side supremacy. For half a
century suburban evenings responded constantly to:

Be good sweet maid, and let who can be clever,
    Do noble deeds nor dream them all day long,
And so make life, death and the Great Hereafter,
    One glad sweet song.

The only rival this had for the favour of practical young women
whose sentimental inclinations were confined to song was another
example of Kingsley's whimpering mood, "Oh! that we two were
Maying", though rarely complete with his last verse:

Oh! that we two were sleeping,
    In our nest in the churchyard sod.

There might have been a feeling that he was a trifle morbid but even then, as in "The Sands of Dee", his lines were known. Composers went after him. A. M. Pares composed the setting for "Airly Beacon", and J. C. Herbert for "Sing heigh-ho". John Hullah's tune caused this to be sung

> For men must work and women must weep,
> And there's little to earn and many to keep

as part of everyday conversation when the housewife was preparing to go shopping.

How remarkable Kingsley's vogue was, and how eloquent of the common mind, becomes clear when we compare it with the songs of his contemporaries. Some plausible explanations which suggest themselves are unconvincing: certainly there was a 'blossoming of episcopalian romance' which sentimentalized clergymen as the heroes of love stories, but to offset this it must be asserted that the singers of his songs did not always know that he was a clergyman. Allowance may be made for childhood memories of *The Water Babies* and boyhood regard for *Westward Ho!*, but here again we may be sure the singers did not come under any such sway. No, "Be good sweet maid"—with words slightly altered from what Kingsley wrote originally—was loved for its own sake, and Kingsley was remembered in gratitude for it.

Throughout that same half-century we regularly sang the songs of another novelist whose name was never mentioned except by an older generation. This was Whyte-Melville. In his youth he was a Guardsman until he retired with the rank of captain. A few years later he left England to serve in the Turkish army during the war in the Crimea. While writing between twenty and thirty books, notably *The Gladiators* and *Satanella*, he took enthusiastically to a country life, and died in 1878 through injuries caused by a fall while hunting. All his novels remained on the active list of lending libraries to the end of the century and after, and a few of his verses were still as familiar as any set to music, but without a thought of their authorship. The one that bore his stamp so plainly as to be unmistakably his lost its place in the general repertoire—"The Clipper that stands in the stall at the top", a fine piece of plain-speaking verse with music by Hatton:

> When the country is deepest, I give you my word,
> 'Tis a pride and a pleasure to put him along:

O'er fallow and pasture he sweeps like a bird,
   And there's nothing too wide, nor too high, nor too strong;
For the ploughs cannot choke, nor the fences can crop,
The Clipper that stands in the stall at the top.

Last Monday we ran for an hour in the Vale,
   Not a bullfinch was trimmed, of a gap not a sign,
The ditches were double—each fence had a rail,
   And the farmers had locked every gate in the line;
So I gave him the office, and over them—pop
Went this Clipper that stands in the stall at the top.

I'd a lead of them all, when we came to the brook,
   A big one, a bumper and up to your chin!
As he threw it behind him I turned for a look,
   There were eight of us had it, and seven got in!
Then he shook his lean head, while he heard them go plop,
This Clipper that stands in the stall at the top.

Ere we got to the finish, I counted but few,
   And never a coat without dirt but my own;
To the good horse I rode all the credit is due,
   While the others were tiring, he scarcely was blown,
For the best of the pace is unable to stop
This Clipper that stands in the stall at the top.

Although Whyte-Melville is generally named as the author of "Drink, puppy, drink", the published copies state that it is arranged by him and make no mention of author or composer. It was sung on the stage by Jennie Lee in *Midge* at the Royalty in 1880— not an important occasion since her career was dominated by her success as Jo in a dramatization of *Bleak House*, but her song remains a classic:

Here's to the fox in his earth below the rocks,
   And here's to the line that we follow,
And here's to the hound with his nose upon the ground,
   Tho' merrily we whoop and we holloa.
     Then drink, puppy, drink,
     And let ev'ry puppy drink,
   That is old enough to lap and to swallow,
     For he'll grow into a hound,
     So we'll pass the bottle round,
   And merrily we'll whoop and we'll holloa.

From the hunting field to the death-bed of the tall stalwart lancer who asked, "Wrap me up in my tarpaulin jacket", is a normal change of scene. What surprises us in Whyte-Melville's output is an agonized cry from the heart. We are taken aback to find that he is the author of Tosti's "Goodbye", the very ecstasy of that finality-mongering which we associate with inactive celibates by a comfortable fireside. Yet it does breathe the air of the countryside:

> The swallows are making them ready to fly,
> Wheeling out on a windy sky,
> Goodbye, summer, goodbye, goodbye!
> Goodbye to hope, goodbye, goodbye!

What relation it bears to Tosti's "Addio", with Italian words by Rizzelli, I have not discovered. "Goodbye" remains the most celebrated of all the successes of Sir Francesco Paolo Tosti, teacher of music to Queen Victoria's family. He was born in Ortona in 1846, and died in London in 1916.

'Try to be happy and gay, my boys.'

SUNG BY

MR. SOTHERN

IN HIS FAMOUS CREATION OF

LORD DUNDREARY.

ENT. STA. HALL

PRICE 2/6

LONDON. DUFF & HODGSON 20 OXFORD ST & 51 HANWAY ST

'. . . with his whiskers a-taking sly glances at me . . .'

XV

Golden Lads Like Chimney Sweepers

❖❖❖❖❖❖❖❖❖❖❖❖❖❖❖❖❖❖❖❖❖❖❖❖❖❖❖❖❖❖❖❖

> *My name it is Sam Hall, chimney sweep,*
> *My name it is Sam Hall,*
> *I robs both great and small,*
> *But they makes me pay for all——*
>   *Damn their eyes.*
>   W. G. Ross

'GOLDEN LADS AND GIRLS all must, as chimney sweepers, come to dust' applied particularly to mid-Victorian music-halls. Towns that doubled in size needed pleasure; publicans built concert rooms for their customers, labourers who could sing threw up their jobs to turn professional, comedians demanded soaring salaries. A chimney-sweep named Sam Collins ran the hall that still bears his name at Islington. A compositor named W. G. Ross demonstrated with his curses, as a chimney-sweep condemned to death for murder, how a song of low life could make a greater mark than any polite simper over a soldier's tear or soul stirrings over an old oak. Close acquaintance with life as it was known to the publican's customers would always be the popular comedian's stock-in-trade, but this was not evident at first. Labourers suddenly possessed of wealth very naturally wanted to cut a dash, grow luxuriant whiskers, wear ultra-fashionable clothes, smoke cigars, and drink champagne.

George Leybourne, a mechanic from the Midlands, became a favourite at the Canterbury Arms, in Lambeth Marshes, by tunefully advising Sayers to bash the Benicia Boy on the boko at the time of their prize-fight in 1860. Almost overnight his salary went up from a guinea a week to twenty-five, and later to £120. By day he wore a topper and fur coat while seated in his carriage and four, and at night he sang, "Champagne Charlie is my name", and "Gold, gold, gold, how I love to hear it jingle". Similarly the Great Vance, after establishing his claims to a higher salary with, "Vitechapel vos the willage I vos born in", cut his dash with, "Cliquot, Cliquot, that's the wine for me", before turning truly genteel with, "Doing the Academy is quite the thing, you know". *Lion Comique* was the title bestowed on one and adopted by the other. It expresses the envy and admiration they excited among young men with just enough means to hire a dress suit for one evening. Wearing a cut-down waistcoat 'to allow the crimson handkerchief carelessly to protrude', they liked to lounge in a box at the Pavilion or Empire while obsequious waiters took their orders. And yet, when it came to setting a standard for high life, the disclosures of the *lion comique* were mild compared with what Henri Clarke could do,

> She sang like a nightingale, twanged a guitar,
> Danced the chachuca and smoked a cigar,
>   O what a form! O what a face!
>   And she done the fandango all over the place.

Soon the day of rollicking rams and their sprees was done. The desire to reform became evident in Leybourne's "Ting, ting, that's how the bell goes", while confessing his love for a pretty young thing in a café of all places. Then Vance, yielding to a mania for proverbial adjuration, changed his tune to "Act on the square, boys, act on the square". A new age had truly begun, but as moralists they could not compare with Harry Clifton, who told us how to help a weary brother in "Pulling hard against the stream", how to love our neighbour in "Paddle your own canoe", and how to be satisfied with our lot in "Work, boys, work, and be contented", even though he did seem to overdo it in "Try to be happy and gay, my boys". For a change he gave us a holiday from zeal in "The Weepin' Willer":

> Down by the countryside
>   Lives Old Gray the Miller,
> Down by the side of the millstream tide,
>   Grows a Weepin' Willer,
> Under the Willer tree,
>   Sat the Miller's daughter,

Singin' a song and gazin' long,
   Into the bubblin' water—liquid.
Chorus: She sat beside the bubblin' water
         Under the Weepin' Willer Tree.

Tears fell from her eyes,
   Hands she was a-wringin',
First she cries and then she sighs
   And then commenc'd a-singin',
'All the world's a waste,
   'Life to me is o-jous,
'Since William he deserted me,
   'And went and join'd the "Sojers" '——Army.

Then from her bosom she drew
   A piece of needle cover,
And on it wrote a very short note
   To her deceitful lover.
'Take this to William Phipps,
   'Straight to him be tellin',
'His Susan died thro' Suicide.
   'P.S. Please excuse bad spellin' '——Orthography

She look'd at the thimble case,
   Which William false had bought her,
She look'd to the right, she look'd to the left,
   And then look'd into the water;
Then she did prepare,
   Her mortal life to injure,
Her head was bare and the colour of her hair
   Was a sort of a delicate ginger——Auburn.

She look'd at the Willer above,
   And said, 'I'll hang in my garter,
'But what a mistake if the garter break,
   'I shall be drown'd in the water'.
She look'd at the water below
   And her nerves began to totter,
'I'm not very bold and I may take cold,
   'I'll wait till the weather is hotter'——Milder.

Clifton died in 1872 at the age of forty, just when he was recognized
as a singer of merit far above the others. Until then his popularity
had depended mainly on his 'motto songs', full of an overwhelming
concern for the moral welfare of his fellow creatures. No other

kind of doggerel is so bad as the stuff which we like because it is good for us, and Clifton always aroused fervour with

> I gaily sing from day to day,
>> And do the best I can,
> When trouble comes upon my way,
>> To bear it like a man

as one among his many endeavours to bring the week of seven sabbaths into the music-hall. There is not a hint in all these beery-breath hymns of the lilt that inspires his nonsense. His "Pretty Polly Perkins of Paddington Green" is the lament of a milkman, jilted in favour of the bow-legg'd conductor of a twopenny bus, but though it follows the usual pattern set by broken-hearted tradesmen, the rest do not display such freshness in the melody and such vividness in the recording of Victorian everyday happenings:

> When I'd rattle in the morning and cry 'Milk below'
> At the sound of my milk cans her face she would show,
> With a smile upon her countenance and a laugh in her eye,
> If I thought she'd have lov'd me, I'd have laid me down and die.
>> For she was as
> Beautiful as a butterfly and as proud as a Queen,
> Was pretty little Polly Perkins of Paddington Green.

Next came The Great Macdermott, whose popularity was said to be 'perfectly astonishing'. He was no mere man-about-town in the old style but a well-to-do citizen with an outlook of common sense which allowed for a proper appreciation of forbidden joys, and an air of solid assurance even if his songs did relate how 'the wife' regularly caught him out in acts of excessive cheer that had the appearance of infidelity. Under his own name of G. H. Farrell he had once earned his livelihood as a bricklayer, seaman, and dramatist; as George Macdermott he had acted in melodramas and written a dozen of them himself, including an adaptation of *The Mystery of Edwin Drood*. On the halls he wore evening dress and went on the spree in a heavy manner, which made it look commendable, but he was lured into horse-play one Christmas when 'Lord' George Sanger engaged him for a pantomime. In the usual way of the music-hall Macdermott's repertoire was about lodgers, twins, curates, flirtations in hansom cabs with the wife looking on, sea-serpents, tight-lacing, and shapely ankles. Of course, patriotism and rude remarks about Gladstone come into it, but that hardly prepares us for the moment when in 1877 Russia went to war with Turkey. Our interests in the Near East were threatened. Parliament was in two minds whether to act or not. One dark night a hard-up hack knocked at Macdermott's window and Macdermott threw a boot at him without driving him away. Once the visitor had had the chance to read his song it proved too good to be declined, especially by a singer in Tory pay. Anyhow the Great One advanced to the London Pavilion footlights while an unsuspecting throng in top hats—to wear them here was correct—sat at the tables, attended by waiters. They liked to appear nonchalant but dropped the pose as soon as they heard, "The dogs of war are loose", and went wild over the chorus with its defiance of Russia and rhyme:

> We don't want to fight, but by Jingo if we do,
> We've got the ships, we've got the men, and got the money, too.
> We've fought the Bear before, and while we're Britons true,
> The Russians shall not have Constantinople.

'Jingo' acquired a new meaning overnight, to which the Great One replied with, 'If it's Jingo to love honour, then Jingoes sure are we'. Gladstone's windows were smashed and Parliament voted six millions for the movement of troops.

Both the words and music of the Jingo song were by G. W. Hunt, who thus stakes his claim to be numbered among the poets who have influenced the world. But his warlike strains were less widely known than his lullaby:

> Don't make a noise or else you'll wake the baby,
> Don't make a noise or else you'll wake the child,
> Don't make a noise or you'll disturb the infant,
> I feel so awfully, awfully jolly I think I shall go wild

which he wrote for Champagne Charlie, though it was still more to the taste of the mothers of large families who had to keep rowdy ones quiet while latest additions were being put to bed. Hunt also supplied Leybourne with:

> O why did she leave her Jeremiah?
> Why did she go without saying 'adieu'?
> When trouble came she look'd much higher.
> Isn't it funny what money can do?

—yet another of those jilt songs of which the old halls could never have enough. Happy endings to allow lovers to live happily ever after are so rare that I gladly find a place for Harry Rickards'

> For the ship went down to the bottom of the sea,
> There's only one that came ashore and that one's me;
> I came across a whale and I sat upon his tail,
> And it brought me home to marry Jenny Jones, Jenny Jones.

When it came to being simple-hearted the winner was an actor, A. W. Young, who appeared as a seventeenth-century Dutchman in *La Belle Sauvage*—meaning Pocahontas—at the St James's in 1869. In wide-brimmed hat, cartwheel ruff, and bulging knickerbockers, he sang:

> Oh where and oh where is my leet-el wee dog?
>   Oh where? Oh where can he be?
> Mit his ears cut short and his tail cut long,
>   Oh where, oh where is he?
>
> Sausage is good and Bologna also,
>   Oh where? Oh where can he be?
> Dey makes dem of horse, and dey makes dem of dog,
>   And I fear dat dey makes dem of he.
>
> Whenever I see a Bologna I shtop,
>   And I whistle dis bootiful air,
> But the sausages never run out of the shop—
>   So I don't think my leetel dog's there!

The penetrating power of this snippet lay in its appeal to the nursery, where it was chirrupped for thirty years. Its rival was a waltz with vocal obligato, performed with unprecedented success at the promenade concerts, Covent Garden, and re-demanded nightly:

> See-saw, see-saw, now we're up or down,
> See-saw, see-saw-aw, now we're off to London Town,
> See-saw, see-saw, boys and girls come out to play,
> See-saw-aw, see-saw, on this our half-holiday.

How thrilling that 'off to London Town' was can be recalled each time we care to sing it. Possibly it was 'traditional' before A. G. Crowe composed it, and so may "Diddle, diddle, dumpling"

have been before it was published as written and composed by
Arthur Lloyd. I can answer only for the consequences. We all
sang:

> Diddle, diddle dumpling, my son John,
> He went to bed with his trousers on,
> One leg off, and the other leg on,
> Diddle, diddle dumpling, my son John.

Whether I am too gullible or not about these, there is no doubt
that the music-hall supplied nursery rhymes. Since these recall a
happy side of Victorian childhood unlike the notions derived from
Little Lord Fauntleroy, Bubbles, and Dean Farrar's exemplary
Eric, it is as well to be reminded of a happiness that had nothing to
do with 'being good'. Some were originally intended solely for
adults, but others sound as though meant to be taken home by
fond parents for the children. Here is an example written and
composed by Geoffrey Thorn:

> Where the bells of the village go ring, ding, dong,
> And the pigs on the trees sing all day long;
> Where the lambs they go 'boo' and the bulls go 'baa',
> And the pretty little milkmaids they laugh 'ha, ha'.

"The tin gee-gee, or the Lowther Arcade", written and composed
by Fred Cape in 1891, was sung by Fanny Wentworth (at the house
in Cambridge Circus that had just changed from the English
Opera into the Palace) and next by Mel B. Spur, who wrote a
revised version (at the Egyptian Hall, Maskelyne's home of magic,
in Piccadilly). A colonel who rides on the tin gee-gee sobs and
sighs because he is marked one-and-nine while on a higher shelf the
fellow who has neither sword nor horse is marked two-and-three.
A beautiful doll, who turns up her little wax nose at the colonel,
flirts with two-and-three until a passer-by who knows what it is to
love a maiden of high degree, transposes the price-tickets. All this
was a trifle too involved for the understanding of toddlers. The
very considerable popularity of the song clearly points to that
simple-hearted side to our grandparents' nature.

XVI

Kinds of Concert

❖❖❖

A young gentleman one day
O'er the bridge did pick his way,
    The name of the bridge it was Blackfriars;
When he came to the Rotunda,
There he saw it was wrote under:—
'A young lady tonight will sing,
"Gentle moon", "Sad heigho", "The light guitar's
        lament for its string."'

W. Hunneman

WHERE WE MODERNS GO to cinemas our forebears went to concerts.
There were so many of these, distinct from music-halls, that a lifetime of misery can be assured for anyone who determines to set them
all down. One way of making a reckoning would be to list the
ladies and gentlemen who toured their entertainments from town
to town; the other way would be to catalogue the rooms, barns,
spas, or polytechnics they appeared at. That at least one museum
comes into the inventory is indicated by "A legend of the Rotunda",
which Hunneman fitted to music by Weber, for inclusion in
Fleming Norton's one-man show at the Egyptian Hall. The
Rotunda, father of public museums, now serves for the storage of
patent drainpipes. It is an elegant little amphitheatre, hardly large
enough for audiences of a size to make it pay its way. (People who
fancy that Shakespeare has been acted there are thinking of the
Ring that stood, before bombs fell on it, further down the road.)

Among the programmes salvaged for this chapter is one
from the Agricultural Hall, Islington, to celebrate the Abyssinian
Expedition of 1868 with a Grand Volunteer Night. "I dreamt that
I dwelt" and "The Minstrel Boy" may have given it an old-
fashioned air, but a grand descriptive and military quadrille—
note how this term has passed from the ballroom to do warlike

service—was bang, literally, up to date. The St George's Rifles were allowed to mingle their instruments with the bagpipes and drums of the Guards to express such things as formation of the Avenging Army, hurrah for the Dangers of Africa, revels of savages in wild fastnesses with variations for piccolo and clarinet, war hymn of the Beloochees for bassoons, ophicleide, and euphonium, elephants dragging cannon, a march through gloomy defiles, cornet solo of "Home, sweet home" by the expectant prisoners, roseate dreams of deliverance, grand assault and "See the conquering hero comes".

A programme of 1878 for the Royal Aquarium, Westminster, begins with a mermaid or manatee, a live whale, and performing fleas; after an organ recital the special grand concert includes "The village blacksmith" and the Jewel Song from *Faust*, until it is time for Zazel to be fired seventy feet from a cannon. Another programme, dated 1889, is from the London Institution, Finsbury Circus; it is a concert edifyingly disguised as a lecture on modern composers of classical songs with a book of words that bears out a statement made in their midst:

> 'Tis like dead music reviving again,
> That no one ventures to recognize.

Forgotten poets, forgotten composers, forgotten singers, and forgotten halls have left stacks of waste-paper to inform us of their importance to their own world. Even so a shock comes from a glance at the programmes of Mr and Mrs German Reed. What remains of their entertainments in print is neither good enough nor bad enough to be worth preserving. 'Lie hidden with the buried years' catches my eye, but no survey of Victorian song may ignore them. They were vital personalities whose very wraiths are forceful enough to remind us that they are not to be judged by what dry records mean to us but by what their live presence meant to our forebears, and how much they meant is evident in the joyous company gathered round them. What are now mere names were once sparkling wits. Fitful appearances are made by young lions like William Brough—collaborating with his brother, who was also his brother-in-law—whose career would take pages to describe if ever we should grow interested in those theatrical squibs which he, one of the 'busy B's of burlesque', casually flipped out of his ink-bottle at the rate of three or four a year. Then there was

John Parry, son of the John Parry (died 1851) who in his songs
serenaded colleens in a light-hearted Irish style. John Parry junior
made his name as a humorist, but he composed a tune for Charles
Jeffreys' soulful "Bridal Bells", illustrated by a mother bursting
into tears at a wedding. In the song the bride also burst into tears:

> Bridegroom! chide not now those tears,
>   Smile from smile still borrow,
> Do thou calm her bosom's fears
>   She will soothe thy sorrow.

Men of talent flocked round Priscilla Horton directly she followed
the profitable trade of entertainer under her own management.
'Illustrative Gatherings' was the label she used, and German Reed
was her composer. He wrote the music for William Brough's:

> And who can see yon blushing bride,
>   Supreme in beauty there,
> And not proclaim her far and wide,
>   'The Fairest of the Fair'.

After Miss Horton had become Mrs Reed, their 'favourite entertainment' was called 'Popular Illustrations'; in this she sang "Gaily
thro' life wander" from Verdi, with words by George Linley at his
tritest. She was no longer young when they rented St Martin's
Hall, Long Acre, and had put on weight, but this was merely the
start of a long triumphal march. In Lower Regent Street they found
a snug little semi-private theatre which they opened as the Gallery
of Illustration. Sir Charles Villiers Stanford praises Mrs Reed's
singing of "In Cheltenham" and Parry's monologue about a
charity dinner in which he made all the speeches before escorting a
procession of invisible orphans round the table, touching some of
them up with a white wand and boxing the ears of others. What the
Gallery itself was like may be evoked by a tiny letter I treasure:

> Dear Sir, I am much obliged for the trouble you have taken in
> writing me about the nail in the seat—it is a service few would
> take the trouble to render on mere public grounds—all future
> occupants of the seat will be emancipated from the obtrusive
> iron. Thanking you for your complimentary expressions. I am,
> Dear Sir,
>
>   Your obliged, P. German Reed.

There is a pleasant glimpse of her in Stanford's memoirs when he recalls her visit to Cambridge. There was very little space for her figure between the iron posts of the footpaths while she was seeing the 'Backs' of the colleges. She kept telling him, 'Go on in front, my dear, while I squeeze Mrs Reed through'.

Tom Robertson, at the height of his vogue as the author of cup-and-saucer comedies, wrote an extravaganza for them in the very same season that gave us *Caste*. This proves how prosperous the Gallery had become, for it now could afford scenery, costumes, and a supporting company. In *A Dream in Venice* the principals acted the parts of tourists. Reed, as a sufferer from neuralgia, takes a drug that transports him back to the days of Doge and dungeons, and then to the twenty-first century, when his wife has futurist clothes and an as-yet-unknown husband.

In 1874 Mr and Mrs German Reed's Entertainment, consisting of a dozen 'Illustrations', moved to St George's Hall, Langham Place, where it had space enough for its ever-growing swarm of devotees. To step into the shoes of Parry, who died in 1879, there was Corney Grain, similarly gifted. When his large mass sat sideways at the piano he made the keys dance to his fairylike touch. The hall also had a harmonium, but we hear very little about that. Soon Reed retired (he died in 1888 at the age of 70) in favour of his son Alfred; later Mrs German Reed also retired; Alfred Reed and Corney Grain were the responsible managers. Arthur Law was the usual author and King Hall the usual composer of songs about such pleasant topics as floating down the river on a night in June:

> The dip of oars within the stream——
> Recalls the golden dream!

Such sentiments have been regularly uttered though seldom so ably. We keep writing them afresh in order to encourage original talent.

Half-way through these illustrations, Corney Grain had the stage to himself for some new musical sketch—"At the Seaside", "Our Table D'Hôte", or "A Musical Family". In "Our Servants' Ball" he sang his own song, "The Ole Black 'Oss", which reveals his knack of happy nonsense:

> He was nearly thirty-three, and he'd one broken knee,
> And the other one warn't quite sound,

And his two 'ind legs was more like wooden pegs,
    And he couldn't 'ardly put 'em to the ground.
So she says, says Mary Ann, 'er as kept the tater can,
    That's jest the little 'oss for you and me,
Oh! won't he look smart in the little donkey-cart,
    When we drives out on Sunday for a spree.
Refrain: But the ole black oss is no longer in the stall,
Chorus: Drat that ole oss, I'm jolly glad he's gone!
Refrain: He never did no work, and he war'nt no good at all!
Chorus: Drat that ole oss, I'm jolly glad he's gone!
    Oh! Ay! Oh! The stall in the stable's empty!
    Oh! Ay! Oh! And the ole black oss is gone!

'Twas the very same day down Piccadilly way,
    I first saw the ole black oss,
He was standing on 'is 'ead, was that noble quadruped,
    And a playing at a game o' pitch and toss.
He'd a fine Roman nose, and he walk'd on his toes,
    I'll take my apple-davy it is true,
His neck was awry and he'd only got one eye,
    And his tail was all a-swivel and a-skew.
So she says, says Mary Ann . . . . . .

Another Corney song, "He did and he didn't know why", followed
a conventional pattern in its tale of an M.P. who lost his seat he
didn't know when, spent a lot of money he didn't know where,
and was made a peer with the title of Lord . . . he didn't know
what. The words of "The Old Gown" were by Arthur Law, composed and sung by Grain. "Only in dreams those hooks and eyes
will meet as in days of yore", gives the gist of it. And that was how
St George's flourished until 1895 when Corney Grain, Mrs German
Reed, and Alfred Reed died within a fortnight of one another.

By then 'Entertainer at the piano' had acquired the knack of
attracting rich fees which 'witch doctor' had in Africa. Comedians
who could sing at an audience while playing their own accompaniments might each be billed as an evening's amusement in himself
which otherwise was an honour reserved for the highest of the idols
on the halls. In part this prestige had been won by Corney Grain,
in part by George Grossmith, the elder of the name, who filled halls
wherever he chose to play and had received the honour of a royal
command. At the Savoy he had created, as a mere actor, a frenzy
of delight when he gathered up his robes while playing the Lord

Chancellor in *Iolanthe* and danced with a sprightly bounce beyond the powers of the winged sylphs from fairyland. Yet even so great a success as that could not equal his renown as entertainer at the piano, however cramping it must have been for a nimble gnome to stay seated, hands to keys, face to audience. This must have been peculiarly irksome when he described what he himself would look like in a state of violent agitation in the course of his most popular song, "You should see me dance the polka"—words and music by himself. It was full of artful tricks. Half-way through a verse he would ask the audience if they knew what an old maid was—and then declare that fourteen of them wanted to be his wife because they had seen his coat-tails flying as he jumped his partner round. The Queen was amused and commanded an encore, which has become so much a part of history that the public may forget the simple fact that he did write, compose, and sing other songs.

Grossmith had a gift for those nonsense verses which reveal such an attractive side of the Victorian character. In his sketch "How I Discovered America", he sang how we left the baby on the shore, how we found it again, how in our weariness we sat upon it, how it slept as it never slept before, and how we reasoned that it was best to leave the baby on the shore. The humour of his sketch "A Little Yachting" indicates the popularity of the obvious, but his "Happy Fatherland" won a lot of approval in the days when German bands rumbled at street corners by arguing that a musical nation would 'not permit loud vulgar tunes for nothing could be wuss', which was why the Fatherland sent those German bands to us. His "Modern Music and Morals" contained the best burlesque on the prevalent type of agonized love-making in "Oh! yearn of my yearn", and there were many other things in his bag which added to our fun for years on end. His "An awful little scrub", published with the portrait on its cover of an urchin after the style of drawing-room ballads about children in a decline, is a pleasantry about what happens aboard my uncle's smack my mother dear.

These had a great vogue. Yet none was remembered more tenderly than an old comic song, "The captain with his whiskers", which persisted in concerts that travelled from hall to hall. It had been originally written by Haynes Bayly for Emma Nichols's entertainment, *The Old Folks*, whence it passed to Mrs Florence and with her again went the rounds:

As they marched thro' the town with their banners so gay,
I ran to the window to hear the band play;
I peep'd thro' the blinds very cautiously then,
Lest the neighbours should say I was looking at the men.
Oh! I heard the drums beat and the music so sweet,
But my eyes at the time caught a still greater treat,
The troop was the finest I ever did see,
And the captain with his whiskers took a sly glance at me.

When we met at the ball, I of course thought 'twas right,
To pretend that we never had met before that night,
But he knew me at once I perceiv'd by his glance,
And I hung down my head when he ask'd me to dance.
Oh! he sat by my side at the end of the set,
And the sweet words he spoke I shall never forget;
For my heart was enlisted and could not get free,
As the captain with his whiskers took a sly glance at me.

But he march'd from the town and I saw him no more,
Yet I think of him oft and the whiskers he wore,
I dream all the night and I talk all the day,
Of the love of a captain who went far away.
I remember with superabundant delight
When we met in the street and we danc'd all the night,
And keep in my mind how my heart jump'd with glee,
As the captain with his whiskers took a sly glance at me.

But there's hope—for a friend just ten minutes ago,
Said the captain's return'd from the war, and I know
He'll be searching for me with con-sid--er--able zest,
And when I am found . . . but ah! you know all the rest.
Perhaps he is here . . . let me look round the house. . . .
Keep still, ev'ry one of you, still as a mouse,
For if the dear creature is here he will be,
With his whiskers a-taking sly glances at me.

That is not among the songs beloved by the masses, but it took
so firm a hold of the polite world who lived beyond everyday reach
of the theatres—the audiences whom the 'entertainers' catered
for—that it is still more evocative in the shires than any of the
town's songs can ever be in the town.

XVII

Christy Minstrels

✦✦✦✦✦✦✦✦✦✦✦✦✦✦✦✦✦✦✦✦✦✦✦✦✦✦✦✦✦✦

Beautiful dreamer, wake unto me,
Starlight and dewdrops are waiting for thee,
Sounds of the rude world, heard in the day,
Lull'd by the moonlight have all pass'd away.
Beautiful dreamer, Queen of my song,
List while I woo thee with soft melody;
Gone are the cares of life's busy throng,
Beautiful dreamer, awake unto me,
Beautiful dreamer, awake unto me.

Stephen Collins Foster

Ethiopian serenaders strummed and harmonized in theatres and pleasure gardens everywhere from Vauxhall to Washington in mid-nineteenth century. As long as they blacked-up picturesquely it mattered little at first what they played or what instruments they played it on, until the Christy Brothers discovered a young man from Pittsburg with a flair for romanticizing the nostalgia of the Deep South. Stephen Collins Foster is now famous, but at the time of his death in New York, at the age of thirty-eight, on 13 January 1864, millions who had come under his spell had not heard of him. "The old folks at home" was published in England as the work of W. Christy. It was a Christy Minstrel song, which was, at the time, all that mattered. It was the same with "Old Kentucky Home" and "Camptown Races". They seemed to have just growed without human aid for they sounded like it—natural, racy, spontaneous, picked up by anybody capable of understanding notation on any plantation. The name of the composer worried nobody, but it was altogether different with:

> Come where my love lies dreaming,
>   Dreaming the hours away,
> In visions bright redeeming
>   The fleeting joys of day

Dreaming the happy hours,
Dreaming the happy hours away,
Come where my love lies dreaming, so sweetly
Dreaming the happy hours away.

Both that and "Beautiful Dreamer" were recognized as art; the negro songs were merely nature. Possibly Foster saw it that way for sleeping beauty had a lasting fascination for him as he showed in still more songs:

Soft be thy slumbers,
  Rude cares depart,
Visions in numbers,
  Cheer thy young heart.
Dream on while bright hours
  And fond hopes remain,
Blooming like smiling bow'rs
  For thee, Ellen Bayne.

Chorus: Gentle slumbers o'er thee glide,
         Dreams of beauty round thee bide,
         While I linger by thy side,
           Sweet Ellen Bayne.

Another title in Foster's list runs, "Under the willow she's sleeping", but until I find the verses I shall not know whether he means above or below the daisies. In his day sleep did sometimes mean that and no more. In the day of his immediate successors any mention of sleep was simply a good excuse for introducing their favourite subject, which was death. Mourning they could never have enough of—the black on their faces, or so the Minstrels seemed to argue, had to be justified somehow—but for no matter what reason their poets perpetually put people, preferably very young people, to sleep after this fashion:

Close the shutters, Willie's dead,
  Whom we loved so dear.
Like a dream his spirit fled
  From our home now sad and drear.
When the Springtime flow'rs were blooming,
  And the birds sang sweet,
Angels called him to their home
  Up in heav'n where we shall meet.

Chorus: Close the shutters, Willie's gone,
                  Hope with him has fled
              From our home, now sad and lone,
                  Close the shutters, Willie's dead.

Why the lively Ethiopian Serenaders of Jim Crow's day should have changed into the funereal minstrels of the 1860s may be explained by reference to the American Civil War. It would be simpler to say that when they came to London the soot of fogs enveloped them in such a thorough mourning that henceforth they could think of death as a very happy release, but this plausible theory ignores the plain fact that in America they were equally determined to be miserable. Stephen Foster, after setting fashions for plantation songs that could last for ever, was dying in New York. Though he never did belong to Dixie, his verses were now labelled 'Confederate ballads' in England, where they were welcomed by a public whose sympathies were with the South. Minstrels who belonged to the Federal side had to make their allegiance known; they did so with the uncompromising sentiments of these verses, taken from an English song-sheet, which listed them as the Federal Hymn among *The Christys Minstrels Favourite Songs*:

Old John Brown's body lies a-mould'ring in the grave,
While weep the sons of bondage whom he ventur'd all to save;
But though he lost his life in struggling for the slave,
      His soul is marching on.
Oh, glory hallelujah, glory, glory hallelujah.

John Brown was a hero, undaunted true and brave,
Kansas knew his valour when he fought her rights to save;
And now though the grass grows green above his grave,
      His soul is marching on.

He captur'd Harper's Ferry with his nineteen men so few,
And he frighten'd 'Old Virginny' till she trembled thro' and thro',
They hung him for a traitor, themselves a traitor crew,
      But his soul is marching on.

John Brown was John the Baptist for the Christ we are to see,
Christ who of the bondman shall the liberator be,
And soon throughout the Sunny South, the slaves shall be all free,
      For his soul is marching on.

M

The conflict that he heralded he looks from heav'n to view,
On the army of the Union, with its flag, red, white, and blue,
And heav'n shall ring with anthems o'er the deeds they mean to do,
   For his soul is marching on.

Soldiers of freedom then strike while strike you may,
The death-blow of oppression is a better time and way,
For the dawn of Old John Brown has bright'ned into day,
   And his soul is marching on.

Those words are of such historic importance that they have to
be given in full. Formerly they fired passions of such an intensity
that the verses were, for all intents and purposes, suppressed; in
fact, apart from this badly printed copy on browning paper that
smells of age, I have never seen more than the opening lines or
heard more than one verse and a chorus sung. In order to divert
attention from its profound significance, the tune that refused to
remain unsung became "The Battle Hymn of the Republic"—but
the destiny of songs is not as easily controlled as that, and the same
irresistible music also became the setting for the parody of "John
Brown's Baby"* which a new generation learnt in innocence.

   The Civil War was fought on concert platforms in England as
well as on battlefields in the States. One London publisher brought
out *Celebrated Songs of the Confederate States of America*, which
included James Randall's "The despot's heel is on thy shore,
Maryland, my Maryland", while another printed the 'Union
version' which by a few verbal changes made the despotism belong
to the other side. "Bonnie Blue Flag", "God save the South" and
"It is my country's call" were answered by the resounding tunes of
Henry Clay Work. This self-taught musician was born in Con-
necticut, where he lived for fifty-six years, constantly employed in
finding a vent for his strong emotions on matters both personal and
political in melodious song. "Kingdom Comin' " was one of his
earliest celebrations of the war:

   The darkies sing, Ha, ha, the darkies sing, Ho, ho,
   It must be now de kingdom comin' or the year ob jubilo,

followed when the fighting was over by the triumphant notes of
"Marching thro' Georgia", which broke like Bedlam on the ears of

---

* Now I hear of a Young Ladies' Seminary where "John Brown's Body" was a
school song till long after the first world war——yes, in England.

Southerners who still suffered destitution because of the hero of it. Other wars in other parts of the world roused partisans to fury when the music of opposing armies sounded in neutral halls until, at last, a truce had to be called. In this fashion the Minstrels had to collect repertoires that did not summon up the blood. Both Foster and Work were laid aside, and those who took their place had orders to use the soft pedal and the minor key.

As I write this an old fellow with a gramophone in a pram passes my window, and the record he plays now, well past the middle of the twentieth century, is a mid-Victorian song that American minstrels implanted in England. It shows their new spirit at its best—"When you and I were young, Maggie", words by George W. Johnson, music by J. A. Butterfield:

> I wander'd today to the hill, Maggie,
>> To watch the scene below;
> The creek and the creaking old mill, Maggie,
>> As we used to long ago,
> The green grove is gone from the hill, Maggie,
>> Where first the daisies sprung;
> The creaking old mill is still, Maggie,
>> Since you and I were young.
>
> *Chorus:* And now we are aged and gray, Maggie,
>> And the trials of life nearly done;
> Let us sing of the days that are gone, Maggie,
>> When you and I were young.

Of all the Minstrels' classics "The Bogie Man", words by Edward Harrigan, music by David Braham, was held in the warmest affection. It was the chorus that aroused this feeling; hardly one in a thousand of those who sang it knew the verses well enough to know it had not been written as a song for children:

> Your father's going to be a fool,
>> To plaze the family;

'Hush, hush, hush' ran a more seemly version which ended, 'It's only naughty children need to fear the bogie man'.

Where the Piccadilly Hotel now stands there were the big and little St James's Halls, both of which served the turn of the Minstrels. Former members of the Christy troupes settled in the smaller in 1859, and were joined by George Washington Moore, who soon gained control. He wrote the tune of "Little Robin tapping on the pane", words by R. Lee:

> When the snow was falling, falling.
>   On a bitter winter night,
> I and little Mary watch'd it,
>   Wrapping all the world in white.
> Came a little robin red-breast,
>   Hungry, shivering, and in pain,
> And we heard him gently tapping,
>   Tapping on the window pane.
>   Robin's gone to sing with Mary,
>   In my dreams I hear the strain,
>   And I wake and hear the echo
>   Tapping on the window pane.

What else could you expect? According to the Minstrels and any number of other singers, the one purpose on earth of songbirds and infants was to die an early death. The soloists of St James, backed by rows of part-singers, all in black to their burnt-cork faces, insisted on it. "Keep pretty flowers on my grave", "Place a headstone over my grave", "Kiss me, Mother, ere I die", "Ring the bell gently there's crape on the door" and "See that my grave is kept green" are typical of what went on in all their programmes.

Higher flights of poetry did not come amiss. "I have seen thee in my dreaming", words by W. H. C. Hosmer, music by J. R. Thomas, tells of amaranthine bow'rs:

> Where the form, divinely moulded,
>   Is never laid to rest,
> And the pale hands meekly folded
>   On the frozen pulseless breast

which indicates the drawbacks of a soaring imagination—its flights are not always easy to follow. Consequently, the Minstrels liked plain language no matter how lofty their feelings. Odes and elegies had to rely on profound thoughts to move the reader to melancholy but the rhymes that went with the rattle of the bones and tambourines had but one method of causing a good cry—a tale of physical distress. Usually it proved fatal but sometimes the sufferer's life could be spared as long as his hardships were more than he could bear. How well the public responded to this treatment was proved by "Driven from home", the work of Will S. Hays, sung with great applause (according to the sheet) by the Christy Minstrels:

> Out in this cold world, out in the street,
> Asking a penny of each one I meet,
> Shoeless I wander about thro' the day,
> Wearing my young life in sorrow away;
> No one to help me, no one to love,
> No one to pity me, none to caress,
> Fatherless, motherless, sadly I roam,
> A child of misfortune, I'm driven from home

and the last lines were set for a four-part chorus to add somehow to the effect. Small boys who heard that were still singing about wearing their young life in sorrow away at the age of three score years and ten.

Moore was an honest vulgarian who gave lavish parties for the express purpose of telling his guests how much he paid for champagne, but when it came to song he knew what was expected of poetry and what his public expected of it also. The result was that by 1868 his advertisements outside the St James's Hall boasted of 1,050 performances. He described his company as 'The ONLY ETHIOPIAN TROUPE in England acknowledged by the Metropolitan Press, or countenanced by the Public.'

In the centre of the front row sat Harry Hunter, gloves, shirt-front, and buttonhole of white to offset the mourning. He was the Interlocutor who asked the comic 'end men' questions in set form concerning, for example, whether they had been walking down the Strand with a nice young lady, which they answered in the same set form to make sure the question was whether they had been seen walking down the Strand with a nice young lady, and were confirmed in the same words before coming to the point whatsoever it might be. By joining forces with James and William Francis first at the Agricultural Hall, Islington, and then at the St James's, Hunter linked his name not only with the Mohawks but also, to this day, with the well-known firm of publishers. He wrote some popular lyrics, one with this chorus (music by W. C. Levey):

> Brown eyes are beautiful, grey eyes are wise,
> But there's truth in the depths of forget-me-not eyes.

Of all the Mohawks the one to be remembered best is Johnny Danvers, uncle of Dan Leno though only a year or two older. Together they shared the hardships of childhood spent as entertainers in public houses, singing, clog-dancing, and collecting coppers. While Dan watched the life around him for the sake of its humour, Johnny had a romantic streak in him that urged him to the Agricultural, where he wore gay clothes, shook a tambourine, and sang his own song about, "Where the flow'rets grow". Then Harry Hunter wrote a ballad for him, with music by Edmund Forman, provoked by that astonishing social phenomenon, Dr Elizabeth Garrett Anderson, who discovered a new world by breaking into a profession regarded as sacred to the male. It was as the husband of a lady doctor that Johnny Danvers sang that he had 'got the ooperzootic and I don't know where it is', because she had diagnosed it in his parallelogram. 'Ooperzootic' became a necessary part of every affable conversation if you wished to be friendly and up to date—in common with several of the gags that originated with Johnny Danvers. He disappeared from the public view. Years passed. After what seemed a lifetime I asked in print, 'Where is Johnny Danvers now?' The answer came in a letter from Dulwich hospital, where I saw that broad, merry face, still creased with smiles. Whereas he had once made us laugh over the medical term for his fictitious illness, he now made a joke of the medical term for the arthritis that had crippled him for life. Harry Hunter died at the beginning of the new century when there was very little interest left in minstrels, though their vast repertoire had left a considerable number of songs that continued to be sung, Hunter's in particular for he had a happy instinct for sentiment in simple form. He had many successes, but "Over the garden wall", music by G. G. D. Fox, outshone all the rest:

> Just come over the garden wall,
>   Little girl to me,
> I've been waiting a long, long time
> And the wall's not hard to climb;

Minstrelsy enriched us generously; if there is one of their songs to be prized above all the others it is J. B. Lawreen's:

> The moon is beaming o'er the sparkling rill,
>   Who's that a-calling?

The flow'rs are sleeping on the plain and hill,
    Who's that calling so sweet?
While the birds are resting till the golden dawn,
    Who's that a-calling?
'Twas like the singing of one now gone,
    Who's that calling so sweet,
Who's that a-calling? Who's that a-calling?
    Is it one we long to greet?
Who's that a-calling? Who's that a-calling?
    Who's that a-calling so sweet?

Whatever the *feeling* that merges words and music into song, there it is more surely than many poets and composers in partnership have found it. Even though they caused a flood of tears deep enough to wash all the burnt cork off their faces, the Minstrels sweetened life with an even deeper flood of melody, so that such choruses as "Come, birdie, come and live with me", added to the charm from the skies in every home.

XVIII

Souls for Sale

✦✦✦✦✦✦✦✦✦✦✦✦✦✦✦✦✦✦✦✦✦✦✦✦✦✦✦✦✦✦✦✦✦✦✦✦✦

It tells the old, old story,
  Of sadness and of tears,
'Tis dead for ever now beyond recall.
  It is of a daughter fair,
  Now an outcast everywhere,
The picture with its face turned to the wall.

J. P. Skelly

EFFORTS TO WRING our hearts gather force from one end of the nineteenth century to the other. Though the number of blind boys and shipwrecked mariners remains constant, and the number of forsaken maidens shows nothing more than a reasonable increase considering the proportionate size of populations, more and more birds suffer from broken hearts—without counting the one in Gilbert's "Tit Willow"—more and more infants either die or are orphaned, and more and more daughters sell themselves for gold. This last subject sets a problem for professors who specialize in what they call literary sources. "The picture with its face turned to the wall" bears the name of Skelly. He wrote it round about the time when Joseph Arthur, the American playwright, brought out his melodrama *Blue Jeans*, which was acted in New York, 1891, though not seen in England until seven years later. Its scene where a father turns his daughter's portrait to the wall moved an American composer, Charles Graham, to bring out the song, "The picture that is turned towards the wall". Then Charpentier, too late in the day to lay any claim to originality, for he came into the contest at the Opéra Comique, Paris, in 1900, used the idea in his opera of modern life *Louise*.

If a little more were known of Mr Skelly, we should be able to decide who gave birth to the idea and who merely exploited it, but all that has come to light is the fact that he was also the composer of "The old rustic bridge by the mill" and of "A boy's best friend is his mother". The latter was written by Henry Miller:

> Then cherish her with care,
> And smooth her silv'ry hair,
> When gone, you will never get another.

Henry Russell's "The gambler's wife" may be the start, but the man chiefly responsible for making moral fervour the main business of song was Work. Whole generations who have lived and died in Great Britain without being conscious of his name have repeatedly sung at least two or three of the oddly mixed budget that came from his brain. "My grandfather's clock", that stopped short never to go again when the old man died, "Marching through Georgia", and "Father, dear father, come home with me now", are still well known but only connoisseurs are acquainted with his masterpiece, the lament for Lilly Dale. As it is the name Anthony Trollope gave his favourite heroine—in 1864, when the vogue of the song was at its height—we may suspect that he hummed it as he wrote *The Small House at Allington*. Here is the song:

> 'Twas a calm still night, and the moon's pale light
>   Shone soft o'er hill and vale;
> When friends mute with grief stood around the death bed
>   Of my poor lost Lilly Dale.
> *Chorus:*   Oh! Lilly, sweet Lilly,
>   Dear Lilly Dale,
> Now the wild rose blossoms o'er her little green grave,
>   'Neath the trees in the flowery vale.
>
> Her cheeks, that once glowed with the rose tint of health,
>   By the hand of disease had turned pale,
> And the death damp was on the pure white brow
>   Of my poor lost Lilly Dale.
>   Oh! Lilly, sweet Lilly, &c.
>
> 'I go,' she said, 'to the land of rest;
>   'And ere my strength shall fail,
> 'I must tell you where, near my own loved home,
>   'You must lay poor Lilly Dale'.
>   Oh! Lilly, sweet Lilly, &c.

' 'Neath the chestnut tree, where the wild flowers grow,
 'And stream ripples forth through the vale,
'Where the birds shall warble their songs in spring,
 'There lay poor Lilly Dale'.
   Oh! Lilly, sweet Lilly, &c.

Any sequel to a lament so final might seem unavailing but even
grief must obey the eternal law of supply and demand. Before
handkerchiefs had dried, every emporium had stocked "Toll the
bell (reply to Lilly Dale)", which began:

   My Lilly dear is sleeping,
    'Neath the old chestnut tree,

and ended:

   My sad heart now is aching,
    With weary care opprest,
   Oh! may I quickly meet thee
    In that pure land of rest.
  Toll, toll the bell, for gentle Lilly Dale,
  And let its tones echo through the vale;
 Our Lilly dear we've lost, so loving, kind, and true,
  Ring today one sad lay, lost Lilly Dale.

Frequent imitations caused such mortality among attractive young
women that henceforth to be loved was for them, when mentioned
in rhyme, to be doomed. "Milly Clare", words by H. Duffy, music
by S. Potter, is just one of them:

  I've been to the village, I found it in mourning,
   In the little churchyard many villagers were.
  I asked who it was that they buried this morning,
   I was told, heav'n help me! 'twas my Milly Clare.

But this is only one of the models that Work set up for others
to copy. Clocks had never been so popular in song before he
wrote "My grandfather's clock" as they were after, and appeals to
drunkards multiplied because of his. *A Temperance Album* contained
these titles: "Papa stay home, I'm motherless now", "I want to kiss
papa goodnight", "Father bring home your money tonight",
"Father won't drink any now" and "Oh, papa don't go out tonight"
(as well as Offenbach's "Water bright and pure as dew drops").

Nor was it merely a matter of words; the tune of "Come home, father" was so popular that it was arranged as a waltz. Did Work ever foresee how immortal these verses would prove to be or imagine that well-meaning people could laugh at them?

> Father, dear father, come home with me now,
>   The clock in the steeple strikes one,
> You promised, dear father, that you would come home,
>   As soon as your day's work was done.
> Our fire has gone out, our house is all dark,
>   And mother's been watching since tea,
> With poor brother Benny so sick in her arms,
>   And no one to help her but me.
> Come home, come home, oh father, dear father, come home.
>
> Father, dear father, come home with me now,
>   The clock in the steeple strikes two,
> The night has grown colder, and Benny is worse,
>   But he has been calling for you.
> Indeed he is worse and likely to die
>   No doubt before morning shall dawn,
> And this is the message I've come here to bring,
>   'Come quickly or he will be gone'.
> Come home, come home, oh father, dear father, come home.
>
> Father, dear father, come home with me now,
>   The clock in the steeple strikes three,
> The house is so lonely, the night is so long
>   For poor weeping mother and me.
> Yes, we are alone for Benny is dead,
>   And gone to the angels of light,
> And these were the very last words that he said,
>   'I want to kiss Papa good night'.
> Come home, come home, oh father, dear father, come home.

Work lived up to his name. It is pleasant to take leave of him as though his self-portrait were contained in his "Ring the bell, watchman". The hero, full of a vigour that few could excel, proffers no reason for a vigilance available on all occasions. Fix'd is his gaze as by some magic spell while his thin bony hands grasp the rope of the bell:

> Yes, yes! They come and with tidings to tell,
> Glorious and blessed tidings. Ring, ring, the bell.

How very different it is from its English companion piece, Oxenford's "The Bell-Ringer", music by Wallace, which rewards the pull on the rope with nothing better than grief and hope. Yes, yes, all tidings from the death of Lilly Dale to the stand made by father in the four-ale bar, plus the whole of the Civil War, inspired in Work the unflagging zeal which is his trade mark.

At heart these anti-alcoholics felt a compassion that moves us when it is naturally expressed. "Th' little sawt lad", words by Jacob Kershaw, music by Mrs Henry Slade, has this effect when it describes (in dialect) a boy with a load of salt, brick-dust, and scrubbing stones in his donkey-cart who has left a drunken father at home:

> My donkey it stons eawt i'th cowd,
>   It's had nowt yet today,
> But neaw aw've had a bit mysel
>   Aw'll not prolong my stay,
> For th' first farm-heause aw do come at
>   Thea'st have a bit of hay,
> And when that thae hast had thi fill
>   We'll again drive on eawr way.

Other songs of the species that are free from over-seriousness are very hard to find. There was a rigid belief in 'Whatsoever thy hand findeth to do do it with thy might', which brought about that thoroughness which we witness when a father plays with his small son's toy train. The British character suffered from it. The American character suffered from it still more, but so similarly that overwrought songs pleased one nation as much as the other. "After the ball was over", sung on the London music-halls by Charles Godfrey and Vesta Tilley, was accepted as a native product: when Charles K. Harris called his autobiography, *After the Ball, Forty Years of Melody*, his evidence that "After the ball" was American could scarcely be believed. Yet its phrases are odd enough to make us feel that the author belongs to any country other than our own. The trouble starts when a girl says 'I wish some water'. When it is brought to her

> there stood a man,
> Kissing my sweetheart as lovers can.

The glass of water falls, 'broken, that's all', and then long years pass. At last a letter comes from that man to say he was her brother. It is too late. She is dead.

The story is told to a child who climbs on an old man's knee, which was immediately recognized as the way any story of a broken heart should be told. According to Sir Max Beerbohm one of these old men began, 'Shall I tell you a story of giants or in the dell?' and there are others which contain lines equally succinct. According to the wisdom thrust upon us in our defenceless youth the gift is peculiar to Latin authors, Virgil above all others, but it is doubtful whether they packed more into one phrase than the horse-poets of Tin Pan Alley when ballads of drama sold at the rate of thousands a day. Charles Graham seems to have been Virgil's closest rival: when he adopted the plan of the story told to a child in "Two little girls in blue" he said as much in a dozen words as a novel could manage in a chapter. In a vague sort of way the uncle confesses that his unfounded jealousy had wronged a heart that was good and true—'one little girl in blue, lad, became your mother, I married the other, but now we have drifted apart'. Once again the British public imagined this to be their own, and they felt the same way about Harris's "There'll come a time some day". An old man's tears are falling and a child wants to know why. She is his daughter. He fears that she will leave him just as her mother did:

> Think well of all I've said,
> Honour the man you wed
> Always remember my story, there'll come a time.

There is an imposing collection of these appeals to the heart in a volume called *Read 'em and Weep*, by Sigmund Spaeth, published in New York in 1926. Munroe H. Rosenfeld is not a name to conjure with in Great Britain, but he deserves remembrance if only because of "With all her faults I love her still". He contributed "Take back your gold", to one of the revivals of *East Lynne*, and composed the music of Felix MacGlennon's "Oh! Flo what a change you know", barely recognizable in its original form when the name is Jane. "Gold will buy almost anything but a true girl's heart" gives some slight indication of Rosenfeld's progress from strength to strength, until his ballads resembled tabloid grand operas. His moral fervour seems to have driven rivals to desperation. That Charles K. Harris could not compete on such terms is suggested first by the plaintive tone of "My dear mamma would never say, 'always in the way' ", and then by his sudden yielding to the temptation of burlesque. Dropping all pretence of righteous ardour he provided Marie Dressler with the mock melodramatics of 'So ev'ry week you'd better send your wages back to me, for heav'n will protect a working girl'. Some fads may be killed by ridicule but not this one. It was so strongly rooted after a full century of growth that the entire populations of Great Britain and the United States had been brought up with an inborn belief that to be musical a song must be moral as well as melancholy. Still, there were some excesses that could not be exported. Paul Dresser's "The Convict and the Bird" did carry things too far. Each day a bird sings to a convict. One day it finds his cell empty. It chirps all night. At early morn it lays itself down and dies. That was not the climax. When Harris, Graham, and Dresser had done their utmost, a poet named Arthur J. Lamb surpassed them all. He brought the words of "She was only a bird in a gilded cage" to Harry Von Tilzer, who drew tears from everybody round his piano while merely attempting a tune. Hardened sinners brought themselves to the brink of virtue when he came to the bit about a grave with a woman in it who is indeed better dead than 'to have people say when seen'—chorus. Ordinarily any enormous success moves rivals to bring out imitations, but here the original author and composer did it themselves. With "The mansion of aching hearts" they won another enormous success, partly because—such is the power of poetry—people who would have been shocked by the title had no idea what it meant.

XIX

The Traffic Goes Round
and Round

+•+

. . . . you'll look sweet on the seat
Of a bicycle made for two

Harry Dacre

BYSICLES AND TRYSICLES, a Paris correspondent reported in 1868, had been seen in the Champs Elysées and the Bois de Boulogne that summer. According to the Oxford Dictionary this was the first mention of them in print. They were first mentioned in song when Fred Coyne rode a tricycle on the stage:

On the new velocipede so gaily,
You'll see the people riding daily
Everyone should try one, everyone should buy one,
See the new velocipede,

which was written by Frank W. Green and composed by Alfred Lee.

Velocity thus made its coming known. Past fashions in traffic may seem all very leisurely now but it went then at a pace which thrilled. You can tell that from woodcuts on tattered song sheets. Artists who decorated these thought the limit of velocity for human beings had been reached by the fastest gigs and riders on the way to Epsom, so much so that the Derby itself would have been a decided anti-climax but for the current belief in the power of race-horses to stretch themselves in full flight like dachshunds. Put your mind in reverse when looking at faded travel pictures. When thirty miles an hour was terrific, Rotten Row occasionally had the effect on beholders that Brooklands had before 'faster than sound' meant anything outside pseudo-scientific poetic licence. You think of Hyde Park when Dalmatians ran beneath the seats of phaetons—their plum-pudding pattern showing between the revolving spokes of bright yellow wheels—as a place of halcyon repose. You have lost the feel of what was dashing.

'Going the pace' was different then from what it is now in both senses. Compare the modern woman of the race-track with the heroine of the ballad written by Harry Dacre for Fanny Leslie on the subject of:

Pretty little Polly on her gee-gee-gee.

She, of course, had to be followed by a groom every afternoon when she went riding; it was the bysicles and the trysicles in the Bois that summer of 1868 which sent modesty sprawling. The idea that women might sit on them stirred The Great Macdermott to action. He who had controlled the destinies of nations would now see what he could do to order the behaviour of the sexes. In "M'yes", written by George Dance, composed by George Ison, he laid down the law: that a lady may canter around but she 'can't ride a Bicycle like her Papa because she ain't built that way'. Barely had he finished when the penny-farthings were replaced by the safety bicycle, which went whizzing past the phaetons with their Dalmatians in Hyde Park, and suddenly it became not merely permissible but highly fashionable for women to whizz past on them. No groom could play the guardian now; no parental control, no matter how rigid, could supervise every movement of a daughter who had mastered this new means of velocity.

In a curtain-raiser called *The Girls of the Period; or, The Island of Nowarpartickilar*, at Drury Lane in 1869, Burnand contrived a scene for girls on velocipedes—supplied by the French Velocipede Company—who wore jockey colours. To the Velocipede Derby Gallop, composed by C. Levy, he strung a lot of rhyming words like skipping and whipping together to create an effect of 'the pace that kills'. Females on bicycles might be seen in Hyde Park, but they were not so common that they could not be presented as an exciting spectacle on the stage for twenty or thirty years longer. This idea of associating women with the mania for speed took our breath away, even though there was always Boadicea's chariot on the Thames embankment to remind us that an Ancient Briton thought of it first. Many a noble mind had striven to achieve the emancipation of women. Machines were now doing it for them.

There was a great deal more than an idle whim in the cycling

'. . . every man this day will do his duty . . .'

'. . . always afternoon . . .'

'. . . in a wood of Crete . . .'

vogue of the 1890s. It caused a revolution in many things besides
peed. When Katie Lawrence sang "Daisy Bell", written and composed by Harry Dacre, she wore a Norfolk suit (of the kind
associated with Bernard Shaw) which meant that the female might
put on the garment of the male without making herself liable to
immediate arrest. Of course the smart cycling set whose billowy
skirts and leg-of-mutton sleeves fluttered in the spring breezes of
the Park never dreamt of anything so low. Nevertheless, the mere
presence of a bicycle gave a woman the right to dress in a way that
without the bicycle would have been criminal. Horsewomen still
rode side-saddle. And the divided skirts of Mrs Bloomer had been a
failure.

By comparison the motor-car made a conventional start in life.
The correct etiquette for 'a young lady motorist' was to leave
the driving to the male, either her father or his chauffeur. We
may never know who worked out the society-shaking theory that
since it was respectable for a woman to drive a phaeton it must
be equally respectable for her to drive a motor-car. We may never
know this but we do know that the revolution was celebrated in
song. "Riding on a motor-car", written and composed by John
Read, proclaimed that, 'She is an angel without wings, riding on a
motor-car'. But that was forgotten while everybody sang:

> Oh Flo, why do you go, riding alone in your motor-car?
> People say you're peculiar, so you are, so you are.

Sometimes it was the vehicle that changed, sometimes the pas-
senger. Our grandmothers had to be fast hussies in order to take
a cab. Climbing up to get inside was a difficult feat for them,
for their laces and flounces became bedraggled through brushing
against the wheel except when a professional door-opener was there
to affix the wickerwork guard over its filthy rim. Even the fastest
hussy could not mount the steps of the knife-board bus, along the
top of which two rows of top-hatted gentlemen sat back to back:
the footholds of ascent were too far apart for wearers of the tight
skirts that came into fashion with the bustle. "Who'll oblige a
lady?" the conductor's cry to gentlemen inside, became a good
title for songs, one of them written by E. V. Page, composed by
Vincent Davies and sung by Fred Coyne. What happened when
no gentleman would oblige was explained by Marie Lloyd in
"Twiggy Voo". While she climbs the stairs on the outside of the

N

bus, the wind blows and the conductor mutters, 'Railways'. What this word meant was, 'Straight up and down', a term of the severest abuse when public opinion firmly maintained that no female form could be regarded as divine without a plentiful supply of curves. The dogma cannot be dismissed as masculine prejudice. Marie Lloyd herself insisted on the importance of good fat calves. There was a new waitress in attendance behind the scenes. When she asked, at the door of the dressing-room, 'Tea or coffee?' the blaze of indignation which met this charge of teetotalism was followed by the command, 'Lift yer skirts up'. While the poor girl stood still in nervous terror, Marie Lloyd examined her legs and then delivered a verdict. 'Got to see the shape of yer legs before I let yer serve me. You'll do'. About this there was general agreement. Audiences denied a hearing to any new serio-comic whose legs did not resemble those mahogany table-legs that bulged in the middle. If she inclined to railways it was her own fault, for Willie Clarkson, the famous costumier of Wardour Street, kept a cupboard full of hips and calves for any girl who wished to please the public.

Trams were the most tenderly sentimentalized of all transport. George Lashwood's 'Many a miss will be missus some day thro' riding on top of a car' brought romance nearer home than any other chorus of the kind. We did not guess that this was yet another American masterpiece, words by Fred W. Leigh and V. P. Bryan, music by Harry Von Tilzer. The classic of the railway, "Casey Jones", was unmistakably American despite a vain attempt to place it on the line to Dover.

Newton, composer, and Seibert, author, were engine drivers before they set wheels turning in all our heads with 'mounted on the engine and took his farewell trip into the promised land'.

There never was any romance about the growler, brougham, fly, or four-wheeler, which the pro's themselves used on their nightly journeys from hall to hall on a round of London engagements. The songs they inspired kept to knockabout humour. "We all went home in a cab", sung by Charles Bignell, is thoroughly typical: there are five-and-twenty of them; the bottom falls out, they turn the growler upside down, and the horse, who refuses to budge, is put inside. The hansom was different, for it lived up to its descent from the private cabriolets of Regency bucks; ''Tis the gondola of London', Disraeli made one of his heroes say. When The Great Macdermott made melodious confession of marital infidelity a hansom usually came into it somehow, probably because the side-lamps made it easy for 'the wife' passing by to take a good look at the two passengers and recognize one as her husband. Only the carriage out-classed the hansom as the vehicle of passion. Arthur Coombes, in gibus and cloak, used to sing about the lost soul who fell panting at the feet of her betrayer, who bows his head in shame—"Carriage waits, m'lord." Of all that picturesque cavalcade of London traffic only one item remains in fair numbers—the coster's pony cart, and that was constantly sung about.

XX

Humour of the Humble Home

◆◆◆◆◆◆◆◆◆◆◆◆◆◆◆◆◆◆◆◆◆◆◆◆◆◆◆◆◆

He's bought a bed and a table too,
A big tin dish for making stew,
A large flat-iron to iron his shirt,
And a flannel, and a scrubbing brush to wash away the dirt.
And he's bought a pail and basins three,
A coffee pot, a kettle, and a teapot for the tea,
 And a soap-bowl and a ladle,
 And a gridiron and a cradle,
And he's going to marry Mary Ann, that's me!
He's going to marry Mary Ann!

Joseph Tabrar.

WITH OR WITHOUT any share in the making of his songs, the music-hall comedian took the credit for them. The singer was supposed to be all that mattered, while the words and music, which may endure as long as paper lasts, were supposed to have no value at all. Of course those joyous souls who came so near to being worshipped as to be dubbed idols created a legend to last long after the ending of their lives, and many a refrain still preserves a personality. On the other hand, fat budgets of homely stuff, written and composed at a guinea a time, possess merit as the mirror of Victorian life. When the stars are forgotten the scribblers come into their own. With less and less talk of Bessie Bellwood there is more and more of Joseph Tabrar, who provided her with "He's going to marry Mary Ann". Such a gift as his for stuffing our ears with lively jingles after the style of:

Dearly beloved brethren isn't it a sin
When you peel potatoes you throw away the skin,
The skins feed pigs and the pigs feed you
Dearly beloved brethren is not that true?

may not call for a statue but it will be the subject of a learned work from professors of folklore.

Until the day arrives when some truly learned minds get to work on the subject, we must make what we can of this vast array of 'coloured fronts' which reveal the changing fashions in popular humour. No topic ever seems to drop out. It is like watching the Derby, from the commentator's lofty seat, as different colours keep forging ahead. Champagne Charlie falls back after a flying start but still keeps a place in the field alongside Jilted Lover and the Portentous Moralist, a long way behind Happy Family. These music-hall songs carry so much red and green and blue that I must be excused for likening them to jockeys, though I am glad to get rid of metaphor and explain that the change in taste indicates how poets have ceased to look at life in the streets and are now living inside the houses. Revelry itself takes on fresh forms, for in place of dashing men-about-town we have husbands, sons, wives and daughters who are either enjoying a night out or suffering its consequences. The more ordinary the things sung about the more sure the laughter. Sensing this swing round in what was wanted, Bessie Bellwood transformed herself from the reckless daredevil of "What cheer Riah, now Riah she's a toff", into the sweet little innocent, about-to-be-married Mary Ann, delighted by a scrubbing brush.

In order to explain the long-lived popularity of family relations as a topic we may put our trust in the theory that the concern of the music-halls was with the humour of the home and its contents, no matter how humble. The only objection to this comes from some comedians whose songs declare, in effect, that they are not nearly so humble as all that. Such a protest is heard when Harry Randall, whose place was not unduly exalted, complains, 'We are without a servant girl', in the patter of "We've had 'em all Irish, we've had 'em all Scotch". This is odd entertainment for any audience. Consequently I must record that it was written in 1886 by T. S. Lonsdale, composed by Alfred Lee, and given a place in an 'annual' to prove its success. Lonsdale was the author of a classic with an almost undying refrain:

> Tommy make room for your Uncle,
>   There's a little dear,
> Tommy make room for Uncle,
>   I want him to sit here.

Both in jest and in earnest popular singers had to come to grips with life. Most of them mocked the hardships they had experienced themselves so that tattered coat, battered topper, and red nose formed the emblem of good fun. Such pothouse ragamuffins may not have been as dominant as we now suppose, for they were outnumbered by 'geysers' in black bonnets and shawls acted all the year round by men who were the dames of pantomime. But the prevalence of alcoholic mirth can still be seen in the numbers of songs on the subject sung by the majority of stars. It was checked when a dignified manager refused to allow "Come where the booze is cheaper" to be sung at the Palace, shortly before we heard the choruses in praise of food. By then the drunkards had had a long innings as part of a resolve to see some joke in squalor.

Where matrimony was concerned audiences laughed at the spectacle of misery. Poverty was more gently treated. It was usually assumed to be a fit subject for jest—but not by Jenny Hill, the Vital Spark, who was the most dearly beloved of all. Very few of her songs are light-hearted. She had known what it was to be a waif, and she preferred to play the part of outcasts, strays, and stowaways, in little dramas to provide some emotional ballad with a setting. She was without a rival, and when she retired through the exhaustion caused by her early struggles her style disappeared. It had been applauded for her sake, whereas merry urchins were liked for themselves. After Nelly Power had finished with this gay outburst:

> The boy I love sits up in the gallery,
>   The boy I love is looking down at me,
> Can't you see, there he is, a-waving of his handkerchief,
>   As merry as a robin that sings on a tree

it served the turn of another impudent minx—Marie Lloyd. She expressed the joys of a lowly life because she had no use for any other. She did not change at heart, and she did not change in social graces either. She kept to the ways of humble homes, which is why puritans described her as coarse. Where an overwrought novelist would want to write a feverish chapter, Marie Lloyd winked, and the righteous who gauged what she meant with exactitude discovered, when resolved on denouncing her, that they had no word, grimace, or gesture to denounce. As she herself sang, 'To cut it short is best, you can let them guess the rest', with the result that

we remember her in snatches in the manner of, 'Every little movement has a meaning of its own', rather than in complete performances. Few of her songs, nearly all written by experts, have any life
left in them; the titles of "How can a girl refuse?" "The Naughty
Continong", "The Wrong Man", "You can't stop a girl from
thinking", "Actions speak louder than words", "Never let a chance
go by", "Keep off the grass" and "Then you wink the other eye"
give an idea of their contents and explain why a special eloquence
was needed in the singing of them. Considerably more is needed
to help us to understand why any normal gathering of human
beings could have tolerated, "Poor Thing", words by Richard
Morton, music by George Le Brunn, described (on the cover that
shows the singer in the dress of a small girl) as 'sung with the
greatest possible success'.

'Before she was seven her ma was dead, and then her pa went off
his head', introduces Sal Smith, who loved a husband despite his
infidelities. He knocked her down the stairs:

> Her salt tears notwithstanding
> He shoved her off the landing

then left her to sob as if her heart were broke; and as the climax
of a tale, intended as a source of innocent merriment, she makes a
hole in the sea so as to be free from tussles down among the mussles,
added to which there is a comic illustration to show her lying face
downwards like a corpse at the foot of the stairs. So many other
songs exhibit the Victorians in amiable moods that we feel a jolt
on being reminded that they prided themselves on some kinds
of insensibility. The desire to shock, natural in very small boys,
overwhelmed them. Fired by this impulse some of the 'artists'
who depicted Marie Lloyd on covers made her look like a harpy,
with bloated cheeks, goggle eyes, and protruding teeth. Little trace
remains of her warm-hearted humanity, or of that side of her nature
which she herself described in E. W. Rogers' "The Barmaid":

> Lor', Bill, she fairly made me blink so
> Rorty bit o' crackling, don't yer think so?

Yet she is now chiefly remembered by the place she gave herself in
the family circle—first as the bad child in "There they are the two
of them on their own" who has to be bribed by the lovers to go

away, then as the innocent in "Oh, Mr Porter, what shall I do?"
next as the eager young thing in Tabrar's

> I shall say to a young man gay,
> If he treads upon my frock,
> Randy pandy, sugardy candy,
> Buy me some almond rock

then as the coster girl in E. W. Rogers' "Garn Away":

> D'yer think I'd ever go upon the stage and show my legs?

and at last as the harassed housewife on moving day in "Can't find
my way home" and "One of the ruins that Cromwell knocked
abaht a bit".

Similarly Vesta Victoria, as a child who impudently borrowed
the Queen's name, was content at first with the appeal of girlhood.
Tabrar wrote for her, "I've got a little cat and I'm very fond of that,
but I'd rather have a bow-wow-wow", when she wanted to carry
her kitten in a basketful of flowers on the stage. He tried a sequel,
"My Daddy's bought me a bow-wow", but that was asking too
much of a soft-hearted populace. When she changed her tune to
"Our lodger's such a nice young man", she mastered the art of
the smooth voice and blank expression now known as 'dead pan'.

From the man's view nothing but misery could be expected
from married life. Even Tom Costello, usually an heroic figure,
became abjectly hen-pecked in order to express agreement with this
when Fred Gilbert provided him with both words and music of
"At Trinity Church I met my doom".

That paired off with "Why did I leave my little back room?"
supplied by A. J. Mills and Frank W. Carter to Alf Chester in the
closing years of the nineteenth century. It made history in the
South African War as the unofficial marching song of the British
Army, which always prefers the mournful to the gay. At that time
it was unfortunate in its choice of generals, and one of them
ordered the song to be banned. 'It's nice to have a home of your
own as happy as a king upon his throne' was the sentiment put
into Harry Anderson's mouth by A. E. Lawrence and George
Lester, but only the first line ever stuck in the mind.

With "Young men taken in and done for"—the work of Harry
King, arranged by Le Brunn—Dan Leno joined the ranks of the
hen-pecked; in his song of a seaside holiday he was the overburdened

father of a family; and as time went on he entertained us with his trials at the hands of more and more relations. He was every man according to his trade, the butcher observing the waistcoat buttons on the side of pork, the grocer sifting evidence concerning the freshness of eggs, the policeman, the postman, and the railwayman. Nothing much of his songs could be whistled or hummed; the tunes were lively but they did not matter; what did was the patter, in which respect they bear a likeness to Grimaldi's, though there was no tradition to link them. Resemblances between these two greatest names in mirth for a century can be seen in their jokes about food and drink and strings of sausages; both, to borrow what Lamb said of someone else, stood amid the commonplace materials of life. But while Grimaldi, in a romantic age, transformed them into the trappings of the wealthy, Dan Leno, in a realistic age, showed them as they were, unchanged by his humour, so that his songs will serve the future as sidelights on his times.

With Little Tich things were much the same. Some of the types he represented himself to be were not people who belonged down our street but they all, the Queen of the Fairies included, appeared as the people down our street saw or imagined them. He painted their portraits in patter that merely began and ended in song. I cannot remember a single chorus of his that was ever heard in the streets.

Many songs for these idols were composed by George Le Brunn; he wrote the music of "Oh, Mr Porter!" for Marie Lloyd, and of "You can get a sweetheart any day, but not another mother", for one of her husbands, Alec Hurley. For Dan Leno he helped with "The Shopwalker" whose frankness startled us in those easily startled days with his helpful remarks to an imaginary customer who could not bring herself to tell a man what she wanted, 'Yes, Madam, white ones? With lace round the bottoms?' Le Brunn wrote songs by the dozen—he had to in the days when a guinea a time was the customary payment—and he could as easily stir us with "The Seventh Royal Fusiliers" as amuse us with "If it wasn't for the houses in between". Yet the best of his songs was rarely heard. It was one of his earlier efforts—"The Song of the Thrush", for Peggy Pride. Some titles suggest that music-hall poets were not always content with the family circle, but at this date they generally saw life from the domestic point of view. In a more remote past a constable would be mentioned to enliven a tale of disorderly conduct or crime; the new outlook is evident in "If you want to know the time ask a policeman", sung by James Fawn, written by E. W. Rogers, composed by A. E. Durandeau. It begins with the comforting reflection that, 'Every member of the force has a watch and chain, of course', but the compliment ends there. The other verses are about getting drinks when pubs are shut, eloping with housemaids, running away from trouble, and embracing your wife in your absence. There you hear the householder, and you hear him again in another famous song where you might have expected a revival of the *lion comique*—Fred Gilbert's "The man who broke the bank at Monte Carlo". It was sung by Charles Coburn in the character of a very ordinary man who had had a very extraordinary experience; he boasted of strolling along with an independent air, which is so unlike Champagne Charlie's swagger about being good for any game at night, my boys, as to be worth noting. Far from bragging about his love of a spree, Coburn taught the public to chant interminably, "Two lovely black eyes, oh what a surprise", and the nearest he came to revelry was in a series of four-lined verses to serve as cues for the question, 'What's the matter with . . . ?' When the local hero had been named there came the answer, 'He's all right'. It proved useful at elections in those days when politics excited enthusiasm.

XXI

Christmas Pantomime

Let the Star Spangled Banner
And the dear old Union Jack,
For ever together be unfurl'd.

E. V. Page (Drury Lane, 1881-82)

THERE WAS A NIGGER minstrel named Henry Sayers who died at the age of seventy-six in 1934. Fifty years earlier he had stopped outside a low dive in the coloured quarter of St Louis and made notes of the gibberish he heard ascending. As "Ta-ra-ra-boom-der-é", with what was called a stylish French accent, it became a number in a minstrel show which was called *Tuxedo* after the New York club whose members wore the smoking-jacket and re-named it the tuxedo in their own honour. With new verses by B. M. Batchelor, who began; 'Once a young man went to woo', it arrived in London. Lottie Collins accepted it because the music suited her plan for a dance which should start demurely and suddenly change to wild abandon. This she introduced into the Christmas pantomime of *Dick Whittington* at The Grand, Islington, on Boxing Night, 1891. What happened to it when she joined *Cinder-Ellen Up Too Late* at the Gaiety matters less; the fact is that she made it a pantomime song.

Song was less important than dance in early Victorian panto-mimes, which often made old familiar tunes serve for new sets of verses, in the same way that old scenery was taken out of dock to serve new subjects. Yet the shoddy trick added one irresistible chorus to the repertoire of street arabs when ruthless hands turned "Dixie" into an accompaniment for:

> I wish I was with Nancy, I do, I do,
>> In a second floor for evermore,
> I'd live and die with Nancy.
>> In the Strand, in the Strand,
> I'd live and die for Nancy.

and a whole generation regarded this parody as the original and the original as a parody.

Until 1880 the Christmas shows at theatres had been performed by pantomimists, notably the Vokes Family at Drury Lane. They quarrelled with the new manager, Augustus Harris (son of the operatic impresario), and he replaced them with stars of the music-hall who were famous for their songs. His first choice was Arthur Roberts, whose dashing style lent itself to topicality, as he had shown in "What shall we do with Cyprus?" written by Edwin V. Page with music by Vincent Davies, to exploit the feelings of dissatisfaction over the news of ill-health among the first British army of occupation:

> Here's another little baby Queen Victoria has got,
> Another little colony, although she has a lot,
> Another little island, very wet and very hot,
>   Whatever will she do with little Cyprus?

One idea is to make it happy with British income tax, and another is to send them a 'Woolwich Infant' with some powder and some balls,

> And if they're good we'll send a minor Canon of St Paul's,
>   To blow up all the wicked ones in Cyprus.

As a topical poet Page ought to have a place in the history of pantomime. For Fanny Leslie, representing herself to be Robinson Crusoe at Drury Lane during the holidays of 1881-82, he wrote this to the tune of W. G. Eaton:

> England looks with joy and pleasure
>   On her sons across the main,
> While America, the treasure
>   Of her love, returns again.

Hard thinking was not what anybody expected from Old Drury, but in *Sinbad* the next year Page tried it again. He attacked the Press in a seemingly artless little tale of "The Winkle and the Whale", music by F. Stanislaus, which told how electric eels stole the news from submarine wires. Arthur Roberts sang:

> They keeps the best and they alters the rest

to get of-fish-al lyin' telegraphs. Then the whale lashed his tail
and went straight home to tea and that there winkle ne'er returned
to his wife and familee. Yet in shows not intended for children
Arthur Roberts contributed to the repertoire of the nursery. In
Gentleman Joe, the Hansom Cabby, at the Prince of Wales's in 1895,
he started the craze of this jingle by W. S. Laidlaw, music by Ella
Chapman:

> She wanted something to play with,
>   Something to love and adore,
> Now Dolly is dead she's put her to bed
>   For evermore

which lasted for years. Though that was by far the most popular
chorus Arthur Roberts ever sang, he had a large store of others.
"Crutch and Toothpick", written by Harry Adams and composed
by E. Jonghmanns, took many a young man's fancy:

> . . . We're gents and we act as such,
> When parading each one brings his toothpick and his crutch,
>   Tral la la, bon soir, bye-bye,
>   So long, so short, so on,
>   Olive oil, au revoir, I——
>   Shall be happy to see you anon.

Simple little rhymes were the stock-in-trade of Roberts in the days
when we could be shocked at the possibility of double-meanings
even if they were not there. T. S. Lonsdale provided him with:

> This timid little maid was really so afraid,
>   Her sweetheart would come to her,
> So she trotted off to bed and covered up her head,
>   And fastened up the door with the skewer.

But when it came to making infants and octogenarians sing together
there was none to equal Harry Bedford with, "A little bit off the
top will do for me" and "When I get some money, oh when, when,
when, when, when", though even these were surpassed by the song
he composed himself, "When the summer comes again". In his old
age he found he had saved some money; it was as much as his friends
could do to stop him giving it all away.

Social historians may be tempted to ascribe the popularity of
childish songs to the custom of celebrating Christmas with fairy-

tale pantomimes. The actual records show that there was a preference in these juvenile entertainments for such themes as "Sparkling Wine" or the misdemeanours of Mr Gladstone. Principal boys did not quarrel over William J. Scanlon's:

> Baby boy! Baby boy! come from behind that chair,
> Baby boy! Baby boy! I see you hiding there,
>   Oh you rascal!

And it was the United States, ignorant of Christmas pantomime, which produced, music by H. W. Petrie, words by Philip Wingate:

> You can't holla down our rain barrel,
>   You can't climb our apple tree,
> I don't want to play in your yard,
>   If you won't be good to me.

As for "In the sweet bye-and-bye", sung by parents to children who demanded presents, this turned out to be one of Sankey's hymns. "Pull for the shore, sailors", was another. In the end he won the day, for his "Oh, that will be glory for me" was so catchy that it held its own in direct rivalry with songs. But some of these household snatches did come from pantomime. When the hypnotizing tune of "La Mattchiche", a Spanish dance from Paris, was being played everywhere from 1905 onwards, one of the Ugly Sisters in *Cinderella* fitted it with the words:

> If I had smaller tootsies and not so wide,
> I'd wear those little bootsies and be his bride,
>   Ah-ah, ah, ha!

All that has been said about the quantities of music that Victorian publishers poured down multitudes of willing throats applies particularly to coon songs. Catalogues survive that consist of nothing but forgotten stuff, but even the titles which are not forgotten are too numerous for anything but a catalogue. Yet in spite of such rivalry "Little Alabama Coon", written and composed by Hattie Starr, made the name of Nellie Richards—otherwise we would not remember her—and it had a tune we can always recall:

> Go to sleep, my little piccaninny,
> Brer Fox'll catch you if you don't.

This shared the vogue in the early 1890s of "Sweet Marie", words by Cy Warman, music by Ramon Moore, which contained a couple of memorable couplets:

> Come to me, Sweet Marie, Sweet Marie come to me,
> Not because your face is fair, love, to see,

which made a good beginning but was not destined to be so often quoted as:

> All the daisies in the dell know my secret, know it well,
> And yet I cannot tell Sweet Marie.

XXII

Love's New Sweet Song

Though the heart be weary,
Sad the day and long,
Still to us at twilight,
Comes love's old sweet song.

WHAT WE USED to sing round the drawing-room piano may be vaguely divided into the Early Victorian, Mid-Victorian, and Late Victorian. When it comes to separating one lot from another the trouble begins. Any number of people began life before Victoria ascended the throne and went on living after her death. Santley was one of them. The poets and composers who provided fodder for his resonant baritone form a crowd with a considerable overlapping of three or four generations. It was different in the rowdy atmosphere of the music-halls, for there nearly everybody died young, so that we seldom confuse their standards of the 1860s with those of the 1880s or even earlier. No such contrasts existed on the concert platform, where old poets taught young musicians, and old musicians taught young poets, 'What was good enough for my grandfather is good enough for me'. Hence the steadfast loyalty to established forms, particularly the ballad with a jolly first verse, a fairly jolly second verse, and a thoroughly maudlin third verse which demanded the death penalty and could never be satisfied with less. How this happened can be seen when our old friend Charles Swain was provided by his publisher, Boosey and Company, with a promising young composer, James L. Molloy. The consequence was "The Old Cottage Clock", which sticks so closely to the recognized formula as almost to burlesque it. At the start its voice warned old and young:

> Tick, tick, it said, quick to bed,
> For ten I've given warning;
> Up, up and go, or else, you know,
> You'll never rise soon in the morning.

Naumann: Leicht Gepäck.
Nº 829. (5137.)

Play on, play on, play on for evermore.

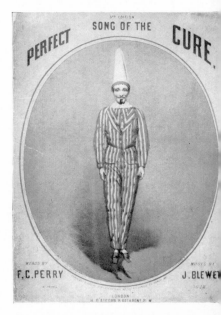

'Still in our hearts thy forms we cherish.'

Half-way through a cross old voice was that tiresome clock as it called at daybreak boldly:

> Tick, tick, it said, quick out of bed,
>   For five I've given warning;
> You'll never have health, you'll never have wealth,
>   Unless you're up soon in the morning.

Finally, while tears are shed for the bright days fled, its hands still move though hands we love are clasped on earth no longer:

> Tick, tick, it said, to the churchyard bed,
>   The grave hath given warning,
> Up, up and rise, and look to the skies,
>   And prepare for a heavenly morning.

Molloy was soon in demand. He composed "The Kerry Dance" for Madame Sherrington, "The Vagabond" for Santley, "London Bridge" for Maybrick, and "Love's Old Sweet Song" for Madame Sterling. His "Tomorrow will be Friday and we've caught no fish today", sung by Barrington Foote, became a tag for closing conversation. Whoever was in a hurry would quote the line not as speech but as a snatch of song.

The difference between topical success and lasting success becomes clear when Molloy's work is compared with the long list of things like "My Pet", "Love but me alone" and "If you love me tell me so" by Harrison Millard, all very popular round about 1880 but not destined to survive. Most of their contemporaries gave us something to remember them by. "Daddy" by A. H. Behrend, comes into the category of once heard never forgotten; there is a record of it in the contralto profundities of Clara Butt which compels tears of a kind never foreseen by singer or composer. But Sullivan, in the list headed by "The Lost Chord", made many an attempt to catch the tear-swilling public. The words of "Looking Back" by Louisa Gray (also a composer) gave him the opportunity for some long-drawn 'loves' and 'ohs' when it ended:

> O ... my love .... O .... my love .... O .... my love. ...
>   O my love I loved her so,
> My love .... that loved me years ago.

What made him choose that lyric is not very plain. For every prize won by insipidity three were carried off by vigour. Theo Marzials

o

wrote his own verses and could turn out the "If only" or "My love is come" sort of stuff with anyone, but while they are forgotten his "Twickenham Ferry" endures along with:

> Oh, we're three, jolly, jolly sailor boys,
> · And we're newly home from South Amerikee,

and it was no mean achievement, when the nights in June are numbered, that his setting of Goring-Thomas's "Have you forgotten love so soon?" should have remained a favourite no matter how many newcomers tackled the same theme. In the robust style there was no author so sure as F. E. Weatherly, librettist of five operas, including the English version of *Cavalleria Rusticana* in the 1890s. He may not have had much encouragement when he turned composer, but when it came to verse he rarely failed. Times change so drastically that we question the truth of his picture in "Masks and Faces" (for Molloy) about a theatrical performance which enthralled the audience:

> Though the real tale of the woman there
> Nobody cared to know

as peculiarly unlike life, but this is not his usual kind of subject. When he paired off with Tosti he stepped into Whyte-Melville's shoes, first with "My dreams" of the day I met you and the light divine, and then, still more, with "Parted", with its questions about how to live without you and how to let you go; but not so much with "Mother", which is a companion picture to "Daddy", whether intended as such or not, since she watches the sun in the west go down. Dusk was the time for tears. "A voice from Heav'n", words by Hubi Newcome, music by Edward St Quentin, referred to a dream in the calm of the twilight with an appeal to childie dear from the angels' shore. "The Link Divine", words by Alfred Hyatt, music by Piccolomini, presents us with a bereft lover who watches the sunset sky 'Tho' your poor soul is dwelling there'. Separation from the living caused a grief that was very much more intense, probably for the very good reason that nothing in the latest catalogues could supplant "In the gloaming" and "Alice, where art thou?" as manifestations of the soulfulness which prevailed in drawing-rooms as the sure foundation of a jolly good musical evening. Tosti's "Goodbye" and Tosti's "Parted" came first in the new crop with a rival from America, which was written and composed by Paul Dresser—he was the brother of Theodore Dreiser, novelist of another temperament—with a title, "Goodbye for all Eternity", that made a bid to outlast all other separations since "Goodbye for ever" by comparison did not seem quite such a long time. Yet in the heyday of finality-mongering yet another time limit was set. Violet Fane's "For Ever", mainly known as Tosti's though Frederic H. Cowen also tackled it, taught us a new language of love:

> My life is curst with thoughts of thee
> For ever and for ever

Both Tosti and Sullivan picked "Venetian Song", written by B. C. Stephenson—part author of the remarkably successful drama, adapted from Sardou, *Diplomacy*.

> The night wind sighs, our vessel flies
> Across the dark lagoon

is how it begins, before passion rears its ugly head with, 'Here am I, to live or die, as you prove hard or kind'. After this, passion was acceptable in song though forbidden everywhere else; in fact, when the word was banned in polite society it became the favourite topic of verse accompanied by music. There was a thrill when it was brought hot from the desert, 'on my Arab shod with fire', by the American traveller Bayard Taylor. Though his main work was the translation of Goethe's *Faust*, he came nearest to immortality with his Bedouin, whose ardour, in Pinsuti's setting, would melt the casque and tasses of the lover in shining armour:

> I love thee, I love but thee,
>   With a love that shall not die!
> Till the sun grows cold, and the stars are old,
> And the leaves of the Judgement Book unfold.

To offset this reprehensible tendency there was a steady flow of lyrics that won the whole-hearted approval of all who believed in the virtues of the open-air. This is where Weatherly excelled no matter how many others may also have seen in it a way to appeal to a larger public. He wrote "The Lighthouse Keeper" for Molloy, with one verse to depict his life, another to maintain that the light-house is the light of love, and a last verse to round things off with death. For Odoardo Barri, Weatherly broke away from the old formula with marching along like "The Boys of the Old Brigade". Then, as a companion picture in honour of the Royal Navy, Weatherly wrote his sea song to the music of Stephen Adam, to maintain that Jack's the king of all, for they all love Jack! This was sung by Michael Maybrick, the outstanding baritone of the rousing type, who had his most suitable songs composed by Stephen Adams, which is not surprising since they were one and the same man. He began as a child pianist who grew up quickly, to be appointed organist of St Peter's parish church of Liverpool at the age of fourteen. While still of school age he wore the morning coat and top hat of a professional man and appeared with great dignity on concert platforms. After eight years of this he was granted leave of absence to enter the conservatoire at Leipsic, where it was discovered that he possessed a voice that would entitle him to a place among the greatest of living baritones. After further training at Milan he returned to England in triumph, which increased when he composed songs admirably suited to himself. 'It is strange', commented a critic, 'that while studying at Leipsic his vocal powers should have been discovered while his talent for composition should have escaped recognition.' But would there be any cause for surprise if serious-minded professors of the art of music refused to listen to popular songs? Added to which is the wonder whether a naturally musical nation would feel the same way about Maybrick's resolve to conquer audiences by storm. Late Victorians had a liking for the powerful; they read powerful novels, applauded powerful acting, and voted for powerful politicians, so that they readily inclined their ears to a baritone's exhortations and other forms of solemnity even when the singer-composer seemed to be making rather free with religion. The consequence was that Stephen Adams' melodies swept the country like a flood. After a time the liking for his "Nancy Lee" slackened, but as long as the love of song lasted in our homes there was always somebody to sing, 'For we'll drink tonight to the midshipmite, sing cheerily lads, yo-ho". Today his near-anthems are thundered forth by radio even though not so regularly as of old at church concerts, where their familiarity with sacred subjects seemed to tremble on the brink of blasphemy. "The Star of Bethlehem" was the first, and "The Holy City", with its resounding call to Jerusalem to lift up her gates and sing, the culminating triumph.

Serenades, which might be expected to resist all attempts at change, had to be adapted to the demands of the new era. Once it had been enough either to address the lady direct with some proposal preferably of an honourable nature, or else to praise her by name, as in the case of Annie Laurie, to the world at large. Now the beauty of a particular face rapidly became of less concern than geography, beginning with Venice. Offenbach's Barcarolle set a fine example, which was followed by a gondolier's offer to a queen of water to go with her a-floating if she would go a-boating. Next came Spain. "In old Madrid", where softly sighs of love the light guitar, words by Clifton Bingham, music by H. Trotère, often reveals its influence.

Swagger songs followed suit with "The Picador", words by Ernest Boyd Jones, music by St Quentin, whose hero was vainly advised to 'staunch now that crimson stream' because this kept to the rule of a mortal finale. Others were more bold and dashing, notably Roeckel's "Stormfiend", while Campana's "Scout", the song of the Uhlan, written for Santley with words by H. B. Farnie, boasted, 'Thousand and more to one, little for odds he cares, rather too many than none! Ha! ha! ha!', in keeping with the standards of our old friend Hybrias who was, however, in no danger of being supplanted. Strictly original songs were so rare that a place must be found for "Moods and tenses bother my senses" by J. E. McArdle, music by G. J. Hoare:

> It's right to say I've written or wrote,
>   But if a foe you've been fighting
> Beware of saying fitten or fote.

All the careers mentioned in this chapter added to the swelling choirs of Victoria's reign but did not end with it. Stephen Adams died in 1913, aged 79, and Tosti in 1916, aged 70—there had been a little confusion when Tolstoy died a few years earlier and George Edwardes had said of the author of *War and Peace* that he would be missed because he 'wrote some good lyrics'. As for Weatherly, after writing "The Ringer" for Herman Löhr and "Beyond the Dawn" for Wilfred Saunderson, he linked himself with the future by supplying the words for "The Little Damozel", by a promising young composer named Ivor Novello. Weatherly took his well-earned rest in 1929, leaving us the legacy that could be accounted rich if it consisted of "Boys of the Old Brigade" alone.

XXIII

Music Wherever We Go

•••••••••••••••••••••••••••••••••••••

Darling, I am growing old,
Silver threads among the gold
Shine upon my brow today,
Life is fading fast away.

E. E. Rexford

'BALLAD VOCALIST' is an odd label. It was applied to singers of the concert type imported into programmes when the old music-hall was being transformed into the palace of variety. What this constituted was not simply a new entertainment but a new public. It contained a vast number of aunts and curates all determined to be broadminded. They seem to have been the same kindly souls who took small boys to see the Minstrels, and as I was one of those small boys I ought to know. I can't think where the girls were taken— probably Kew Gardens, since botany was so excessively feminine— but anyhow there was money to be made at half-term matinées, especially when even girls were allowed in, and variety programmes contained more and more ballad vocalists in the diabolically mistaken belief that they were good for children. Genuine music-hall turns yielded to the new influence, so that there was less and less of the old comically sprawling stuff, full of the sights, sounds, and smells of life down our street, and more and more of the formally shaped ballads. If you catch the Minstrels in their less funereal moods you will recognize in some such American jewel as "Silver threads among the gold" (words by E. E. Rexford, music by H. P. Danks, with different names on pirated copies) a pattern set for middle-class audiences, distinct from the early Victorian division between rich and poor.

Where these songs came from is of minor importance. Where they got to is the test. They filled our homes with song. At the break of day, as we awoke to the clank of pewter milk-cans, the milkman and his boy, holding unwashed ·empties at the churn in

their two-wheeled chariot, taught us the latest choruses. The
butcher, high up on his meat-box which was then the fastest thing
on wheels, sped not too fast for the strains of another favourite
to reach us. People on buses sang, the drivers and conductors sang.
Housemaids, charwomen, and errand boys sang, and what wasn't
sung was whistled. Men might growl over breakfast but they
always sang in the bath or under the lather. Mothers did sing to
their children—not some pretty little lullaby but the latest choruses.
Why these should change was a problem for there were whole
series on similar topics. Before we had finished with silver threads
among the gold there was Harry Dacre's, "As your hair grows
whiter", with its catchy bit about although your footsteps falter
my love will never alter. And there was an unending stream of
successors to the Minstrels' most insidious tune from America—
"Won't you buy my pretty flowers?" by A. W. French, music by
G. W. Persley.

> Underneath the gaslight's glitter,
>   Stands a little fragile girl,
> Heedless of the night winds bitter,
>   As they round about her whirl;
> While the hundreds pass unheeding,
>   In the ev'ning's waning hours,
> Still she cries with tearful pleading,
>   'Won't you buy my pretty flow'rs?'
> *Chorus:*   There are many, sad and weary,
>   In this pleasant world of ours,
> Crying ev'ry night so dreary,
>   'Won't you buy my pretty flow'rs?'

With absolute unanimity the entire English-speaking world
accepted "Won't you buy my pretty flowers?" as the perfect
'pity me' song, for whose sake they were resolved to forsake
dozens of others. Yet so strong is the emulative instinct among all
who are concerned with song that those experienced veterans,
Weatherly and Molloy, chose the subject of brother and sister, she
with her flowers, and he with his broom. "Tatters", a little later,
told the tale of a little crossing-sweep and a little flow'r seller who
fall in love until death interferes, as usual, in the last verse. Horrible
little boys everywhere were taught to sing it; in the words of quite
another song, 'And I was one of them'.

Waifs were common ground for all classes, music-hall, drawing-room, and fairly superior concerts. Otherwise the types of song intended for each kept distinct. In satisfying the middle public Harry Dacre set his own words to his own music at a good pace, though never too fast to imprint them on the whole population's memory. Even if Leslie Stuart's "Sweetheart May" could not be surpassed, Harry Dacre could equal it exactly with "I'll be your sweetheart, if you will be mine". How many songs he wrote would be hard to calculate, but from 1892, when "Daisy Bell" revealed his gift, he regularly set everybody singing. Katie Lawrence sang his, "Sweet little Rosey-Posey, all in your Sunday clo's-ey", and Harriett Vernon, statuesque principal boy, his "She only answered, 'Ting-a-ling' ". At the same time Fanny Leslie was singing his, "Jolly little Polly on her gee-gee-gee!" and Dan Leno of his day at the seaside, where he drew his feet from the sea with the resolve, 'The next time I wash 'em, I'll wash 'em at home!' which, of course, does not represent the style with which Dacre's name was chiefly associated. That he was drawn to the ballad vocalist was evident directly the South African War broke out, for he responded in the new style with, "A patriotic pattern to the world", and still more with, "The lively little lads in Navy blue". This middle-class appeal seemed essentially English, and yet Dacre was preceded by an American. Harry Kennedy was the author and composer of simple ditties that found their way into nooks and corners whether they were grave or gay. One was "Molly and I and the baby"; another, "Say 'au revoir' but not 'good-bye'", was one of those agonizing farewells-for-ever which were then necessary to our peace of mind. Roughly speaking, the idea was that when the yelp was over you felt pleased, as you looked at your spouse, that you hadn't got to say good-bye at all.

Bennett Scott made his name, as the twentieth century was dawning, with the lower middle classes. By avoiding life down our street on the one side and the glut of birdsong amid the roses on the other, he provided tunes for those who heard them at the pantomime and then took them home. He also has his place at the end of the Henry Russell tradition, for Scott wrote the last of the widely popular emigration songs. His "I've made up my mind to sail away", with its final promise of coming back a millionaire, is rosy with the flush of Victorian romance.

This insistence of the middle classes on their right to songs of their own made itself still more strongly felt in the kind of music

they listened to in the theatre. Earlier in the nineteenth century the
musicals were devised by literary gentlemen who followed the
hoary tradition that new tunes were unnecessary as long as there
was a good supply of the old. H. J. Byron, for example, seized
"The Sea" for this parody—one among many hundreds written
by himself and the other busy B's of burlesque:

> The Tea! The Tea!
> Refreshing Tea.
> The green, the fresh, the ever free
> From all impurity.
>   I may remark that I'll be bound,
>   Full shillings six was this the pound—
>   Full shillings six was this the pound.
> I'm on for tea—I'm on for tea!
>   For the savour sweet that doth belong
>   To the curly leaf of the rough Souchong,
> Is like nectar to me—nectar to me—nectar to me.
> Let others delight in their *eau de vie*,
> What matter, what matter, I'm for tea.

There is no dodging the thing the Victorians mistakenly called
burlesque. Sometimes it was performed with songs, sometimes
without, but it stayed ever present in their musical life. To understand it requires an effort, because it has become more remote to us
than a war dance of savages. What adds to our bewilderment is
that when the worst specimens are picked out of its printed texts
they often prove to have been the most successful. Sir Francis
Burnand, who wrote them at the rate of two or three a year throughout the second half of the nineteenth century, is the most puzzling
figure in the whole history of wit. What was accepted as his sense
of humour appears to have been nothing more than geniality.
When he engaged in the prevalent love of verbal horseplay, he
could not even pun; a fair sample of how hard and unavailingly he
tried occurs in his parody of the Mohawk Minstrels' "Conductor of
the fav'rite bus":

> By road, by river, or by rail, by hansom cab or 'bus,
> We'll go right through and mean to do the great Metrolo*pus*.

Elsewhere he makes his verses fit other people's tunes by the
liberal use of 'Tiddley um' and 'lardy do, lardy do, all day',
and he was eventually knighted for it. Some excuse for the en-

couragement bestowed upon him may be found in our pleasure
when octogenarian great-great-grandfathers make an annual joke
strictly for the benefit of their families. Theatres then were largely
attended by family parties, whose presence argues that they
listened to Burnand's affabilities in the spirit of devoted offspring.
The only other explanation is that any author whose name began
with 'B' held an indisputable claim to write burlesque, but this
is an unfair slight upon H. J. Byron, who gave us Buttoni in his
burlesque of Cinderella and the Widow Twankey in his burlesque
of Aladdin.

To infer from our forebears' delight in misrhyming and mis-
pronunciation that they were mentally deficient in their fun is,
of course, misguided. The audiences which treated Burnand in his
prime as though he were a toothless, hoary-headed old patriarch,
left his mangled verbiage behind them in the theatre. The verses
they brought home from other burlesques to sing to their children
are cherished as a feast of nonsense. Over a dozen celebrated wits
could be named who wrote songs for a livelihood and yet never
produced one worth remembering between them. On the other
hand, the stray ballads which were interpolated into the feasts of
mirth which they wrote for the theatre frequently took root as
firmly as "Ta-ra-ra-boom-de-ay". Gaiety burlesque, which gave
this to the fashionable part of the town, consisted mainly of puns
and fleshings; its songs were usually collected from almost anywhere, so that the title of composer was bestowed upon Meyer
Lutz partly as a joke. "Little Jack Sheppard"—the criminal was
now called little out of compliment to Little Lord Fauntleroy, hero
of the current best-seller—was written for the Gaiety at Christmas,
1886, and revived there eight years later. It deserves to be remembered for one song, "Botany Bay", for even though its tune comes
from the Irish, "Mush, mush, mush", its words have the authentic
ring of cockaigne:

> Farewell to Old England for ever,
>   Farewell to my rum culls as well,
> Farewell to the well-known Old Bailee,
>   Vhere I used for to cut such a swell.

The printed copy, as sung by David James, is not as good as the
one I remember, the one my father sang to the swish of his razor.
There is another classic from burlesque—nonsense verse of the

felicity peculiar to a generation that had to obtain relief from its
own prodigious solemnity:

> Hard trials for them two,
> Johnny Jones and his sister Sue,
> And the peach of em'rald hue,
> That grew, that grew,
> Listen to my tale of woe.

'She took a bite and John a chew and then the trouble began to
brew a trouble that the doctor couldn't subdue; under the turf
where the daisies grew they planted John and his sister Sue, adieu'.
This, written by Eugene Field and composed by Hubbard T.
Smith, was sung by Johnny Danvers.

Opera, by the time Verdi came on the scene, had become so very
grand that only very grand people could tackle it, or rather bits of
it, in their own homes. There is a drawing in *Punch* by George du
Maurier which shows how this was done. While everybody is being
attentive to everybody else, the tenor by the grand piano is bawling
his head off without attracting the slightest notice. *Il Trovatore*
was translated soon enough to be sought after for favourite airs,
and "Wrong not the Gypsy" came readily to the pianoforte, but
that happened in the 1850s. After that, opera was the prerogative of
professionals and the family party turned to operetta, opera bouffe,
burlesque, and extravaganza—not the music-hall for fear of being
vulgar.

Sullivan, Offenbach, Planquette, and Meyer Lutz basked in the
favour of a vast public, for now the great plague that has gone
unrecorded by history had broken out in London—the great, the
overwhelming plague of pianos that for a century remained an
unavoidable part of a citizen's existence. The music-hall served the
working class, comic opera the middle-class. We enjoy it on its
merits now. We no longer realize the excitement of it when there
was mockery in the words to offset the artless idealization of the
tunes. Sometimes a hint of the joke would be heard in the music:
audiences recognized in Sullivan's call for *Iolanthe* the notes from
Mendelssohn's horns of elfland faintly blowing in *A Midsummer
Night's Dream*.

The succes of *The Sorcerer*, *H.M.S. Pinafore*, *The Pirates of
Penzance*, and *Patience* at the Opera Comique in the years 1877
to 1881 led to the building of the Savoy Theatre, where *Iolanthe*,

Princess Ida, *The Mikado*, *Ruddigore*, *The Yeomen of the Guard*, and *The Gondoliers* founded a cult of worshippers until 1889, and then by means of revivals onwards. That is a very familiar tale. Amateur operatic and dramatic societies, crowds round band-stands, and concerts in church halls never-endingly swelled the chorus of praise, while the D'Oyly Carte Company took the Gilbert and Sullivan repertoire round the country on a continuous tour. Above all else it was Gilbert and Sullivan who were the carriers of the piano plague. Hymns Ancient and Modern were not much better known. There were no signs of any revolt yet. To be allowed to sing "Take a pair of sparkling eyes" was every young man's dream no matter what his register.

Rivals were shut out, Planquette among them apart from *Les Cloches de Corneville*. For *Rip Van Winkle* he wrote a song of the tobacco-pipe, and for *Vanderdecken* he composed another about being rocked upon the billow that delight anyone with an ear for melody. *Rip Van Winkle* was by Henry Brougham Farnie, music by Robert Planquette, original libretto by H. Meilhac and P. Gide, Comedy Theatre, 14 October 1882. The refrain of "My Pipe" runs:

> Then breathe full south,
> From thy cool amber mouth,
> Let my fond grasp entwine,
> Thy slim figure divine.
> Thy kindling eye and thine odorous sigh,
> Are more rapturous far,
> I find, than a love told by light of the star.

The setting is of a love song.

That these should have been neglected indicates how thoroughly the vocal chords of the middle class were now monopolized by the Savoy operas. Offenbach was no longer appreciated by a generation so deaf to his wit that the can-can from *Orphée aux Enfers* was separated from Jupiter's exquisite minuet, which gives it point. "The sabre of my sire", from *The Grand Duchess of Gerolstein*, was occasionally heard, but the only tune by Offenbach that never died, apart from that can-can, was the gendarmes' duet:

> If we find some helpless woman,
> Or little child that does no harm,
> We run them in,
> We run them in,
> Just to show we're bold gendarme

which a humorist chose for the regimental march of the United
States crack corps of Marines.

That one song from an operetta refused to be overwhelmed
by Sullivan is proof of witchery. It was by W. G. Wills, called
King of Bohemia, crowned by a shabby bowler and old wig over his
bald head. He was the nearest approach to Shakespeare that the
1880s could boast, for he wrote poetic dramas for Irving at the
Lyceum. Here all that matters is that he wrote—to the music of
Frederick Clay*—a serenade which is labelled as from *Lalla
Rookh* though deluded readers seek for it there in vain. There
were several dramatized versions of Tom Moore's poem, and
Wills wrote this for one of them:

> I'll sing thee songs of Araby,
>   And tales of fair Cashmere,
> Wild tales to cheat thee of a sigh
>   Or charm thee to a tear;
> And dreams of delight shall o'er thee break
>   As rainbow visions rise,
> But all my song shall strive to wake
>   Sweet wonders in thine eyes.
> In those twin lakes where wonder wakes,
>   My enraptured soul I'll sink,
> And as a diver dives for pearls
>   Bring tears bright tears to their brink.

When the enthusiasm for Gilbert and Sullivan became the
monopoly of the middle classes, the Savoy's business manager,
George Edwardes, went to the Gaiety in order to keep 'the sacred
torch of burlesque' burning with Meyer Lutz as musical director.
Both stalls and gallery supported him so wholeheartedly that he
continued with this policy and allowed an operetta entitled *Dorothy*
by B. C. Stephenson, composed by Alfred Cellier, to pass out of his
hands and make the fortune of a rival manager. In this piece
Hayden Coffin sang "Queen of My Heart" to an adoring public
which was not at all sure whether it ought not to be shocked by

> Then why should we wait till tomorrow
>   You are queen of my heart tonight.

* Composer also of "She wandered down the mountain side", words by B. C.
Stephenson, the tale of a maiden seeking for her dead lover.

Out of the profits of *Dorothy* the Lyric was built in 1888. There it continued to run until *Doris*, by the same hands, replaced it. The lesson was not lost on Edwardes. Though the Gaiety remained faithful to old custom he speculated elsewhere with musicals in modern dress, beginning in 1892 with *In Town*, by Adrian Ross and J. T. Tanner, music by Osmond Carr, at the Prince of Wales's.

His next experiment turned on a fountain of melody that ran for years. This fairly describes the songs of Sidney Jones. As a very young bandsman he had composed the tune of "Linger longer Lucy". Edwardes entrusted him with the score of *A Gaiety Girl* by Owen Hall—the name adapted by James Davis when he was 'owing all'—at the Prince of Wales's in 1893. There was no mistaking the hold of this partnership over the public. When Augustin Daly gave up his ambitious plans at his own theatre in Leicester Square, George Edwardes ran Daly's as a fashionable headquarters for Sidney Jones. From the February of 1895 to the end of the century his songs were sung there regularly. The series consisted of *An Artist's Model*, *The Geisha*, *A Greek Slave*, a revival of *A Gaiety Girl*, and *San Toy*. The last libretto was by Edward Morton; Owen Hall worked with Jones until 1899, when he went to the Lyric to write the words of *Florodora* for Leslie Stuart. At the Shaftesbury *The Belle of New York*, by Hugh Morton (C. M. S. McLellan), with music by Gustav Kerker, had added to our granary of tunes, and at the Gaiety musical comedies with 'girl' in their titles had revealed the gifts of Lionel Monckton and Ivan Caryll. Authorship became more and more involved as more and more lyrics by other hands were added to libretti. When the century ended in this resounding outburst of song, Leslie Stuart busied himself with a mock-glory number. As war was imminent he changed his mind and re-wrote "The Soldiers of the Queen" in a manner to aid recruiting instead. Albert Christian sang it first, and then Hayden Coffin.

XXIV

The Coster's Laureate

+·+

Such ikey 'ats an' feathers, green,
Red, yeller, pink and blue.

Albert Chevalier

OUT OF THE TAPROOM into sunlight was the way the singers of the music-hall went. While the fun of life down our street was still full of zest, usually against the backcloth of a street-corner so quiet as to hint at an eternal Sunday afternoon, while tales of brokers' men, mothers-in-law, and amorous lodgers had yet to face a yawn, while parterres retained the tables at which revellers in top hats ordered drinks, there was a change in the regular round of jokes about Irish funerals and cockney weddings. Albert Chevalier, one of the actors belonging to the new generation which eschewed effects that were not natural, established himself in a night— 2 February 1891, at the London Pavilion, Piccadilly Circus— as the coster's laureate. There was poetry and music in him as well as an artist's eye for expressive movement when he observed the habits of those London aborigines who adorned their clothes with rows of pearl buttons to proclaim themselves 'pearlies'. All this was his own. Where he influenced others was in his love of fresh air. That first audience of his was taken by surprise by the new note of tenderness in "The Coster's Serenade", written by himself with music by John Crook. Love songs had been warbled in London dialects nightly, sometimes pleasantly, but nobody else had made the voice of Romeo come from 'the Welsh 'Arp, which is 'Endon way, where Juliet prods me gently with the winkle pin'. To music by the same composer he wrote " 'Appy 'Ampstead". With Charles Ingle, his brother, as composer, he wrote "Wot Cher! or, Knock'd 'em in the Old Kent Road". To his own accompaniment he wrote, "The future Mrs 'Awkins", dwelling on the refrain, 'Oh! Lizer! Sweet Lizer!' until Katie Lawrence appeared as Liza to deliver a sharp reproof. Then with Ingle again he dressed as an old labourer minus pearlies and sang "My Old Dutch", at the Tivoli in the November of 1892; and it was with Ingle in 1892 that he brought out, "Our Little Nipper", who stands by the bar when two pots are filled and asks, 'Wot! ain't mother goin' to 'ave none?' which topped the list of favourite quotations. In two years he justified his laureateship so well that there seemed nothing more to be said. He gave us another quotation in 1894, "Wot's the good of hanyfink? Why nuffink!" and possibly another one still in, "It ain't exactly *wot* 'e says, it's the nasty way 'e says it", but in all his songs during the next twenty years there is hardly one to set besides the early ones which he went on singing to the end. He sang at fashionable gatherings, toured concert halls for fabulous fees, appeared in operettas, and acted in a play, *My Old Dutch*, at the Lyceum in 1920, which was applauded enthusiastically. Despite all such successes his main achievement was to put fresh life into popular song by taking it out of a smoky atmosphere. This was not brought about solely by whisking us off to Hendon and Hampstead, for his song about Hampton Court (not his authorship) sticks to the old humour in its tale of a bride so big that she bursts the boat. Even down our alley, when a toff tells him that his rich uncle has popped off, we are in the open—unaware that we are listening to him within four walls when he "Knock'd 'em in the Old Kent Road!" Technically that is interesting because it is a comic song without a joke. The old practice was for the performer to hand a pencil to his poet with the demand, 'Show me where I make 'em laugh'. The art of Albert Chevalier was to make 'em smile.

As a cockney who saw humour in character Gus Elen belonged to the taste that was fashionable in the 1890s. Yet the London types he acted were as old as the times of Dickens. Towards the end of his life, when he came out of retirement to perform exactly as he had always performed, the clothes he wore as market porter or dustman were such as had never been seen in our streets within ordinary memory. Yet there was such an air of authenticity about him that you felt sure these were what he had faithfully observed in his early, his very early, childhood. Some of his songs were written by Edgar Bateman and composed by George Le Brunn, and these included, "If it wasn't for the 'ouses in between" and "It's a great big shame" that the likes of 'er should put upon the likes of 'im. What sticks in our minds has far less to do with technical skill than with its value as human experience. We often quote, "I'm glad we 'ad a nice quiet day", sung by Gus Elen as a footsore postman after a dreary outing with the whole of his family, and only an expert eye sees less in that than in the skilful rhyme and rhythm of Frederick Gilbert's song that Elen sang:

> Away went Polly
> With a step so jolly
>   That I knew she'd win.
> Down the road——
>   The pace was killing,
>   But the mare was willing
>   For a lightning spin;
> All the rest were licked
>   And might as well have ne'er been born.
>   Woa, mare! Woa, mare!
>   You've earned your little bit of corn!

Compare that not only with what had gone before but with what came after as well and you will see how remarkable were Gilbert's inventive talents. Though intricate, any audience could sing it.

By the time the new spirit arose in the music-hall Vesta Tilley was already a veteran. As a chairman's tiny daughter she had been bred and born to the old humour of alcoholic orgies, nights out, coming home with the milk, domestic strife and amorous lodgers or curates. When her adult wit observed humanity she told the truth about masculine pretensions as a male impersonator in such variety that she let any number of masterpieces slip into the past. It is now necessary to insist that Burlington Bertie, a masher who lived up to his name, was her creation. There was a 'reply' song about a pathetic scarecrow called, "Burlington Bertie from Bow", which Ella Shields always sang because she never found anything better. She never attained the prodigality of Vesta Tilley, who discarded a repertoire that would have kept a dozen idols before the public for a lifetime. We have scores of songs to remember her by but the liveliest, not necessarily the best, was undoubtedly—words by Fred W. Leigh, music by Kenneth Lyle—"Jolly good luck to the girl who loves a soldier!" Cold print causes a shock to see how little there is left when we have lost that alert little figure in red tunic with a stride worthy of the Guards. But the performance, cheering

P

to the heart though it is, was not such a masterpiece as the weedy little recruit of 1914, in ill-fitting khaki and outsize in boots, who told us, "I joined the army yesterday so the army of today's all right".

Meanwhile there was still a powerful insistence in popular songs that departures from normal life had to be mocked. Under this heading came the Salvation Army as an easy first, teetotallers and vegetarians, the clergy, coppers, and Jews, all foreigners but more particularly the French, Germans, and Italians, tramps and toffs, landlords and lawyers, and any female who was not a fine figure of a woman. The list is very nearly complete, but even so it becomes difficult to see how a hall could find enough normal people to supply audiences when as a final item 'the married' are added. I had a brother, little more than a year older than myself, who at fourteen years of age had a knowledge of the halls that was not merely comprehensive but almost exhaustive. We were taken away from his favourite haunts to an expensive palace in town. There a Scot sang "I'm the saftest of the family" while we stayed silent. On the journey home my brother regained speech with an effort in order to declare very firmly, 'It won't do'. Even after Albert Chevalier and Vesta Tilley had brought about a revolution in taste Harry Lauder came as a challenge to the accepted notion of what was funny and what was not, and, even more, what was entertaining and what was not. When he sang "I love a lassie" he won. Henceforth we were to be charmed. It meant that the balance between illusion and effect, which operates in every form of fiction, would favour those who copied life. Lauder made his first London appearance at Gatti's in Westminster Bridge Road, which survived as an empty shell until 1950. I passed it by as the walls were being demolished, and each morning, as his health grew worse, they sank with him. His old haunt vanished with him day by day. The last bricks were displaced at the hour of his death, and I must confess that this, a simple coincidence, shook me. Yet that was less saddening than a radio quiz a year or two later when a group of Scottish children could not supply the missing word in the song title, " . . . . in the gloaming", and when told what it was, murmured in full agreement that they had never heard of it.

Reminiscence keeps carrying me off the track: my business is with the early years of the twentieth century, when the new idols of variety seemed to sing under an open sky, which may or may not have had somethig to do with the invention of sliding roofs for the auditorium. Old Harry Bedford contributed the words and music of a happy warble called "Three pots a shilling"—otherwise known as "When the summer comes again"—which Kate Carney sang as a coster with practical plans for work in the country. Gertie Gitana made a folk song of Nellie Dean by the flowing waters, and brought us a whiff from the Sussex Downs with "When the corn is yellow on the hillside". And yet it was Eugene Stratton's face, blacked with burnt cork in the old Minstrel manner, which conjured up the vision of open spaces still more freshly, in part because of his own skill, in part because he sang the effortless melodies of Leslie Stuart. The fascination of the darkie whom Stratton embodied in shapeless hat and sloppy clothes was that he seemed never to have been on the stage before; he held you because you thought he might suddenly run short of inspiration and dry up. Unlike the thousands of buskers and amateurs who had a go at his songs, he did not let himself float along on the even flow of the accompaniment. He unburdened himself of love, for love it nearly always was, as though blurting it out with feelings so wistful as to be almost painful. What the seaside pierrot poured out as amorous bravado—'No one's got to kiss dat garl but me!' came out of Stratton's pursed lips like desperation. It *seemed* to happen like this: since there was music rising from the orchestra he had to tell us what was on his mind in rhythm and rhyme and therefore his soul was in labour. It never, for a moment, sounded as though anybody had written those words for him. You would regularly hear the gallery girls exclaim, 'Isn't he natural?' You never thought of Stuart at the actual moments when Stratton was singing his songs: you never thought of anybody but Stuart when anybody else was singing them. There existed between them an affinity stronger than any other friendship of singer for composer. Some clue to it is in the bond that links one inveterate gamester to another.

From first to last, throughout the history of Victorian song, Scotland, Ireland, Cockaigne, and Dixie have been unfailing. There is no exhausting them. Memory is filled with them—"On Mother Kelly's doorstep down Paradise Row", which George A. Stevens wrote for Fred Barnes, "Little Annie Rooney", written, composed, and sung by Michael Nolan, "I like your apron and your bonnet and your little Quaker gown", words by John P.

Harrington, music by Alf. J. Lawrance, sung by Mabel Green, exert an uncomfortably powerful spell.

Yorkshire and Lancashire specialized in songs of simplicity. George Formby, who must be called the elder owing to the widespread affection bestowed upon his son, gave Simple Simon a northern upbringing and the name of John Willie, with the unfortunate result that people who possess a Lancashire accent have found it difficult to get themselves taken seriously ever since. As author and composer of "John Willie, come on", Formby must be given much of the credit. He was the same in "I was standing at the corner of the street", with this refrain as the explanation of all the things that happen to him, but a change came over him when he began to boast to the tune of "Since I parted my hair in the middle". The phrases he now used recalled the Rollicking Rams of the *lions comiques*: he was 'One of the Boys' engaged in 'Playing the game in the West', and he had become 'Such a hit with the girls'. But he was still John Willie, still wearing shapeless hat, boots, and clothes with a muffler round his neck and a simper spreading into his cheeks. All this time he was dying. He made a joke of the cough that racked him—'Coughing better tonight. Coughing summat champion.'

Underdogs had become the kind of comic singer the public liked best. They were a small band that effected a mental balance. As far as numbers go gay dogs seemed to rule, for the old blatancy persisted when dudes made hymns out of their delight in 'the Girls'. There was always some readiness to join in such jubilation, pandering to the inner wish of respectable persons to think themselves less innocent than they were, but the more subtle pose was to sympathize with the henpecked, the half-witted, the unlucky, the butt, and the botcher. Tabrar, keeping abreast of the times, wrote and composed, for Jack Smiles to sing, the ballad about what was not likely to happen again for months and months and months, which became proverbial. The refrain became a catchword though not to the same extent as "The rest of the day's your own", which continues to be the proverbial retort to overwork. It was written and composed by Worton David and J. P. Long for Jack Lane, who ended each verse not with the customary chorus but a chant to explain his daily duties in the house and on the farm, until he got confused about milking hens and shaving the cat. It was Jack Pleasants who inspired the greatest number of imitations at the piano in homes. George A. Stevens and Charles Ridgwell were responsible for "I'm shy, Mary Ellen, I'm shy", the most frequently heard of all. Feelings not unlike 'Blessed are the meek' may be read into this, but that theory is upset by other samples. *Sancta simplicitas* on the halls never ruled out pride, arrogance, and boastfulness. It might be a pitiful brag in some but it was a trifle over-bearing in others. Take Billy Merson, a merry, sturdy figure, usually engaged in romantic burlesques of a pirate or revengeful lover. To match this song—all his own work—he gave a very purposeful study of inexperience at grips with life in "I've just broke a window, and had a small port". Unlike the others who stuck to this style because they found it profitable, Billy Merson suddenly tired of it, discarded his wig and false nose, and appeared as his good-looking self in musical comedy at Drury Lane. His immediate success was his final undoing. As a natural comedian he was one among dozens. As a broadly comic simpleton he had had a niche of his own. Even if he had wanted to return to it, the door or gate, or whatever it is that is possessed by a niche, had closed. Simple Simon belongs to the tradition of Victorian song, and in the 1920s that was rapidly coming to an end.

XXV

Heroics

✦✦✦✦✦✦✦✦✦✦✦✦✦✦✦✦✦✦✦✦✦✦✦✦✦✦✦✦✦✦✦✦✦✦✦✦✦✦✦

Nearer it crawls to me,
My trigger I pull it,
It's accepted my bullet,
He'll never more breathe again.

Sung by Charles Godfrey

"HERE UPON GUARD AM I", written by Harry Adams to the tune of E. Jongmans, reads like a sequel to "Let me like a soldier fall", for the foreigner looks for trouble upon some open plain and accepts it with breast obviously expanding for the ball. When the singer says:

Take heed, ah, yes, at last, at last
One's found its way in here,

the accents of civilian satisfaction in warfare are more emphatic still. Hence the difference between the war songs of Queen Victoria's subjects and the war songs of today. There has been nobody to take the place of those red-ink-stained heroes who once stood so high in public regard.

Charles Godfrey, the singer of "Here upon guard am I", enjoyed so much personal popularity that it killed him as surely, though more gradually, as a bullet. All who lived in the old country while the Zulu and Sudanese Wars were being fought wanted to meet Charles Godfrey and most of them wanted to stand him a drink; quite a number of them succeeded. He was the nation's hero— most mimic heroes were, while real heroes had a pretty thin time of it. Puce-faced patriots, one of them a notorious swindler, won glory by persuading schoolboys to lie about their age to the recruiting sergeants. It is just as well to bear in mind what kind of world it was that rejoiced in such glorious sentiments.

As long as fighting was kept far away, the one smell that pleasure seekers loved even more than that of horses was the acrid stench of gunpowder, and Charles Godfrey gave them more of this than any other performer outside the tent of Lord George Sanger, who understood its spell-binding power equally well. But while the circus kept up to date, even to the extent of making Nile gunboats to fit neatly round horses whose heads stuck out of the decks, the music-hall deemed it better policy to hark back to the Crimea. With his index finger on the public pulse George le Brunn got to work on the verses of a promising youth, Wal Pink, and handed to Godfrey the manuscript of "The Seventh Royal Fusiliers", a tale of Inkerman forty years ago. Its tale of a streamlet that runs dry and a dam that has to be cut falls flat, but the chorus, with its boast of carving a way to glory, is irresistible to anyone except men actually on active service.

Having served his apprenticeship as a melodramatic actor in the East End of London, Godfrey liked to display his versatility in comic songs, swashbuckling songs, and songs of revelry, but what the public demanded from him was death or glory. Wal Pink wrote a military sketch for him called "Balaklava", which concluded with a magnificent tableau, "Into the Jaws of Death", of the Charge of the Six Hundred, in which Godfrey rode a horse which was shot under him amid shot and shell, or rather smoke and smell.

When Godfrey died in 1900 his place had to be filled; the South African War continued, and as it could not be ignored some stalwart figure had to give voice to patriotic fervour on the halls. Out of several claimants, all well qualified for the post, Leo Dryden was chosen as 'the Kipling of the halls'. As a Canadian Redskin he sang "Great White Mother" to a transparency of Queen Victoria, and as a rajah he gave "India's Reply" to any query about throwing in her lot with the Empire; and he sang the praises of the Dublin Fusiliers and the Gordon Highlanders. To reflect the change in the mood of patriotism he laid less stress on showing the enemy who was master and more on the bonds between kinsmen in different parts of the world. In this style, blending the old nostalgia and calls to emigrants into a new appeal which stirred the heart most strongly, he became the singer of the hour with "The Miner's Dream of Home". On the published copies we read, 'written and composed by Leo Dryden and Will Godwin'. According to *The*

Oxford Dictionary of Quotations this is the hint of a remarkable
story for it puts

> 'Twas a night that should banish all sin,
> For the bells were ringing the Old Year out
> And the New Year in

down to William Godwin, the philosopher, Shelley's father-in-
law, whose life ended before gold-fever caused miners to dream of
home to any great extent. Of course, I do not question this authority, but I gladly add to my own astonishment by pointing out that
Will Godwin also wrote a jolly little thing, sung by Bessie Bellwood when having her wildest fling, called, "Hi diddle diddle um",
which extols the drunken frolics of certain gentlemen who dance
upon their hats and throw their boots at old tom cats. I trust room
will be found for this in the next collected edition of works by the
author of *An Enquiry Concerning Political Justice* and *An Essay
on Sepulchres* just to brighten things up. Otherwise it is a sad story.
Some twenty-odd years after the South African War, Leo Dryden
was singing "The Miner's Dream of Home" in the streets until he
appeared in a county court where he told the judge, 'I am on my
beam ends'. At the Star, Bermondsey, and at Collins's, Islington,
he was welcomed back to the boards, not only for his own sake by
those who remembered him but also by many who had never till
now heard his name but to whom his song was so familiar as to be
well beloved.

The mantle of Godfrey might also be claimed for Tom Costello.
While loved by many for his humour in "At Trinity Church I met
my doom", he was admired by still more for "Comrades", written
and composed by Felix McGlennon. From the same source Costello
obtained "The Ship I Love", which won greater favour at the time
though it did not last so long. If a little over the heads in the
nursery, it was very much to the taste of small boys, with its
refrain about going down to the angry deep 'with the ship I love'.
I sang that chorus before I was taken out of my loathed skirts and
breeched; consequently I always looked on Tom with awe when, as
friends, we sat together in Broadcasting House revising his scripts
to allow for his knack of emphasizing the last word in every
sentence after the fashion of "The Ship I Love". He was tall,
strong, and handsome, capable of carrying the girl he loved up
several flights of stairs to his attic, where a formidable landlady

would say, 'And now, Mr Costello, will you kindly carry her down again'. These were *lions comiques* though never given the title. George Lashwood was the handsomest of the lot, with rather more of the lover in him, as you can tell from "Riding on top of the tram". His military spirit was shown in "The Last Bullet", a drama of the relief of Lucknow; in the same turn he sang "The Tipster" and "My Poll".

By now Kipling's attitude was making itself felt when rhymes were found for shot and shell. Heroics may not have altered much on the halls even though a greater interest was being taken, under his guidance, in outposts of Empire. But he was not competing with the popular school of patriotic poets when his turn came to be sung. He stepped into the favoured place once occupied by Tennyson and Longfellow. Directly *Barrack Room Ballads* were published in 1892 they were claimed for the concert hall and drawing-room, where they startled people. We who are used to the shock tactics of 'tough' fiction in every shape or form are prepared for any of its manifestations, but in the 1890s the first acquaintance that most audiences made with it was Kipling's advice to the young British soldier to blow out his brains when the women of the Afghans come out to 'cut up what remains'. That was pitching it too strong for ears long accustomed to romanticism, and this particular item was reserved for smoking concerts in the special meaning of the term then current. But no such objection was taken to "Mandalay", and its swinging melody was a favourite until superseded. To raise funds for army charities Kipling wrote "The Absent-Minded Beggar"—and Sullivan composed a march to match it—which was sung on the halls, whence its chorus floated to all the places where music-hall choruses were sung. It immediately got mixed up with choruses belonging to a different war altogether, simply because Britain had become a profitable market for them. It's an ill bang that blasts nobody any good.

Tin Pan Alley did not start the fighting in South Africa—a remark which may seem uncalled for on the face of it. What compels me to make it is the diabolical plot that might be read into the facts. With our minds trained from infancy not to believe in the innocence of those who make large profits, we could easily construct a thriller out of the manner in which a war gave publishers the chance to export music no longer needed in their own land. The Spanish-

American conflict of 1898 was over so soon that the songs of good-bye were supplied with last verses about the homecoming of the army minus a particular hero. By 1899 these had about as much interest as out-of-date newspapers, and the United States would weep over them no more. It was then, month by month, that trouble became inevitable in the Transvaal. With ample time for preparation, publishers on both sides of the Atlantic arranged for the performance in Great Britain of the stuff that had sprung from minds under the real stimulus of war. The transfer of patriotic outbursts from one country to the other succeeded zestfully. Without the slightest suspicion that the goods they were consuming were second-hand, the audiences of English music-halls and panto- mimes enthusiastically cheered ballads in honour of imaginary heroes who had already died, in an entirely different cause from the one now under consideration, for the sake of profitable fiction.

Before any of London's idols could be fitted for their uniforms as Indian Rajahs or New South Wales Lancers, or provide the band parts for rhapsodies to the greater glory of the Empire, Hamilton Hill in plain clothes had taught the whole country to sing the words of Will D. Cobb to the tune of Paul Barnes, until the name of New York's "Dolly Gray" was certain to be associated for ever with Mafeking and Ladysmith. It was Mr Hill also who sang "Blue Bell", companion picture from the same city, words by Edward Madden, music by Theodore F. Morse. Both told of a hero who died in battle thinking not of fame or glory but of Dolly Gray in one case and Blue Bell in the other. At the end of each the war was supposedly over, but this was of no importance to the multitudes whose sole concern was the overpowering impulse to join in a topical chorus as relief to their feelings. "Break the news to mother" had been written by Charles Harris as a flashback to the Civil War, and he gave it the same shape as his dramatic narratives about passion and jealousy. For domestic use it was rather too powerful, but in Christmas pantomime it was treated to a scene by itself. There was a mention at the start of 'the boys in blue', by which Harris meant the Federal uniform, but a public ignorant of this remembered that Sir Redvers Buller's relief column included a Naval Brigade. In the first verse a boy is mortally wounded while saving the flag; in the second 'a noted general' cries, as the captain turns away to hide a tear, 'It's my son'. War or no war English class-consciousness was very much alive, and it disapproved of this. In our drawing-rooms small boys were taught to sing a polite version of much the same story—"The King's Own", words by Herbert K. Crofts, music by Theodore Bonheur, was about a merry little drummer who dies unheeded and alone for the king has claimed his own.

While American songs that proclaimed their origin, after the fashion of Paul Dresser's "On the banks of the Wabash", were almost unknown in London, those that did not do so frequently made a wide appeal. Both "I can't tell why I love you but I do-oo-oo" and "Do have some pity, Kitty, tell me you'll be mine" were thoroughly naturalized by Lil Hawthorne. Many a song that was regarded in the United States as typically American was the pirated edition of an English composer's work, and Harry Clifton's "The dark girl dressed in blue" became a New York folk song when some reference to 'the park call'd Central' had been introduced. Geography teaches us in childhood to loathe places we do not know and this may explain the pains that were taken to change names—Frisco into Dover, for example—when verses left their native shores. As plays had to undergo a still more rigorous adaptation there does seem to have been a period when fancy itself was insular. Even when *The Belle of New York* set us all murmuring:

> She makes all the Bowery
> Fragrant and flowery

experts held that audiences did not want to stretch their imaginations beyond their own shores. Florrie Forde came to London from Australia but she never sang about Australia. She exercised her gift for making everybody except the lions in Trafalgar Square chant her choruses, mainly in favour of the Isle of Man, which had to be freely translated for American purposes into 'the Emerald Isle'. She taught Britons many American choruses—striding along by the footlights while facing audiences by means of a triangular marching step mastered only by herself—before the turn came of Von Tilzer's "Under the Anheuser Busch". The refrain was an obstacle to be overcome before the lilt of the tune and the liveliness of the other words could stand a chance. Poets were puzzled until an office boy, who had whistled most of the chorus, burst into full song with "Down at the Old Bull and Bush, Bush, Bush", so that if our reference books wish to acknowledge authorship they should not name VonTilzer, who had never heard of the pub at Hampstead.

While "The Old Bull and Bush" was clinging so tightly to London life that a professor quoted it as a cockney ballad, a British composer, Leslie Stuart, made Idaho as well known to his countrymen as Pimlico. Songs that could not be altered gained a hearing, though we never heard who was responsible for

> I can hear the warders calling,
>   Sing-Sing, my native home

or learn more than the refrain of

> Just becas she made dem goo-goo eyes
> I thought I'd won a home and copp'd a prize

or of

> Come along ma honey, bring along your money,
> Put your Sunday clothes on and come alonga me

but when R. G. Knowles arrived with his song about the Bowery— 'I'll never go there any more'—he made it Brighton, whereupon this became half-way house to a better land, for evangelists altered it to "Heav'n" with other changes, naturally.

XXVI

Moonshine, Laughter, Coo-oo-oo

+‑+

There are fairies at the bottom of our garden.
                                    Rose Fyleman

VICTORIA DIED. Then and there, it might be argued, song ceased to be Victorian. That is reasoning by calendar and clock without proper regard for the awkward fact that the past will always persist into the present. Aspidistras continued to bifurcate, and the ideal they represented of green leaves in every home was further upheld by palms in pots on specially designed pedestals. Much of the ordinary Edwardian home elaborated ideas of comfort and elegance, supposedly outworn, that were just as venerable. This misdirected effort in taste takes the form in my memory of a 'dressing-table set' given to my sister, which included trays and pots and bowls, a thing for hanging rings on, another thing for putting hairpins into, and candlesticks, though candles had gone out of use: we spent a happy hour smashing it piece by piece not just to improve the look of her room and save a lot of housework, but out of the sheer joy of destroying objects so brand new and yet so musty. Our lives were still regulated by Victorians from swaddled infancy to fussy funerals. The day still began with the clank of those evil-smelling milk-cans and ended with the sniff of gas, while the hours between reeked with variegated stenches. And everything still happened to music. The milkman woke you up with "Molly, Molly, always so jolly", your father sang to nerve himself for a cold bath, school began with "New every morning is the love" and ended with "Now the day is over", one part of the evening was given up to music lessons and another part to learning songs for some performance at a party.

As long as horseshoes and iron-rimmed wheels clattered over macadamized roads, nobody in good health could reasonably complain of noise: invalids had cartloads of straw laid down, which prompted the joke of the child who 'didn't know babies came in so much packing'. German bands, barrel-organs, and the Italian bandit with a monkey on his hurdy-gurdy could be bribed to go into the next street, but the most persistent turmoil of all was caused by the plague of pianos which steadily grew as more and more instruments in ever worsening condition were to be bought cheaply second-hand or twelfth-hand. As long as waste-paper had no value, the quantity of sheet music available to the multitudes of pianists, taught, self-taught, and untaught, was immeasurable, and all the songs ever published had a chance to be heard anywhere from Mayfair to Ratcliff Highway. There was such a strong affection for old songs and fresh collections of them were being issued so frequently, that sentiments belonging to a new era stood little chance of being widely heard at first. What gave the Edwardian song-writer his first public was a pretty custom among the young women, as soon as flappers put their hair up, of singing to each other through their idle afternoons with a fancy to outdo each other in choosing the latest thing in the style of roses feeling shy when they heard her nigh.

Music shops in every high street thrived on the sales of Liza Lehmann's setting of "There are fairies at the bottom of our garden", Teresa del Riego's "O dry those tears", Montague Phillips's "Sing, joyous bird", Paul Rubens's "I love the moon", George Aitken's "Maire, my girl", Frank Lambert's "God's Garden", Guy d'Hardelot's "Because", Dorothy Forster's "Dearest, I bring you daffodils", Hermann Löhr's "Little grey home in the west" and "Where my caravan has rested", Haydn Wood's "It is only a tiny garden", and Sheridan Gordon's "Love could I only tell thee". Titles swarm like bees when you think of sunlight printing the pattern of lace curtains on the carpet round a piano adorned by girls in white blouses, long skirts, high lace collars, and plaited hair along the napes of their necks. At the sound of your key in the front door they would call to you, and before you could hang up your silk hat one would be playing the opening bars of *your* song, Leslie Stuart's swaggering "I am the bandolero", Eric Coates's "Green hills o' Somerset", Graham Peel's "In summertime on Bredon", or Robert Coningsby Clarke's "Blind

Ploughman". The musical evening was no longer what it was, for the sense of tribal duty was lacking, but still we all sang.

And song was still part of every day in every season. In summer it was strong because the seaside was the inescapable holiday, and there claims were staked on the sands by the Nigger Minstrels, the Pierrots, and the Children's Special Service Missions, who borrowed profane tunes. The general rule was for the beach to take its repertoire from the music-halls; in the evenings the concert parties, who prided themselves on being more than a little superior, would instal themselves in pavilions or bandstands, and they would sing the stuff of drawing-rooms except when they allowed their funny man to be slightly vulgar. In this way all the latest published numbers permeated the whole nation, since even puritans who never went to the theatre were sure to hear them, if only wafted along a summer breeze, while on holiday.

But no tune, here amid the excitements of the seashore, could take so enduring a hold on remembrance as those woven into a fairy tale on the stage at Christmastime. The magic of the panto-mime owed much of its spell to its choice of music in the Victorian mode. The more sentimental these were the more certain they were to be sung by the Principal Boy in the scene of the forest glade, in whose unseen depths lurked a male voice choir to harmonize soulfully in solemn chorus. Early love in these verses was sur-rounded by birds, blossoms, and bees, as in "The shade of the old apple tree" and "The honeysuckle and the bee". Many of these had the good luck to have been 'introduced to the public' in a show with Ellaline Terriss as its heroine, and she enriched our studies of amorous botany by telling us how all the little pansy faces look at you with eyes of love. Though less thought was given to the moral as a rule, the appeal of "Little Yellow Bird", by C. W. Murphy and William Hargreaves, came from a sparrow's resolve to freeze rather than share a canary's cage of gold. C. W. Murphy supplied the tunes for some of the verses of Harry Castling, who outdid the Victorians both in fun and tenderness; together they wrote "On the Isle of Anglesey" and "The girl in the clogs and shawl" as well as "Let's all go down the Strand". This last was sung by Charles Whittle, the new kind of comedian who tried not to be as comic as he could but as elegant as he could in silk hat and grey morning suit, while directing the efforts of the audience with his cane in an opulent manner. Fred Godfrey composed the music for a simple-hearted ditty by Castling about Jenny with her eyes so brown, which has a haunting sweetness. It brings back to mind the morning when I met Castling in the office of a publisher who wanted the public to be made aware of what was owing to this veteran of their trade. I went enthusiastically to consult my friends in Fleet Street, until they made me realize their interest never went farther than singers. And by then no life was left in the traditions he had upheld.

While we were contentedly sentimentalizing over "Beautiful garden of roses", and the scores of similar idylls conjured up both in the United Kingdom and the United States, the rude blast of a new craze that would shatter them began by blowing down the happy-go-lucky fancies that went with burnt cork, banjoes, and bones. America applauded a song of dislike for them minstrel folks and the end-men's jokes; the change of fashion made itself known in the realism of a negro lullaby of reassurance to a baby that it would be kept safe from 'All der udder black trash sleepin' on de flo' ', which was sung to the accompaniment of Sousa's Band. The outlook of black mammies became a paramount influence when H. Cannon wrote "Bill Bailey, won't you please come home?" The date of its copyright in the States is 1902, which has to be mentioned because there are disputes about the time it was first heard in England. When I was at school in 1906 the master asked an absurd question which caused us to ask 'Who?' He joyously told us, 'Bill Bailey', and as we knew this to be the title of Victoria Monks's song we tumbled to it that this was the latest catch-phrase and took it home to try on innocent adults, who could make neither head nor tail of it. From that time forward thousands of questions were asked everywhere, so that people could have the satisfaction of saying 'Bill Bailey' when their victims said 'Who?' In America the success of the song caused a vogue of appeals by remorseful black mammies to good-for-nothing men who had been turned out-of-doors and were now flaunting their independence. One of these, written by Von Tilzer, had a hero named Alexander, who got entangled in the craze for ragtime. Irving Berlin, then a young emigrant from Russia, took him as cue for his song "Alexander's Ragtime Band", which was published in 1905. At that time songs made a habit of slow travelling, so that the latest arrival had often been ten years on its way. While the favourite cornet solo from bandstands was still "Take a pair of sparkling eyes", a style of ultra-sentimental ballads

made itself known in "Sing me to sleep", words by Clifton
Bingham, music by Edwin Greene, dated 1902, followed by "The
sunshine of your smile", plus Edwin Greene's setting of Ella
Wheeler Wilcox's "Come cuddle your head on my shoulder, dear".
One summer in the reign of George V, with the world at peace and
grass turning yellow under a blue sky dazzling in glare and heat,
the plague of pianos engaged in civil war, on one side the sunshine
of your smile, on the other the ragtime band. But though Victorian
song, having shown such an obstinate unwillingness to die, was
being murdered, its last breaths would go on for a long time yet.
Millions who sang still did not know the meaning of syncopation.

Victorian melancholia persisted in ballads that gave expression
to what we now know as inferiority. 'Alone by the telephone'
became a recurring theme in modernized versions of 'Why should
you treat a poor maiden so' year by year. Whatever pleasure was
to be had from singing them was nothing compared to the rapture
of sitting in the front row of the gallery and having them directed
straight up at you, as though you were the gay Lothario who
scorned the love of the gorgeous soprano. That is my theory, but
it was shaken when I heard a gallery boy, fresh from the receipt of
this sign of favour, depart on his way parodying a celebrated
Irving Berlin inferiority ballad somewhat after (I have had to
change a word or two) this fashion:

> And though you left a tear
> On the chiffonier,
> It's withered up, I fear
> Ma's aspidistra.

While starting life in 1911 as reporter for a country paper, I
listened to amateur concerts two or three times a week, when trades,
friendly societies, religious bodies, stamp-collectors, municipal
employees, vegetarians, social reformers, naturalists, and other
happy bands of brothers found it impossible to meet in friend-
liness without encouraging each other to sing whether able to sing
or not. Since all the necessary business of their association was
speedily dismissed at the start, more particularly when it was
political, I wondered whether the disputes of governments could be
avoided by making music the final item on the agenda. It was a
world of song. The people who went to music-halls to join in the
choruses went to church to join in the hymns. They went to one

Q

another's homes for one purpose or another, but whatever this might be at the start they invariably stood round the piano at the finish. Whist was regarded as mildly wicked and Bridge as the beginning of vice, and card tables were brought out with the firm intention of packing them away again before the evening was very far advanced. The feeling was that song alone held people together. They had not yet acquired the habit of dashing into the country every Sunday wet or fine, and they still went to matins and vespers regularly as the normal behaviour of every community. In their music they paid strict regard to what was fit to be sung on the Sabbath and what was not; while they heartily disliked the Victorian desire for religion on week days they had so little wish to secularize the day of rest that 'sacred ballads' had a steady sale. Many devout people, innocent of any desire to evade the Fourth Commandment, maintained that music was holy. Despite the outcry of prophets who foresaw what this would lead to, the tolerance that had been reluctantly extended by our apprehensive grandparents towards orchestral concerts on the Sabbath now became an excuse for the National Sunday League to gain permission for concerts of popular songs on the Sabbath. 'Good' tunes were, or so ran the argument, indeed 'good'. It was John Wesley who first said that the devil should not have all the good tunes and General Booth who is given all the credit for the idea because he quoted it. Some unknown parson on a holiday beach put it into practice by teaching children to sing, "We'll all go to heaven, hurray, hurray", to the tune of, "Yip-i-addy-i-ay-i-ay", at a time when George Grossmith junior had created a rabid frenzy over this doggerel among the population of the British Isles.

There was no more significant figure in Edwardian song than the little George Grossmith's very tall son. When we have finished being impressed by the love of heaven expressed in so many contemporary ballads, we may turn to the love of sinless merriment blissfully expressed in others. To replace his father's praise of the polka, the son and heir bounded into musical comedy with "Waltz me around again, Willie", which excited shrieks of delight by rhyming a reference to shouts from a tram with 'I don't care a . . . . . bit.'

It was not until he went to the Folies Bergère that the astounding quality of his appearance was noted. In a polite reference to the contrast between the gaiety of his legs and the gravity of his face,

French critics drew attention to an incongruity far more remarkable than that—he was the conventional personification of death. His face had the normal amount of flesh upon it without letting you forget that it covered a grinning skull, and the dictates of fashion insisted on narrow cylinders for arms and legs, so that his clothes seemed to contain a fleshless framework. Listening to the clack of a voice which suggested the impact of bone on bone, Max Beerbohm declared that Grossmith raised banality to the sublime: the silliest lines of a librettist's chit-chat had the awful tone of mortality when he uttered them with fixed stare and majestic self-assurance. Whole generations had grown up in the belief that the name of Grossmith meant frolic, and in this deep-rooted conviction the British public accepted the new bearer of the name as a jester and never took a purely objective look at him. If it had his style of entertainment would have been limited to the macabre, the dance of death in every movement of his dangling arms and flying legs, to the delight of the diabolists, and the horror of the unthinking who had seen Mephisto so often as a well-fed actor or singer on the stage as to be incapable of associating Death or Devil with charnel house. Yet here was dissolution itself, fastidiously clothed in glossy silk-hat, starched linen, suède-uppered boots and all the other bits and pieces of opulent attire, ghastly in its implications of 'in the midst of life we are in death'—and singing its way into the heart of the nation at its freshest as well as its silliest. His power of 'putting over a song' never left him. That apparition came down to the footlights, that lipless voice sounded its first hollow note, and the next moment even the dispassionate observer who saw skull-and-crossbones in immaculate tailoring sat spell-bound. . . . 'Dancing time is any old time for me' it aptly was, for at a touch a skeleton will dance, but you did not think of this at the time. You simply heard the song.

Unless you are afraid of philosophizing too much you will see a butterfly on a skull as the emblem of that decade. Otherwise, ignoring the pessimism of despair which underlies both its wit and its sentimentality, you can see in its forced gaiety nothing but the revolt against Victorian solemnity. 'All together with a fa-la-lay-fa-la-diddle-diddle' sang bass and baritone in an endeavour to keep up with the tenor's sigh over the love-life of a rose and the soprano's joy in fairies and sunlit gardens full of birds, beasts, flowers, and insects all heavily under the influence of human amorousness. Trills, ah-has, tra-la-las, cries of wake-up, wake-up, wake-u-up, and shrill cuckoos sought to attain ecstasy where words failed, although seldom so successfully as coo-oo-oo in a dearly loved ballad which required the singer to avow her resolve to be ever true to it, whatever that might mean. No difference was noted between the light-hearted and the light-headed. Any amount of the stuff then published looks like an orgy of unabashed silliness—but only to the coldly critical eye. There is barely a line of its vacuous whimsy about the behaviour of roses when excited by lovely woman that is not somebody's treasured souvenir of a heedless existence. Some of the songs then being composed in England still rank among the best, for very rarely can music add to a poem so deftly as when Vaughan Williams took

> An' there vor me the apple tree
> Do lean down low in Linden Lea

from the Victorian poet in Dorset dialect. At the time it was not so popular as the songs of Samuel Coleridge Taylor, the negro whose life of hardship and early death in London made everyone responsive to his pathos. You have only to compare his setting of "Onaway, awake beloved" with any other to understand what a mastery he possessed over a style that eluded all the composers who breezily, heartily, religiously, or whimsically yielded themselves up to the spirit of the hour.

People wanted what they called 'romance'. Whether plaintive, nostalgic, maudlin, wistful, tender, and miserable, or coy, jubilant, merry, hilarious, mischievous, and hysterical, it is what they saw in those photogravures that covered their walls with visions of idealized home life, and it was what they heard in Continental waltz songs that held a delight not less than intoxicating. At the risk once more of being over-philosophical I must state that they belonged to that same Vienna whose witty cynicism inspired comedies far too adult for the rest of the world in the new century's first fourteen years. Half a century had to pass before we could laugh at the play that became the film *La Ronde*. But we were very ready to welcome Viennese music—after Lehar's delicate operettas had been transformed by tomfoolery into musical comedies. Only a slight exaggeration would be needed to say that his songs were listened to in a swoon. In their native city, where every intelligent person clearly saw the writing on the wall, such distraction was

accepted as a drug. In London it was part of a code which condemned mental exercise as bad form. Proof of this occurred when
Shaw's *Arms and the Man*, as plain a warning as the most realistic
politician could utter, was ignored as a play but wholeheartedly
applauded as a musical that contained the voluptuous appeal of
"Come, come I want you only". The score, by Oscar Straus,
came from Vienna, where the methods of contriving that seductive
swirl—and how seductive it was cannot be explained now—might
well be likened to the making of champagne in France. Nothing
like it could be produced elsewhere. As a melodist Lionel Monckton
displayed his unfailing gift in *The Quaker Girl, Our Miss Gibbs,*
and in all the songs he composed for Gertie Millar, without
attempting the sensual strain. Though she appeared in Leo Fall's
Gypsy Love he stuck to the open air style which excelled in comedy
and avoided the passionate.

But though the musical was ignorant of reality the music-hall
was not. War was one of its subjects when disregarded almost
everywhere else. Among twenty turns in a programme at the
Oxford in 1911 there was "The Roll Call", with Crimean and Indian
Mutiny veterans, and a 'Powerful Chorus of Boy Scouts', to
support George Leyton when he sang, "Boys of the Chelsea
School", which foretold how 'in a few years' the children of that
day would be heroes brave. More direct references to ominous
events were made by Arthur Reece in "Sons of the Sea", one of
those songs that made history. It began by stirring a patriotic
impulse to do 'something about it', just as the jingo song had done.
This time the crisis occurred through the rivalry over naval
armaments between Great Britain and Germany. The national
pride taken in the unprecedented size of the Dreadnought had a
setback when the Kaiser ordered the Kiel Canal to be enlarged
so that the fleet which passed through it from North Sea to Baltic
could contain battleships of a still larger size. The British public,
accepting the news as a warlike challenge, responded by chanting
Arthur Reece's chorus, with its declaration that 'they can't build the
boys of the bulldog breed', like an anthem. There were processions
along the Thames Embankment with banners to proclaim a desire
for a bigger Navy. Henceforward on all momentous occasions
crowds always sang, "Sons of the Sea". One night in the early
August of 1914, Arthur Reece stood by the railings of Buckingham
Palace while a shout went up for the King. Suddenly the vast

crowd burst into song—that same chorus which for six years had accompanied the threat of the disaster now imminent.

Even then, in the midst of horrors, serious consideration was given to what we ought to sing, what we would like to sing, and what we were actually singing. Parsons plugged "Onward Christian Soldiers" until Church Parades became a penance while the British Expeditionary Force chose "It's a long way to Tipperary" as its marching tune. It indicated a return to the Victorian vogue of the nostalgic. Poilus, who enlivened their souls with "Madelon" listened with astonishment to inexpressibly sad strains of "The trail of the lonesome pine" and "There's a long, long trail". As long as the Army remained cheerful its high spirits found expression in doleful tune. It was not until that war became intolerably depressing that the popularity of 'smile, smile, smile' began. Meanwhile London theatres owed much of their prosperity to performances with songs that wedded merry words to wistful tunes. "Any time's kissing time" in *Chu Chin Chow* and "A bachelor gay" in *The Maid of the Mountains* sounded heartbreaking when played by a string quartet, and probably were in their associations to many who were then listening. At the Gaiety *Tonight's the Night* contained a tender duet with the refrain, 'And when I told them how wonderful you are', which acquired a touch of the macabre from the ghoulish presence of George Grossmith, whose fixed stare and mirthless smile never hindered him from presenting himself to subalterns and their young women as an ideal lover. He demonstrated as no one else could the power of song.

As the twentieth century got into its stride the change in the appeal of popular music became more and more evident. A tune that sets us all by the ears one month may be, and often is, completely forgotten the next. We have to fall back on old stuff to express deep feelings; after serving this purpose at the Armistice of 1918, "Sons of the Sea" was brought back into use in 1939 and again in 1945. Where are the songs of the second world war? Some, like "We'll hang up our washing on the Siegfried Line", are forgotten for good reasons, but others, like "The Sergeant-Major's Stores", are set aside because we habitually scrap yesterday's joys.

EPILOGUE

Covent Garden in the Morning

+-

Cherries so red, strawberries ripe,
At home, of course, they'll be storming;
Never mind the abuse, you have the excuse,
You went to Covent Garden in the morning.

THERE IS A BELIEF that tunes once heard in happy surroundings
will always be heard gladly, but the truth is not nearly as simple
as that. Many of us who heard Gilbert's comic operas among our
earliest joys of the theatre now cannot listen to Sullivan without
a feeling that windows need to be opened; due acknowledgment of
their merits in wit and melody cannot overcome the claustrophobia
caused, perhaps, by associations of unalloyed bliss. On the other
hand, many other people respond so wholeheartedly to the
Victorian appeal, whether the singing is good or horrible, that
their enthusiasm drives any member of the opposite way of feeling
out of the theatre. Any hope of applying some theory based on age
groups becomes hopeless when you inspect audiences which
represent mixed generations. Whenever this problem is raised there
is a tendency to get round it by laying the blame on Gilbert, as
though his humour were bad enough to create nausea, but it is rarely
bad and often brilliant. In a steadfastly inquiring mood we must
conclude that we attach too much importance to early associations
when explaining the power of old songs. By themselves they
decide nothing in particular. We all know what it is to be
unaccountably moved by a Victorian song we have never heard
before.

The vogue of old songs began shortly after the first World War.
There was a music-hall mimic, Barry Ono, who also deserves
note for the collection of Penny Dreadfuls which his widow
presented to the British Museum; he gave a turn consisting of well-
known songs as they were sung by idols of the 1890s, and it roused

the old frenzy for joining in the chorus. Next came the 'Veterans of Variety', dearly loved idols who seemed to have returned from a forgotten world although they merely brought to the 1920s some memories of the 1910s. It was Leo Dryden's "The Miner's Dream of Home" which meant most—more than it had ever meant before now that its simple homesickness had turned into remembrance of all the young men who had gone singing to war. Among such there had once been a dialect spoken by those who went to the halls, full of such catchwords as 'Wotcher, me old brown son' and 'Who were you with last night?' and now every chorus raised by variety's veterans recalled the former way of life in a glittering haze. Over and above all this gilding of the past there was the real and immediate sense of goodfellowship in such happy souls as Tom Costello and Harry Champion. Present mirth still had present laughter where they were. They called themselves veterans but they were not so very old; not a lifetime, nor even half a lifetime, had gone by, but merely half a dozen much too eventful years. Ada Cerito still looked dangerous when she sang:

> I want another old man to begin
> Where the other old man left off

though at the celebration after the show she was concerned with her shopping bag. We saw her home to Brixton, and set her down in the garden outside her front door. After good-nights had been said and we had driven away, we went back to make sure she was safe. There she was, collecting parcels strewn all over the grass, in the light from many open windows—she had broken into the wrong house.

Yet it was neither the music-hall stars nor the music-hall songs, however hard they tugged at our heartstrings, which proved the most evocative. We were not overwhelmed by the sense of things gone beyond recall until we let it catch us unawares while we were busily guying them. This was the experience of all, including the very young as well as the very old. There was no deliberate intention of mockery. The beginning was an intelligent impulse to create the atmosphere of Thackeray's 'Cave of Harmony' as an entertainment to cater for the sudden interest in night life. Harold Scott, who incubated the idea, lavished on Mid-Victorianism the delicate zeal that other connoisseurs have devoted to the *Quattro-cento*. Aided by three or four others, including Elsa Lanchester and

Matthew Norgate, he ran a little club in Gower Street, and then down a disused sewer of Seven Dials, where supper was served at tables while the ballads beloved of an older generation were sung. It was exquisitely done and duly admired. But what might have been appreciated as an artistic achievement had a great success as a craze for derision, which made Miss Lanchester's singing (later) of "Please sell no more drink to my father" the talk of the town. And it was when we were laughing that we became aware that if we stopped laughing we might weep.

Meanwhile, in their different fashions, other actors were trying to provide London with intelligent amusements at night, more especially Peter Ridgeway—so rare a soul that when he appeared as Charles Lamb on the stage, he was by general consent said to have matched the part. In his own home he had tried out new plays until he discovered that any attempt to collect funds for expenses would offend the law. In his search for licensed premises, so to speak, he walked into the historic mansion in the north-east corner of Covent Garden Market whose basement had once housed the song-and-supper rooms known as 'Evans's, *late* Joy's' and had then, more recently, been fitted up for fights by the National Sporting Club. It was the attic, over the offices of a firm at work in the Market, which interested Ridgeway, for it was a private theatre in need of a tenant. Here he installed his Players' Theatre and struggled, as his predecessors had done, to excite an apathetic public in unknown actors and unknown authors. Aided by Leonard Sachs he carried out all the tasks that ought to have been left to a staff, even to scrubbing floors and cleaning lavatories, rather than forsake his ideal. Still the public stayed away, while Ridgeway grew weaker and weaker, until he could not eat and knew that he was dying. In order to gain a little rest he was thankful to hand over his theatre for a fortnight to Harold Scott in partnership with W. L. Hanchant, who expertly prepared a programme reminiscent of those presented at Evans's, *late* Joy's. There was never a doubt about it—this was what the public would want. There were choir-boys to sing, "I'd like to be a daisy if I could be a flower", there was a descriptive fantasia to illustrate the Relief of Lucknow, there was a recitation of Sims's "Ostler Joe", and there was a singer of such power as to revive the terrors of "Sam Hall" in sinister tones at which nobody could laugh. For a fortnight that attic was packed. The season ended but still the people came. A similar programme was hastily put together, partly out of the previous one, but as the copyright was infringed this would not do. Word went round that here was an opportunity for any player with an old song and ability to sing it, and in they came, though not always with material to match. Both Robert Eddison and Peter Ustinov used original material, while Archie Harradine proved that comic songs of almost any date did equally well, and Alec Clunes revived "Villikins". For his last appearance on any stage Peter Ridgeway, in a Victorian suit of pale pink and pale blue, like a shimmering ghost in the haze of tobacco smoke, sang two choruses. One was "Covent Garden in the morning" and the other

> Oh! the fairies! Whoa! the fairies!
> Nothing but splendour and feminine gender!
> Oh! the fairies! Whoa! the fairies!
> Oh! for the wings of a fairy queen!

Here at last was success, unending, unmistakable success, even though an unruly lot of enthusiasts kept him running round like a policeman to see that glasses were emptied at the close of licensing hours. Without any complaint or railing against fate that is how he ended his life, content that the show he called, *Late Joys*, was wanted. Under Leonard Sachs it did not stop at the outbreak of war. When the Blitz began it went into Evans's cellarage, and when that was no longer habitable it found a basement deep enough in Albemarle Street where the audience could bring its blankets and bed down for the night. It was then that the custom began of toasting Queen Victoria and denouncing that enemy of mankind, the King of the Zulus. *Late Joys* had become part of London life. When peace arrived fresh quarters were found in the old music-hall, Gatti's-Under-The-Arches, beneath the railway at Charing Cross. Here, with Don Gemmell as chairman, the style broadened into merriment belonging to comic songs of the past in any kind, and it was worth noting that those who thought they were guying Victorians laughed loudest when outraged by the forced gaiety of Edwardians.

Victorian music sounded now from another quarter. In Canada a male-voice quartet, named the Four Gentlemen, won a hearing all over the North American Continent until they had won the right of a regular relayed service to Great Britain. Their success was due to a repertoire which was, at first, unerringly evocative, with "Alice, where art thou?" as their master stroke. Just as their place as radio stars seemed supreme they broadened their style and the spell broke. Every now and then fresh attempts are made to capture this emotional magic; either those who make it are too young to know what they are about or else it proves singularly elusive. But one thing is plain, Victorian song had some formula which is a secret we have lost.

INDEX OF SONGS